Women in Ancient China

Women in Ancient China

Bret Hinsch

ROWMAN & LITTLEFIELD
Lanham • Boulder • New York • London

Published by Rowman & Littlefield
A wholly owned subsidiary of The Rowman & Littlefield Publishing Group, Inc.
4501 Forbes Boulevard, Suite 200, Lanham, Maryland 20706
www.rowman.com

Unit A, Whitacre Mews, 26-34 Stannary Street, London SE11 4AB

British Library Cataloguing in Publication Information Available

Library of Congress Cataloging-in-Publication Data

Names: Hinsch, Bret, author.
Title: Women in Ancient China / Bret Hinsch.
Description: Lanham, Maryland : Rowman & Littlefield, [2018] | Series: An
    Asia/Pacific/perspectives series | Includes bibliographical references and
    index.
Identifiers: LCCN 2017060918 (print) | LCCN 2018020059 (ebook) | ISBN
    9781538115411 (Electronic) | ISBN 9781538115404 (cloth : alk. paper)
    ISBN 9781538158340 (pbk: alk. paper)
Subjects: LCSH: Women—China—Social conditions. | Matriarchy—China.
Classification: LCC HQ1767 (ebook) | LCC HQ1767 .H54 2018 (print) | DDC
    305.40931—dc23
LC record available at https://lccn.loc.gov/2017060918

Contents

List of Figures

Introduction

Research into the history of Chinese women has made impressive strides in the past few decades. As late as the 1980s, few historians bothered with gender matters, relegating women to the margins of China's historical narrative. Since then, however, the female experience has become a major focus of historical inquiry, and the resulting insights have reshaped standard representations of China's past.

Although the academy has embraced the history of Chinese women, research focuses on the most recent eras. Historians interested in women's issues usually study the Ming and Qing dynasties and especially the twentieth century. The recent past holds obvious appeal for scholars, as the sources are copious, accessible, and more readily comprehensible. Moreover, its impact on today's China is readily evident. Nevertheless, the preponderance of China's history, including many milestones involving women, occurred long before the Ming dynasty. Indeed, the most basic characteristics of Chinese gender relations emerged in antiquity. Generally speaking, the more fundamental an idea, the earlier it appeared. The most basic practices, such as separation of the sexes and gendered division of labor, date back to the high antiquity or even prehistory. More recent gender norms often consist of iterations of ideas and customs first conceived long ago.

Historians conventionally define Chinese antiquity as the long stretch of time prior to national unification in 221 BCE. Seen from the perspective of contemporary China, life so far back in the past seems alien in almost every respect. The enormity of these differences challenges anyone hoping to comprend such a distant era. Until recently, historians frequently used the recent past to understand more remote eras. They would use information from the late imperial era to construct general models about historic China, then project these back into time, assuming that certain conditions remained timeless. In recent years, however, this homogenized view of China's past has come under harsh critique, exposing it as condescending Orientalism. Careful scholars now emphasize the fact that life in ancient China differed considerably from the late imperial era and must be understood on its own terms.

Instead of using the recent past as a template for understanding antiquity, historians now tend to emphasize the vast disjunctions between the remote past and more recent times.[1] In contrast to Ming and Qing, ancient China as yet lacked tea and soy sauce, chairs and porcelain, paper and monks. And yet however distant and unfamiliar that era might seem, it gave rise to basic characteristics of Chinese civilization. Early society saw the emergence of agriculture and commerce, Confucianism and Daoism, bureaucracy and codes of law. And the ancient era culminated with the unification of China as the most populous polity ever established, a monumental event in world history.

As society became more complex, communities established increasingly inclusive and effective institutions capable of regulating complicated social interactions. In response, people had to adapt their behavior to suit changed circumstances. The practices and ideas that resulted from this interaction formed the substrate of Chinese relations between the sexes. Many features of prehistoric and ancient gender norms continued until the end of the imperial era, and some endure today.

Increasing social complexity stimulated large-scale administration, economic productivity, and social stratification, causing male and female roles to diverge. Documentation from every early civilization shows that men usually took on the most prestigious activities and ranks. Official ideology glorified male pursuits such as warfare and ritual. Men dominated emerging specialized professions. And men served as rulers, officials, and soldiers, providing them status, connections, and remuneration.[2] In contrast, women found themselves increasingly excluded from the most powerful and prestigious roles. So as society became more complex, the sexes became increasingly unequal. This book details the process of growing sexual inequality as it unfolded in China.

Scholars often refer to gender hierarchy as patriarchy. This term can be misleading, as it implies that the inequality of men and women comprises a single institution.[3] Yet generally speaking, gender status encompasses three dimensions.[4] First, members of one sex can have a higher authority or worth within a culture. Second, gender hierarchy can describe a relationship of dominance and subordination which does not necessarily relate to prestige. Finally, even in a society where the sexes are unequal, women can still control some aspects of their own lives and the affairs of others. Because gender hierarchy encompasses varied ideas and practices, it makes no sense to simplistically describe the status of women as either high or low, or to see gender relations in absolute terms. Power and prestige took many forms and involved different aspects of life, making the relations between the sexes complex and inconsistent. A woman might defer to her father-in-law yet dominate the lives of her children; a queen could issue orders to powerful men yet feel obligated to obey her father.

Women could often manipulate a male-dominated system to purse their own interests. When men claimed superior status, women could contest domination, seek alternate sources of prestige, or exert power differently. So even as growing social complexity depressed female status in many respects, it also brought new opportunities. Increasing social complexity in ancient China gave rise to a dual prestige system. Men and women could both obtain respect, but each augmented their social standing differently.[5] For example, Shang dynasty men monopolized leadership positions, key administrative roles, and specialized occupations. Yet because kinship formed the foundation of this aristocratic society, women from the most important families enjoyed immense wealth, controlled important domains, and even led armies into battle.

The conquest of Shang by the Zhou people and their allies in 1046 BCE brought about an abrupt political and cultural transition that transformed female life. Archaeologists have unearthed numerous inscribed bronze ritual vessels that document the activities of Western Zhou queens and noblewomen. These texts describe queens conducting state rituals and presenting gifts to the nobility, thereby helping to bind together the Zhou realm. The *Shijing* (*Classic of Poetry*) collection supplements inscriptional evidence by describing the lives of ordinary women, village customs, and even stereotypical female emotions.

The Eastern Zhou saw a marked decline in the participation of women in public matters. Comprehensive administrative institutions upheld by sophisticated bodies of thought emerged during this era. As political ideologies became increasingly refined, men drew on these ideas to exclude women from the halls of power, criticizing female participation in affairs of state as unwarranted meddling. Even so, political marriages between the noble families of different states placed women in an intermediary position between powerful men, allowing them to influence the relations between father and husband. And educated women could employ their knowledge of rhetoric and ritual to guide important events.

This book covers millennia of prehistory and early civilization. The immense time frame and vast geographic scope of Chinese antiquity can seem daunting. Yet examining the past through such a lengthy timespan has advantages. Limiting research to a shorter period, such as a single dynasty or reign, obscures larger trends that only become evident within a broader chronological framework. By looking at how the relationship between gender and political power shifted over the *longue durée*, the historian can perceive how growing institutional complexity affected female rights and privileges.

A steady increase in social complexity constitutes the most fundamental trend in ancient history. Social development influenced gender relations in varied ways. For example, as society stratified and powerful male leaders emerged during the Late Neolithic era, some people would sacrifice a woman and place her in the grave of a deceased ruler to accompany him to the afterlife. In contrast, during the Shang dynasty a small number of elite women exercised power by virtue of their kinship ties. And Western Zhou monarchy allowed a queen to gain authority and prestige by serving as her husband's surrogate. Because women's power grew out of the underlying systems binding society together, their status and authority fluctuated as institutions changed. The basic conditions of each era circumscribed female agency in different ways. Yet in each period, even as society's norms constrained certain actions, they also provided space for women to creatively pursue their interests.

In conducting research, the historian must study the available material, reenvision what took place, then use language to construct a simulacrum of the past. Because most evidence about life in remote antiquity disappeared long ago, scholars have no choice but to judiciously utilize imagination to supplement the available information. When dealing with remote antiquity, reimagining becomes extremely problematic. As the role of imagination increases, it becomes more likely that historians will unwittingly introduce anachronistic ideas and values.[6] When discussing gender relations, it is tempting to read later norms into the earliest circumstances, potentially downplaying the importance of women. For example, standard interpretations of Neolithic society usually concentrate on male activities, ignoring the possibility that women also made important contributions to the community by acting as socializers and transmitting traditional wisdom. And sometimes an archaeologist will assume that only men performed an important task without any evidence that this was the case. Was every Neolithic stone tool made or used by a man?[7] Did only men go hunting or work in the grain fields? People today should approach these questions with an open mind.

Moreover, even as certain tasks became associated with gender, past peoples did not necessarily consider male occupations more important or prestigious than those of women. Although archaeologists traditionally emphasize the importance of hunting over gathering, women in some non-agricultural societies contribute substantially to sustenance. Between

60 and 80 percent of the diet of the !Kung people, hunter-gatherers in the Kalahari Desert, consists of wild foods gathered by women.[8] In some prehistoric societies, women likely had a similar role in provisioning. Moreover, when male hunters captured game, the meat did not necessarily go to feed their family. Anthropologists have found that male hunters tend to share their kill with the entire community, whereas women usually keep most of the food that they gather for their own household.[9] In light of evidence from anthropological fieldwork, it seems that women's economic contributions to the household in prehistoric and ancient China might be underappreciated. On the other hand, wishful thinking about gender equality should not lead historians and archaeologists to exaggerate the importance of women's roles. Cautious and mindful interpretation of the evidence should guide the investigation of early gender history.

The advent of writing marked the transition from prehistory to history. Although written evidence allows for a far more detailed understanding the past, it also presents methodological quandaries. As genres of writing evolved, texts provide new kinds of information and relate it in changing ways. Most anciently, laconic Shang dynasty divinatory inscriptions provide insights into the lives of a small group of women at the apex of society. Western Zhou bronze inscriptions record the politically significant activities of queens and noblewomen. Ancient poets sometimes described the lives of ordinary women. And authors from the Eastern Zhou era composed long and abstract texts encompassing a range of subjects, including gender.

As writing and literature developed, perspectives on ancient women shifted considerably. Changing viewpoints can easily mislead the historian. What appears to be a major change might be the result of more detailed documentation or a different style of writing. Moreover, written sources imbed descriptions of women within the prevalent ideological matrix, which also altered over time. Rather than discussing each woman as a unique individual, ancient authors tended to understand women in terms of the normative family roles of daughter, wife, and mother.[10] The historian must strive to extricate the ambiguous realities of female life from these simplified ideological ideals.

Geography presents additional interpretive challenges. In antiquity, the region of Chinese culture occupied a much smaller area than the expansive borders of the People's Republic of China. As a result, some artifacts unearthed within China's current boundaries lack a direct relation to the development of historic Chinese culture. The magnificent "goddess temple" at the Niuheliang site in Liaoning province exemplifies how the boundaries of early Chinese civilization sometimes differed from current borders.[11] This large structure originally contained statues depicting a pantheon of goddesses, including a large female face inset with striking jade eyes. Although the Niuheliang site has attracted intense interest, it belonged to the northeastern Hongshan culture (4500–3000 BCE), which differed considerably from prehistoric societies farther south. Most likely this temple was built by the progenitors of the Eastern Yi (Dong Yi) peoples who repeatedly fought against Shang and Zhou.[12] Many other artifacts unearthed within China's current borders, however splendid and intriguing, must likewise be excluded from discussions of the evolution of Chinese gender.

I begin this book with a critical discussion of a vexing methodological problem. Marxist scholars have aggressively promoted the theory that the earliest societies were matriarchal. The Chinese academy treats this assumption as orthodoxy, and ideas about ancient matriarchy continue to inform research on early society. Only by understanding the details of this theory and appreciating its immense impact can outsiders decode the implicit assumptions underlying mainstream Chinese scholarship about ancient gender.

The body of this study follows the conventional periodization scheme for Chinese history. Women's lives in each phase of prehistory and antiquity differed considerably, so chapters 2 through 5 each covers one of the major eras of antiquity: the Neolithic period, Shang dynasty, and Western and Eastern Zhou eras. Finally, an epilogue explores the gradual emergence of anti-female ideology in antiquity. When read in tandem, this sundry evidence reveals the many contributions of women to the rise of Chinese civilization.

1

~

The Myth of Matriarchy

The theory of matriarchy, long dismissed by Western academia, has steered research on ancient Chinese women to such a degree that no one can comprehend the subject without first understanding this interpretive model. Matriarchy briefly became a popular topic in Western intellectual circles during the nineteenth century. For a time, influential European and American scholars assumed that the earliest and simplest societies were all both matrilineal and matriarchal. They used this assumption to try to reconstruct the origins of humanity and even attributed examples of female power in the ancient historic era to lingering influence from a primal gender system that favored women. Although Western academics soon discarded matriarchy theory as baseless, it subsequently won over key Chinese intellectuals, and many Chinese scholars still use this framework to interpret early gender practices.[1]

Since the mid-nineteenth century, when China opened up to the outside world, intellectuals have had to manage successive waves of ideas coming from the West. Some of these imported notions, Marxism in particular, have had an immense impact on the way Chinese think about their nation's past. Because nineteenth-century Marxists embraced the theory of ancient matriarchy, this idea also gained currency in China. Many Chinese historians and archaeologists believe that all societies, including China, initially passed through a prehistoric matrilineal phase prior to developing patriarchal institutions. A great deal of Chinese research about early women rests on this assumption.

The embrace of matriarchal theory did not mark a complete departure from China's own intellectual traditions. Centuries ago, some authors vaguely referred to distant countries dominated by women. Rumors spoke of a "kingdom of queens" somewhere far to the north, where women ruled over men. However, "no one has ever been there."[2] Nebulous Tang dynasty accounts mentioned far-away kingdoms ruled by a queen or populated solely by women. These stories seem to have stemmed from the misapprehension that rule by a woman constitutes matriarchy, even though a female monarch can exercise power within a patriarchal system. Interestingly, rather than seeing matriarchy as normal or acceptable, imperial authors derided strange lands with powerful women, seeing female rule as proof of barbarism.[3]

The modern theory of matriarchy came to China from abroad, having originated in Europe. Eighteenth-century European thinkers discussed the importance of mothers in remote prehistory, and the Swiss thinker Johann Jacob Bachofen (1815–1887) crystalized this idea into a coherent schema. In a detailed account of prehistoric social development, he asserted that all societies initially go through a phase of primitive matriarchy before establishing more advanced patriarchal institutions.[4] The scion of a wealthy family, Bachofen initially taught Roman law at the University of Basel. However, he soon discovered that he preferred research to the petty aggrevations of the classroom, and he renounced his post to dedicate the rest of his life to unraveling the origins of society. Unfortunately, archaeology and anthropology had only just begun to emerge as serious academic fields, so Bachofen had access to very little reliable information about social development. Lacking hard evidence, he revived an antiquated methodology. Assuming that mythological tales relate garbled accounts of early society, he analyzed them for clues about prehistoric social conditons. In 1861 Bachofen published *Mother Right (Das Mutterrecht)*, in which he set out his theories in detail.[5] He argued that as humanity first emerged from absolute savagery, a system dominated by women brought a degree of order to society. However, because matriarchal institutions were so primitive, they could never endure. As society developed, men gradually accrued power. They eventually overcame female resistance and established the patriarchal institutions that have endured ever since.

The erudite Bachofen couched his ideas in confident and persuasive prose, and his book had a major influence on the emerging field of anthropology. Many scholars accepted Bachofen's model as a reliable description of society's origins. Most importantly, the pioneering American anthropologist Lewis Henry Morgan (1818–1881) adopted Bachofen's theory of primitive matriarchy as a cornerstone of his own research. In *Ancient Society* (1877), Morgan proposed that all societies pass through a series of uniform developmental phases, gradually ascending from savagery to civilization.[6] Like Bachofen, Morgan believed that the earliest and most primitive societies throughout the world were matriarchal.

Over time, social development led people to abandon female rule for the more advanced patriarchal system.

Friedrich Engels (1820–1895), Karl Marx's patron and intellectual collaborator, read Morgan's work with interest. Engels borrowed the idea of uniform social evolution and made it the basis of a new account of early social history, published in 1884 as *The Origin of the Family, Private Property, and the State* (*Der Ursprung der Familie, des Privateigenthums und des Staats*).[7] In this influential work, Engels followed Bachofen and Morgan in identifying matriarchy as the initial stage of social development in all societies. However, Engels reinterpreted it according to Marx's materialist ideology, attributing the rise of patriarchy to the emergence of private property.

Because Engels accounted for social evolution in materialist terms, his writings entered the Marxist canon. As Marxism began to influence the Chinese academic world, many intellectuals accepted Engels' theory of prehistoric matriarchy. Because this vision of powerful ancient women cast doubt on traditional gender restrictions, radical thinkers welcomed this novel paradigm.[8] Matriarchal theory began to guide academic research as well. In 1937 Chen Dongyuan (1902–1978) published an influential overview of women's history in which he declared matrilinealism to have been the earliest phase of society, integrating Marxist matriarchal theory into Chinese historical discourse.[9]

The Soviet Union adopted prehistoric matriarchy as a key tenet of the orthodox Marxist version of history, giving it a further boost. As communist ideology gained ground in China, this point of view became increasingly widespread. After the founding of the People's Republic of China in 1949, the Chinese Communist Party ordered historians to teach the Marxist account of history and to use it as the basis of their own research.[10] The prominent historian Guo Moruo (1892–1978) led the effort to reorient discourse about prehistory and antiquity around the theories of Engels and Morgan. In the end, matriarchal theory became a central component of the orthodox narrative of China's distant past.[11]

When Marxism became China's official dogma, scholars in various fields strove to apply this framework to their own research. They followed nineteenth-century authorities in conflating matriarchy (rule by women) with matrilinealism (tracing descent through the female line), assuming that the two systems always appear in tandem. Opinions over the dates of China's alleged matriarchal period vary widely, ranging from the middle Paleolithic era to the Shang dynasty. Although some scholars consider matrilinealism to have been an era of gender egalitarianism, most envision it as a time when women dominated politics and the economy.[12] They describe matrilineal societies as the simplest form of human organization, with primitive technology and low productivity.[13]

Matriarchal society as yet lacked the division of labor, and the clan served as the primary economic unit.[14]

The warm reception that matriarchal theory received in China contrasts with its unhappy fate in Western academia. Soon after Morgan and others posited matriarchy as a universal phase of social development, this theory came under intense criticism.[15] When anthropologists began conducting systematic fieldwork, they soon realized that societies do not pass through a uniform series of evolutionary stages. Each society follows its own trajectory as it becomes increasingly complex, conditioned by environment, contingency, and agency. Common economic and social processes can give rise to a spectrum of outcomes.[16] Moreover, early anthropologists soon realized that even though matrilinealism and matriarchy sound similar, in fact these two systems have absolutely no relation.[17] Not only do men dominate all matrilineal groups, but some of these societies display extreme male privilege.[18] Men dominate matrilineal systems because this type of kinship is not organized around women themselves, but instead link men to one another via their female relations.[19] Critics of matriarchy theory also emphasize the universality of patriarchy. Ethnologists have yet to discover a society in which women have more power than men overall, casting doubt on the possibility that a true matriarchy has ever existed.[20]

At first female intellectuals in the West embraced the theory of prehistoric matriarchy, portraying it as a lost utopia.[21] Some appealed to matriarchy to emphasize the potential flexibility of gender roles, arguing that one day women might once again become as important as men. In contrast, some men used the the belief that primitive societies practice matriarchy to legitimize patriarchy. The nineteenth-century model of human development portrayed the emergence of patriarchy as social progress, making male supremacy a fundamental characteristic of civilization.[22] Over time, feminists grasped the misogynistic implications of this theory and began to condemn it as hopelessly sexist and reactionary.[23] Contemporary Western writing about prehistoric matriarchy uniformly portrays it as an antiquated Victorian myth.

Despite the abandonment of matriarchal theory in the West, it continues to hold a respected place in Chinese academia. To this day, many historians and archaeologists assume that women dominated early society, and this belief informs their research. Even so, a few dissenters have raised their voices in protest. Some Western scholars with close ties to Chinese academia have criticized uncritical acceptance of an archaic theory. They also point out how this model distorts the analysis of archaeological data.[24] Even some Marxists have expressed their reservations. In the 1940s, Soviet scholars began to criticize theories of matriarchy. By the 1970s, it had become common for Soviet intellectuals to disparage

Morgan's errors, including his belief in prehistoric matriarchy, and these criticisms seem to have affected some Chinese scholars.[25]

After the Cultural Revolution ended in 1976, critics of the disgraced radical Jiang Qing accused her of having personally propagated the doctrine of matriarchy to selfishly bolster her own power.[26] Since then, a handful of Chinese academics have publicly criticized the matriarchy paradigm for lacking any empirical basis. They point out how numerous archaeologists and historians have distorted their conclusions to force them to conform with this theory.[27] Even so, the number of overtly dissenting voices remains small. Presumably some scholars have quietly dismissed this model, as it fails to appear in many important works about prehistory. Yet because matriarchal theory has become entrenched as state orthodoxy, skeptics usually avoid overtly attacking it.

Matriarchal theory continues to exert an immense influence over Chinese portrayals of past women. Although some archaeologists believe that society had already become patriarchal as early as the Yangshao era, many employ this paradigm to describe all phases of the Neolithic.[28] Historians who see matriarchy extending into the Early Bronze Age use this belief to interpret Shang dynasty gender relations. Proponents point to the privileges of royal consorts such as the famed Fu Hao as proof that matriarchy still influenced fundamental institutions during the Shang.[29]

Scholars have subjected aspects of ancient religion to a matriarchal interpretation as well. Numerous scholars have tried to interpret the flamboyant designs on Yangshao era ceramics through matriarchal theory. In numerous books and articles, authors construe painted fish and flowers as symbols of female genitalia, circles and whorls as vaginas, and straight lines as phalluses that presage the rise of patriarchy.[30] Writers also frequently invoke the matriarchal paradigm to interpret mythology. Some have asserted that legends about Fu Xi, Nü Wa, the sage ruler Yan, and the Zhou female ancestor Jiang Yuan embody the values of a society dominated by women.[31] Sacrifices to female ancestors by the Shang and Zhou supposedly reflect remnants of the matriarchal system.[32] Ancient goddess worship has also been attributed to matriarchy.[33] And scholars have asserted that the ancient veneration of gourds, seen by some as tokens of female fecundity, reflected the supposedly exalted status of women at the time.[34]

The theory of matriarchy has also had a major impact on investigations of early Chinese kinship.[35] Some historians have declared that ancient veneration of female ancestors preserved memories of a distant matrilineal age.[36] And various studies refer to matrilinealism and matriarchy in analyzing descent practices, marriage, and incest taboos.[37] This line of inquiry has even affected archaeological methodology, as some archaeologists claim to be able to detect signs of matriarchal marriage customs in burial patterns. Due to influence from matriarchal theory, the interpretive techniques of Chinese archaeology sometimes differ from those used elsewhere.[38]

Matriarchal theory has also guided the study of early language and literature. A large body of philological research precedes from the assumption that matriarchy constituted the earliest phase of Chinese society. Many scholars have pointed to certain surnames and other characters with female components as alleged proof of matrilinealism.[39] And in the realm of intellectual history, it has become common to attribute the origins of female-friendly Daoist thought to ideas and values that emerged from matriarchy.[40] Specialists in ancient literature also resort to matriarchal theory in their readings of early texts. Some consider the prominent feminine imagery in *Shijing* (*Classic of Poetry*) and *Chuci* (*Elegies of Chu*) residues of women's original dominance.[41]

The impact of matriarchal theory has extended far beyond studies of remote antiquity to influence depictions of every period of China's past, even those considered patriarchal. Various historians have construed almost any indication of female power as a vestige of matriarchy.[42] For example, some explain the powers of Han dynasty empresses dowager and their kinsmen as lingering matriarchy.[43] And because matriarchy characterizes primitive society, many historians attribute it to the societies of northern steppe peoples. They then use this supposition to account for the impact of conquest dynasties on medieval Chinese society.[44]

Even today, Chinese anthropologists contend that some minority peoples in Yunnan province, such as the Mosuo, practice matriarchy. Although the Mosuo themselves know this to be untrue, they nevertheless embrace the matriarchal tag because they find it a useful way to attract tourists. The Mosuo present their culture to each group of outsiders differently, titillating Han men with intimations of sexual license while pandering to foreign feminists by exaggerating the authority of women.[45]

In sum, few fields of academic inquiry carry an ideological burden as weighty as the history of ancient Chinese women. The myth of matriarchy has distorted research about prehistoric and ancient Chinese women for decades, affecting both specialized studies and popular accounts. To move forward, researchers must cast off this archaic enumbrance and reexamine the original sources without preconceptions. Reconstructing early Chinese women's history on an empirical foundation reveals an understanding of women's lives in the remote past that is not only far more reliable, but also much more remarkable.

2

~

Neolithic Era

Physically modern humans have resided in East Asia since at least the Late Paleolithic era, yet very little evidence about humanity predates the invention of agriculture. Anthropological fieldwork about hunting and gathering societies can help fill this lacuna. Even though material remains reveal nothing about Stone Age gender relations in China before the invention of agriculture, foraging societies througout the world share certain characteristics in common, and people in Mesolithic East Asia probably had similar customs as well.

Most fundamentally, foragers strive to maximize their food resources and ensure that children receive adequate nutrition to guarantee the survival of the band.[1] Women and men tend to form stable monogamous ties for life, as polygyny, divorce, and remarriage would create conflicts of interest between family members. Multiple generations live together so that parents and grandparents can help nurture the young. Although small-scale foraging socies are basically egalitarian, they nevertheless distinguish men from women and associate certain roles and tasks with one sex or the other.[2] In foraging societies, men typically hunt large game while women gather plants and capture small prey, although the specifics of gendered labor differ according to environment and custom.[3] Many foraging cultures celebrate hunting as highly prestigious, thereby encouraging men to face danger to obtain valuable supplies of protein.[4]

Although embryonic agricultural practices in the region now known as China might date back more than twenty thousand years, Neolithic societies centered on cultivation began to emerge about ten millennia ago. The earliest agricultural societies had very simple material culture and nascent social organization. Even so, the shift to agriculture altered almost every aspect of life. This new way of obtaining food stimulated the invention of a range of novel technologies that included ceramics, architecture, spinning and weaving, and new stone tools.

Archaeologists classify Early Neolithic cultures primarily according to their unique styles of pottery, and use the place name of a characteristic site to represent each culture. Nascent agricultural societies did not develop uniformly. Each community followed a somewhat different trajectory, and the pace of change varied. Through this uneven process, over time societies in each region became increasingly complex, productive, and stratified.

Burial customs reveal some features of Early Neolithic social organization. In the early phase of the Laoguantai culture (6500–5000 BCE) of northwest China, people buried the dead both singly and in groups. One typical group burial includes five sets of remains: two men and three women[5] (Fig. 2.1). Each of the deceased has similar grave goods placed beside the feet or legs. As each sex received similar mortuary treatment, it seems that women and men had roughly comparable status while they were alive. In this young agricultural society, egalitarian economic organization fostered parity between the sexes.[6] Where food is shared, power tends to be shared as well. In a society with minimal social distinctions, a person's age and clan likely determined primary social identity.

Mortuary practices varied across north China. Some communities buried men and women differently, such as positioning the bodies of each sex in distinct ways. In one Early Neolithic cemetery, women lay on their side with legs flexed while male bodies are supine and extended.[7] Although we have no way of knowing what these burial positions meant, it is significant that people in some early agricultural communities had already begun to inter the dead differently according to sex. Even in a relatively egalitarian society, gender already constituted a fundamental element of individual identity.

At some sites, the remains of men outnumber those of women, hinting at the inauguration of gender bias. One cemetery from the Peiligang culture, dating to about 4700 BCE, contains the remains of 1,853 adults.[8] Of these, 1,170 are male and 683 female. The proportion of male to female remains increases with the age of the deceased. Of the 239 skeletons of young people, 104 are male and 135 female. But of the 1,534 people who died in the prime of life, 1,009 are male and only 525 female. And only twenty-five skeletons of the eighty-two elderly people are female.[9] Given such clear disparity between the sexes, it seems likely that people in this community valued men more than women, as they more often considered them worthy of a formal burial.

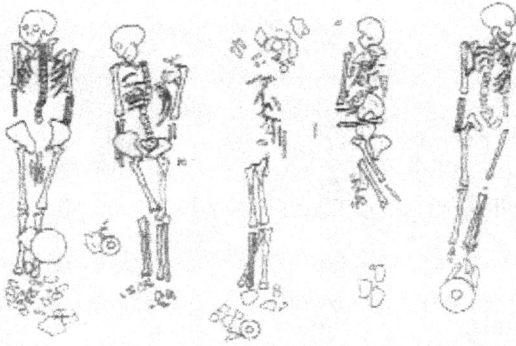

Figure 2.1. Early Neolithic Egalitarian Burial of Three Women and Two Men
Zhang Hongyan, "Weishui liuyu Laoguantai wenhua fenqi yu leixing yanjiu," Kaogu xuebao 2 (2007): 174.

As the economy developed, labor became increasingly specialized. Concentrating on a smaller number of tasks allowed people to perform each job more effectively, raising individual productivity and making society more prosperous. Some Early Neolithic sites show nascent signs of division of labor by sex. Anthropologists theorize that prehistoric women tended to specialize in tasks they could perform while simultaneously taking care of children, such as domestic work.[10] Allocating different work roles to women and men changed the way people conceptualized gender difference. After a few key work roles became gendered, many other tasks became randomly assigned to either women or men, eventually leading to the association of virtually all important activities and places with one sex or the other.[11] In this way, gender became closely associated with distinct work roles.

Not only did the gendering of work transform the economy, but division of labor also provided practical reasons for individuals to enter into stable marriages, and for clans to divide into families. The earliest kinship units consisted of large groups either descended from a common ancestor or constructed through fictive kinship ties. Men and women lived and worked together in these groups, which constituted their primary social identity. However, the gendering of labor roles made it economically rational for one man and one woman to form a close and stable bond. A pair of spouses could carry out both stereotypical female and male tasks, thus providing a family with everything they required. In this manner, gendered division of labor turned the family into the basic building block of society.[12]

Specialized male and female work roles emerged extremely early, as attested by mortuary evidence from the Peiligang culture (7000–5000 BCE) in present-day Henan province. Graves of men and women contain similar numbers of burial goods, suggesting that they enjoyed roughly comparable status while alive. However, different items were interred in the grave of each sex.[13] Men's graves contain agricultural implements such as stone axes, shovels, and sickles, whereas women were buried with stone querns used to prepare millet. Because millet had to be laboriously husked before cooking, grinding grain was an important and time-consuming domestic chore. Women's graves also contain vessels used to store, prepare, and serve food, such as pottery beakers, jars, and bowls. No single Peiligang grave contains both querns and agricultural tools, implying that women performed most domestic chores while men labored in the fields. Even though men and women were buried with different kinds of items, all of their main grave goods were related to the production and preparation of food, underscoring the fact that both male and female labor were necessary to provide sustenence. A reciprocal exchange between the sexes made each meal possible.[14] Men provided millet from the fields, and women husked and cooked it to feed the family.

Peiligang graves show evidence of other types of gendered labor as well. Stone axes (used to clear land for new fields) and spindle whorls (for making thread) usually do not appear together in the same grave. So in addition to grinding grain, it seems that women also spun thread and wove it into cloth to provide their family's clothing. Archaeologists laud the invention of textiles as a revolutionary advance that exponentially increased humanity's adaptive capacities. In China, this key technology was primarily a female domain.[15]

Other Early Neolithic sites in northwest China show similar distinctions between the grave goods of men and women.[16] At one settlement belonging to the Laoguantai culture of the sixth millennium BCE, many men were interred with stone shovels whereas women's graves lack burial goods. And at a cemetery of the Beishouling culture in Shaanxi province, male graves contain arrowheads and grinding stones whereas women were often buried with pigments and ornaments. Although the items interred with each sex varied according to region, people in many Early Neolithic communities manipulated material culture to differentiate the sexes and display gender identity. As culture grew in complexity, symbols and practices, not just biology, increasingly distinguished male and female.

The gradual emergence of a more complex way of life marks the beginnings of the Middle Neolithic era. Dwellings became bigger and more varied, settlements larger and more numerous, and communities practiced more elaborate rituals. Agriculture spread over a much larger area, giving rise to a wider range of cultures. Although the Yangshao of northwest China represents the most famous Middle Neolithic culture in the region, and archaeologists often use it to represent the entire period, distinctive societies in other places had reached comparable levels of complexity.

Investigations by osteoarchaeologists have yielded information about the lives of people at this time. At a Middle Neolithic site in Henan, women began to bear children at around fourteen or fifteen years of age. The average woman gave birth to between two and seven children who survived infancy.[17] Because each woman bore so many children, families tended to be large. A family usually had between three and eleven members, with an average of seven.[18]

Osteoarchaeology also reveals details about the physical condition of the deceased. According to an analysis of skeletons uncovered at another Henan site, at the end of the Middle Neolithic era, men had an average height of 165 cm and women 154.3 cm.[19] At a Dawenkou culture site in Jiangsu, adult men averaged 167.6 cm while women reached 150.7 cm.[20] A study of remains at a Dawenkou cemetery revealed that both men and women there died at an average age of thirty-six, while at another settlement both sexes lived to about twenty-seven or twenty-eight.[21] Archaeological data from other regions of the world shows that Neolithic men and women elsewhere usually had similarly brief life expectancies.[22] Only when society stratified into social classes did members of social groups have extremely different lifestyles and diets, resulting in unequal life spans.

Middle Neolithic graves have yielded numerous body ornaments, providing clues as to how people may have appeared in life. Both sexes used items made of stone, pottery, horn, bone, tooth, and shell to decorate their hair, forehead, ears, wrists, neck, chest, and waist.[23] Most Dawenkou women and men had some teeth pulled during their teenage years, likely as a rite of passage.[24] In addition, some people may have ornamented themselves through tattooing, scarification, or body painting, common practices among tribal peoples around the world.[25]

Many communities apportioned labor roles according to sex. At the Yangshao culture Banpo site in Shaanxi, male remains are accompanied by numerous and varied stone agricultural tools. Except for a small number of stone adzes, female graves lack items related to agricultural labor. However, the graves of both men and women contain querns for grinding grain, suggesting that some kinds of basic domestic work had yet to be associated with either sex.[26] Similarly, male graves from the Daxi culture of the Three Gorges region have large numbers of stone agricultural tools, whereas those of women include numerous stone awls.[27] At a fourth millennium BCE site of the Majiabin culture, stone adzes and axes were interred exclusively with men and most spindle whorls with women.[28] Similar gendered division of labor can be seen at sites from the Dawenkou culture (4300–2600 BCE) of the Lower Yellow River region, where men's graves have agricultural tools and those of women contain spindle whorls, needles, and awls.[29] These differences in burial goods suggest that in many places men specialized in agricultural labor whereas women made cloth and performed domestic chores.

Differentiated work roles did not necessarily bring about an immediate decline in female status. At one Majiahong culture (5000–4000 BCE) cemetery in Jiangsu, men's graves have pottery vessels and agricultural tools while those of women contain a much more diverse range of burial goods, including pottery vessels, combs, adzes, and spindle whorls.[30] The inclusion of a similar or even greater number of items in women's graves suggests comparable respect for both sexes. For a family to thrive, both husand and wife had to perform their appointed tasks.[31] In a primitive economy lacking commercial exchange, a man had to find a woman willing to make his clothes and prepare his food or else he would suffer cold and hunger. The necessity of female work roles made them respectable. And even if women did not tend grain fields, they still might have contributed significantly to their family's diet. In addition to cultivated vegetables, which women may have grown in a kitchen garden, people still ate wild plants that might have been gathered by women.[32]

Although men undertook demanding labor in the grain fields, women's work was not necessarily any easier. One analysis of Middle Neolithic skeletons unearthed in Henan studied the dimensions of the humerus (upper arm bone), which reflects arm muscle mass. Investigators discovered that the average woman had slightly more upper body musculature than men. However, the tibias (knee bones) of women had slightly less muscle.[33] Whatever work women performed, it involved heavy lifting. Most likely, women developed heavily muscled arms by carrying pots of water to supply their family's needs. Because people did not yet know how to dig wells, it was necessary to carry water long distances in pots every day for cooking and cleaning. In this community, women likely had responsibility for this strenuous task.

Burial practices provide clues about the bonds between women and men. Mortuary customs had yet to standardize, and the forms of burial varied considerably. People in some places, such as the Dawenkou culture of eastern China, interred their dead in several ways, even in the same cemetery.[34] Elsewhere some people laid the deceased to rest in a uniform manner. Bodies at a Yangshao cemetery in Luoyang were buried singly, usually without grave goods.[35]

Many Middle Neolithic burials consist of a small pit containing a single occupant. Although these graves often lack burial goods, sometimes people placed pottery vessels, tools, and ornaments beside the deceased.[36] The amount of pottery in each grave varies significantly. In some cemeteries, female graves have far more pots than their male counterparts. However, this does not necessarily imply that women had higher social status. People of the time may have considered pots mundane utilitarian items. If so, large amounts of pottery in a grave would not have conveyed social superiority.[37]

Occasionally two people, often of the same sex, were buried together.[38] Most likely they were blood relatives, as kinship constituted the primary social tie. Sometimes, however, a man and woman were buried in the same grave. Although these pairs may have been spouses, archaeologists assume that they were more likely siblings or other close blood kin. Overall, mixed sex burial eventually went into abeyance. In some places, the number of dual burials gradually increased but never became the most common mortuary practice.[39] Some joint graves contain burial goods, most likely common property of the deceased.[40]

Some communities buried large numbers of people of different ages and sexes together in large pits. At the Yangshao Banpo site and elsewhere, ash pits used to burn or bury sacrifices to the deceased surround large common graves. Funeral rites seem to have been undertaken by the entire community.[41] The number of people buried together in each pit varied. In the Shijia phase (4300–4000) of Yangshao, each pit held between three and eighty skeletons, with an average of twenty. Osteological analysis has revealed shared phenotypic traits among the skeletons in each grave, which differed from the skeletons in other pits. In other words, people were interred with their blood relatives, and each pit contained an extended family or the members of one branch of a clan. The fact that a woman was buried with her natal kin instead of her husband's relatives suggests that the community considered the marriage bond less important than blood kinship.[42]

In some places, people practiced secondary burial, temporarily interring a body in one place until the flesh decayed, then moving the denuded skeleton to a final resting place. The remains of both men and

Figure 2.2. Pit Burial
Zhang Chi, "Yangshao wenhua xingsheng shiqi de zangyi," Kaogu yu wenwu 6 (2012): 21.

women were sometimes given a secondary burial. Treating both sexes similarly after death suggests that they held fairly equal positions in life.[43]

Increasing social complexity eventually sent egalitarianism into decline. Individuals and groups began to take on different roles and hierarchical statuses. As social identity became more diverse, pit and secondary burial declined and single burial became the norm. The emergence of single burial of the deceased shows an emphasis on individual identity, which began to vary. Rising inequality spurred social development, allowing people to occupy different social roles. In assuming different roles, people performed increasingly specialized tasks, allowing a community to become more productive and undertake projects of greater scope and difficulty.

A few women benefited from initial stratification and assumed a privileged position. Archaeologists have unearthed the tomb of a Dawenkou woman that is far larger and more richly furnished than the average burial in the area. Her grave goods include the most finely crafted objects in the entire cemetery. This woman clearly held an elevated status and might even have been the highest ranking person in her community.[44]

The Yangshao cemetery at Yuanjunmiao reveals traces of a very different type of female privilege. Although this site has relatively few children, most child graves belong to girls. Some girls received a more elaborate burial than the adults interred in the same cemetery, and were laid to rest with lavish quantities of pottery and ornaments. Archaeologists speculate that these girls may have served as shamans and enjoyed a high position due to a unique religious role.[45] Alternatively, elaborate child graves might show the emergence of hereditary ranks. Young girls would not yet have had the opportunity to distinguish themselves with individual achievements, so their elevated status might have come from association with a prestigious family or clan.[46]

In spite of a few examples of women who assumed high positions, growing social inequality depressed female status overall by spurring the rise of patriarchy. In this era the sexes began to assume extremely different degrees of wealth and power. Within a clan or family, the authority of each spouse depends largely on the value of contributed resources.[47] Because men controlled access to staple food, they assumed preeminince in the domestic sphere. Outside the home, men monopolized prestigious ranks and roles and relegated women to lesser positions.[48] Men also began to take control of the products of female labor.[49] These developments spurred the emergence of patriarchy, also described as sexual stratification, sexual asymmetry, and gender hierarchy.[50] Divergence in the power and prestige of each sex marked the beginning of a long-term trend that would have fateful consequences for women, affecting gender relations down to the present day.

The mortuary treatment of women and men became more distinct in the Middle Neolithic period, reflecting the increasing importance of gender to social identity. In some cemeteries, the bodies of people of each sex are arranged in the grave in different positions. For example, in some dual Dawenkou graves, a man is laid out straight in the center of the grave and a woman's body lies in a flexed position by his side.[51] Other Dawenkou burials have a man lying on his left side and a woman on her right side.[52] In a group of burials from the Majiahong culture (5000–4000 BCE), all of the male bodies are flexed with limbs extended. However, female bodies are arranged in a variety of ways: 62.5 percent straight, 25 percent flexed, and 12.5 percent on their side.[53] Although the connotations of these burial arrangements cannot be known, people in these communities clearly assumed that men and women should be treated differently after death. Because each sex was buried in distinct ways, presumably they were also treated differently while alive.

Figure 2.3. Middle Neolithic Ornaments
Original drawing by Allen Y. Yu.

At some burial sites, the remains of men far outnumber those of women. For example, most of the skeletons at the Shijia site in Shaanxi are male.[54] Initially pit burials at the Yangshao Jiangzhai site in Shaanxi had roughly equal numbers of men and women. But in later eras, the ratio of men to women increased to 1.68:1. At the Yangshao era Yuanjunmiao cemetery, also in Shaanxi, men outnumber women by 1.5:1. At the Dawenkou Sanlihe site in Shandong the ratio of male to female remains is 1.65:1.[55] And at many cemeteries containing secondary burials, male skeletons far outnumber female remains, sometimes by a large margin.[56] The reason for the decline in female burials remains a mystery. Perhaps mourning customs varied according to age, and women tended to die younger than men due to the dangers of childbirth. If so, this would explain the different postmortem treatment of the sexes. However, most likely funeral rites had begun to vary according to sex, and the remains of men received more elaborate handling after death.

Differences in the richness of burial goods further attest to male ascendency in the Middle Neolithic. Dawenkou graves of men contain far more items than those of women. For example, among a sample of graves from Dawenkou period I, women have an average of twelve burial items whereas men have twenty-three. In a mortuary group from period II, women have twenty-two items and men have thirty-five.[57] The difference in burial goods suggests that men enjoyed a higher status and controlled more wealth than women.

Evidence from northwest China reveals a strikingly similar trend. At the Banpo site, men had more of every kind of grave item.[58] In phase I of the site, men had 1.93 times more burial goods than women. And in phase II male graves had 2.89 times as many objects. Moreover, only male graves contain luxury goods such as jade and turtle shell. None of these valuables have been found with female remains. Men controlled the rarest objects, which presumably symbolized power and status. As in other regions of the world, luxury goods were likely used when conducting ceremonies. So by monopolizing ritual paraphanalia, men could exclude women from prestigious rites.[59]

Social stratification eventually gave rise to a highly privileged elite who controlled much of the community's resources. Some tombs begin to stand out from the rest by their size and rich contents, and almost all of these belong to men. Among a group of elite tombs from the Shijia area, all except one contains male remains.[60] Changing mortuary practices show that as social differentiation fostered hierarchy, men monopolized the highest ranks. In sum, growing social complexity fostered patriarchy in two ways: giving men a higher status than women overall, and reserving the highest positions for men.

During the Late Neolithic era, exemplified by the widespread Longshan culture, much larger and more densely populated settlements emerged in north China.[61] Some nascent urban centers became more important than others and served as the focus of religious, military, and administrative activities, as well as the redistribution of resources. People in rival settlements frequently fought to control wealth, land, and people, making war an important activity. Late Neolithic graves often contain weapons, and urban centers have high walls and other defensive facilities. Warfare and large-scale building projects attest to the rise of government institutions and a political elite.

Not only did settlements diverge in importance, but each community became increasingly stratified as well. Some kinship groups controlled more power, prestige, or wealth than others, so people assumed different ranks. Chiefs ruled some settlements with the aid of key followers who constitued a hereditary elite. Some chiefs used war, exchange, and ceremony to dominate surrounding areas. By either conquering their neighbors or else enticing them to participate in a more advanced system, ambitious men established embryonic polities.

Some aspects of gender relations show an intensification of earlier trends. As division of labor intensified, specialized occupations emerged. For example, professional potters achieved a high level of technical prowess, manufacturing opulent ceramics. Leaders used exceptional ceramics and other luxury goods to symbolize their elevated status. As in archaic polities elsewhere, men usually owned more prestige goods than women.[62] Elite men also exerted increasing control over society's productive capacity. Because men tended to dominate the most important social, political, and economic roles, as well as the items symbolizing high status, intensifying stratification and division of labor widened the gap between the sexes.[63]

Men and women continued to perform different tasks. As before, male graves often have agricultural tools while those of women contain items relating to textile production.[64] As population density increased, hunting and gathering declined into marginal activities.[65] Men working in the grain fields provided most of the food supply. Late Neolithic peoples also consumed many kinds of domesticated animals, including pigs, dogs, water buffalo, and cattle. Women may have had a hand in animal husbandry, as people probably raised animals close to the home.[66]

Life expectancy shifted during the Late Stone Age. Although data from earlier eras suggest roughly equal life spans for both sexes, during the Late Neolithic women tended to die at a younger age than men. Analysis of graves from the Majiayao culture (3100–2700 BCE) in west China indicates that women had a shorter life expectancy. Not only did they face the dangers of pregnancy and childbirth, but they probably had access to fewer key resources than men.[67] So as the social positions of the sexes diverged and men gained more control over food and manufactured items, female life span contracted in comparison with men.

Comparative studies of a large number of Neolithic sites from across China show that male remains generally outnumber those of women by a wide margin.[68] Because women tended to die earlier, some may not have receive a formal burial due to their youth.[69] But most importantly, the decreasing number of female graves likely reflects a general decline in women's status. As society stratified, women lost prestige, so they were likely less likely to qualify for full mortuary treatment.

Due to social stratification, Late Neolithic graves varied in size and richness. In many cemeteries, people of each rank were buried very differently. Some cemeteries even contain two or more distinct sections that segregated people of different status. For example the Taosi site (2300–1900 BCE), dating to the cusp between the Late Neolithic and the the Bronze Age, has a few large and lavish tombs, but about 90 percent of graves consist of single burials of the simplest kind.[70] Sometimes subsidiary burials surround a large tomb, presumably containing the occupant's dependents and subordinates.[71] Large tombs almost always contain the remains of a man, whereas subsidiary burials are often women and children.

Not only did fewer women receive formal burial than before, but more female remains are positioned in ways that seem to have been intended to express inferiority.[72] In cemeteries of the Qijia culture (2200–1600 BCE) of the upper Yellow River region, male bodies are laid out straight whereas those of women are flexed and often placed facing a man. Archaeologists speculate that this pose might represent female subservience. Some graves contain the remains of one man and multiple women, perhaps attesting to concubinage or polygyny.

Late Neolithic peoples buried their dead in various ways. Although individual burial became increasingly common, sometimes groups of relatives were buried in proximity, emphasizing the enduring importance of blood kinship to social identity.[73] The practice of dual burials of one man and one woman emerged at different times in each region.[74] The Dawenkou culture (3500–2400 BCE) in the east had different-sex burials relatively early, followed by the Majiayao culture (2600–2000 BCE) to the west. Frequent joint burial of a woman and man developed even later in other places. The appearance of male-female burial seems to have been related to fundamental changes in the underlying relations between the sexes, attesting to the growing importance of the marital bond.

In some dual sex burials, the woman and man are laid out in a similar fashion. For example, one tomb from the Keshengzhuang culture of the Wei River valley, dated to about 2400–2000 BCE, contains the remains of a man and a woman.[75] They were placed in the grave in comparable

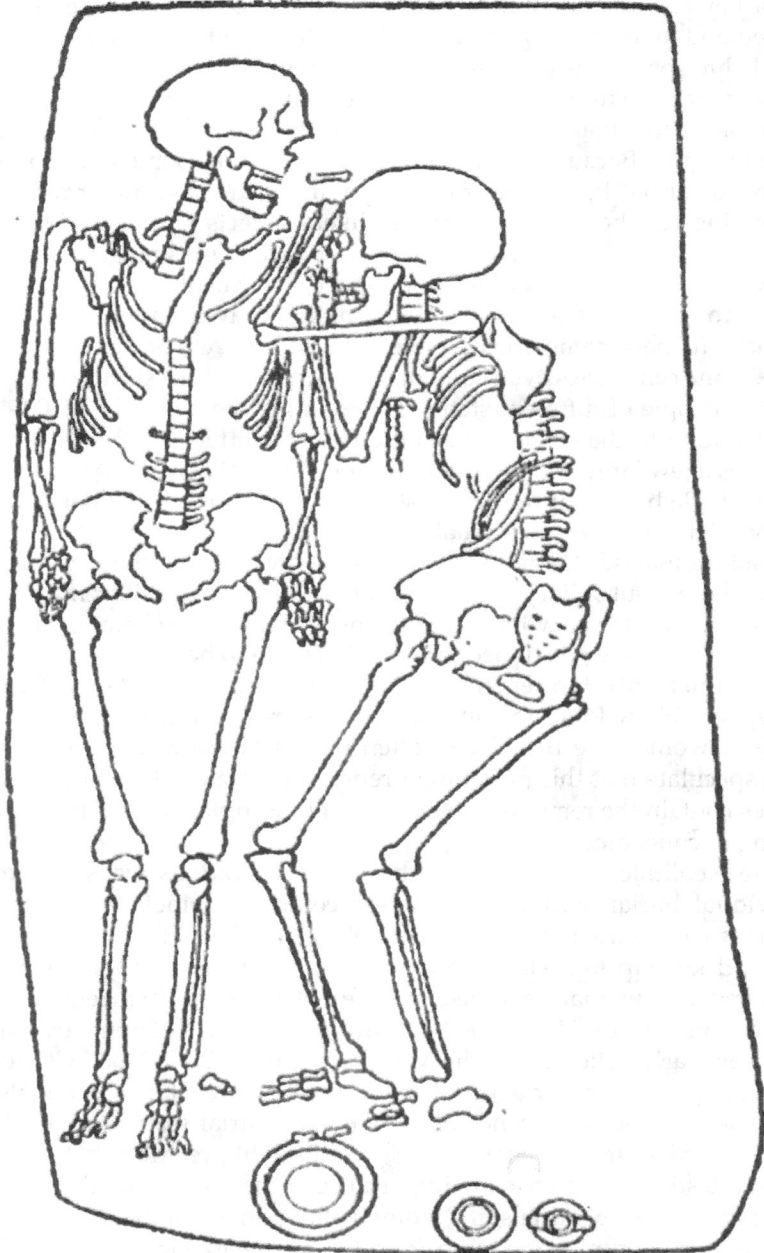

Figure 2.4. Dual Burial of Man (extended) and Woman (flexed)
Zhongguo Kexueyuan Kaogu Yanjiusuo Gansu gongzuodui, "Gansu Yongjing Qinweijia Qijia wenhua mudi" Kaogu xuebao 2 (1975): 65.

positions and accompanied by six pottery vessels. And at a pair of graves at a Majiayao site, a woman and man were each interred with one half of a broken ceramic ewer. Although this pair may have been brother and sister, archaeologists assume that they were most likely spouses, and speculate that the sharing of pieces of a pottery vessel may have symbolized the spousal bond.[76]

Sometimes a man was interred with two or more women, implying polygyny or concubinage. For example, one medium-sized grave in the Taosi cemetery contains the remains of a man and two women, one aged about twenty-five and the other between thirty-five and forty years old.[77] Likewise, many of the mixed-sex graves of the Qijia culture contain a man and two women.[78] It seems that some men had already begun to use their authority over multiple women to demonstrate status and power.[79]

In many dual graves, male and female bodies were laid out differently.[80] In some Qijia graves, the man lies prone whereas the woman's knees are flexed and facing him, which might represent a subservient pose. In other graves from the same culture, the man is encoffined while a woman rests to the side without a coffin of her own. Large Taosi tombs always contain the remains of a man, with women buried alongside in medium-sized or small graves as subsidiary burials.[81]

Growing social complexity affected views of religion and the afterlife, giving rise to more elaborate beliefs and rituals. Toward the end of the Neolithic, some communities began to worship ancestors. Over time the focus of ancestor worship gradually altered.[82] Instead of conducting sacrifices to large groups of deceased kin, people increasingly focused their devotions on a small number of high-status individuals. And in place of rituals conducted by the community at large, a small elite gradually took over the ancestral cult. These changes affected the ritual attention given to deceased women. When the community offered sacrifices to all deceased kin, they venerated female ancestors alongside male counterparts. But as attention shifted toward a small number of key male ancestors, the importance of female forebears receded.

The level of social development in each region remained extremely uneven. Although some communities had become considerably more complex and unequal, others maintained simple egalitarian customs and made few distinctions between women and men. For example, the Majiayao culture interred their deceased in many different ways. Regardless of how a person was buried, however, the number of items in each grave was roughly similar, showing that this society had yet to stratify.[83] And in the Liangzhu culture (3400–2500 BC), women as well as men were buried with jade items.[84]

Yet in spite of lingering sexual egalitarianism in some places, many societies became extremely unequal as the Neolithic era drew to a close, with some groups rising in prominence as others fell into subservience. Stratification did not have a uniformly negative impact on women. A few elite women achieved high status, as reflected by some lavish female tombs. For example, one large and richly furnished tomb at the Dadianzi site in Inner Mongolia belonged to a woman who died in her early twenties.[85] In spite of her youth, she enjoyed a high position in her society. However, high-ranking women were the exception. In general, as social identities diverged, prestige accrued to elite men. Female status increasingly came from a woman's connection with her father or husband.

In this unequal milieu, the elite used conspicuous consumption, luxury, and deliberate waste to elevate their status. For example, privileged groups buried their dead with numerous opulent items to signal their lofty status to the rest of the community.[86] As luxury goods increased in number and importance, they became closely associated with the male elite. Prestigious and ritually significant jade objects such as battle axes and stone tubes (*cong*) were almost exclusively interred with men.[87] A Longshan site in Henan exemplifies this trend. One burial contains the remains of a woman aged thirty-five to forty.[88] Although she was accompanied with an array of pottery vessels, the nearby tombs of men are much more lavishly furnished. Male and female burials from the Qijia culture in west China also show clear disparity.[89] And at the Taosi site, men have far more grave goods than women.[90]

The tomb of a man of the Liangzhu culture in the Suzhou area exemplifies the growing difference in gendered status. He was buried with numerous jade items as well as finely crafted ceramic and stone goods. Nearby are two subsidiary graves of women. Archaeologists believe that these women were considered just another kind of burial good, akin to fine jade, and were killed and placed in the grave to symbolize the man's rank.[91]

The Dadianzi cemetery exhibits a clear distinction between the sexes, as male graves are larger and more elaborately furnished than those for women.[92] Moreover, the economic status of each woman seems to have been related to that of nearby men. Apparently men and women acquired status and resources in different ways. While men seem to have achieved a higher status through their activities, or perhaps through inheritance, a woman's status came from her association with blood kin or a husband.

Human sacrifice presents the most extreme evidence of prehistoric stratification. Because Early Neolithic society was relatively egalitarian, it would have been unthinkable to kill one person so as to elevate the status of another. But as people acquired extremely unequal ranks, the elite gained immense authority over those at the bottom of society. Eventually the most powerful people could kill dependents during the most important rituals, such as funeral ceremonies. Only when a society becomes

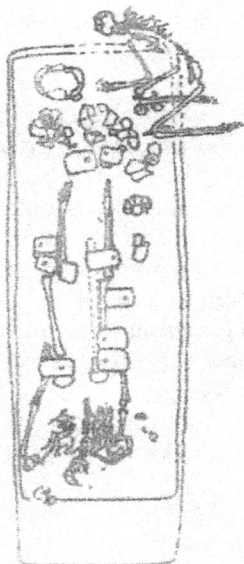

Figure 2.5. Tomb Showing the Sacrifice of a Woman (flexed) to a Man (Extended)
Zhao Ye, "Liangzhu wenwu renxun renji xianxiang shixi," Nanfang wenwu 1 (2001): 32.

sufficiently complex does human sacrifice emerge, so this practice characterizes a highly unequal prehistoric society ruled by a powerful elite. Societies around the world practiced human sacrifices, but the meanings attributed to these rituals varied according to the cultural context, so the precise meanings of human sacrifice in Neolithic East Asia remain unclear.[93] Whatever the putative significance of human sacrifice, it was extremely useful to those at the apex of society. This practice symbolized a leader's political authority and his right to appropriate resources. It reinforced a steep social hierarchy. And the right to kill people of lower status provided the elite with a potent tool for punishing insubordination.[94]

Murdering human beings to accompany high ranking people in death seems to have developed out of animal sacrifices to the deceased, which became common in some places during the Late Neolithic and Early Bronze ages. At Taosi, both men and women were sometimes buried with pigs.[95] Graves at some sites linked to the Erlitou culture (1900–1500 BCE) contain women buried with pig legs and rabbits.[96] And at the Late Neolithic Dadianzi cemetery, dogs appear exclusively in male graves whereas the remains of pigs are found with both men and women. Overall, men buried at this site received about 50 percent more animal sacrifices than women.[97]

The sacrifice of animals to the dead eventually developed into human sacrifice.[98] Women were often the victims. A Liangzhu tomb presents a typical example.[99] In addition to the remains of a twenty-five-year-old man and thirty-nine burial items, this tomb also contains a subsidiary burial of a woman of the same age who lacked any grave goods except for the jade ornaments she was wearing. Her body was positioned at the man's feet in a submissive pose. Archaeologists assume she was killed and added to the man's grave as a sacrifice to his spirit. Sometimes the Liangzhu placed a murdered person in the grave alongside a pig or dog, emphasizing the analogous roles of human and animal in the sacrificial cult.[100] Archaeologists assume that the victims of human sacrifice were people that the deceased had dominated in life, such as a wife, concubines, children, officials, slaves, or captives.

Many Late Neolithic cultures practiced human sacrifice, often killing women to bury them with important men. Some graves at Qijia sites have

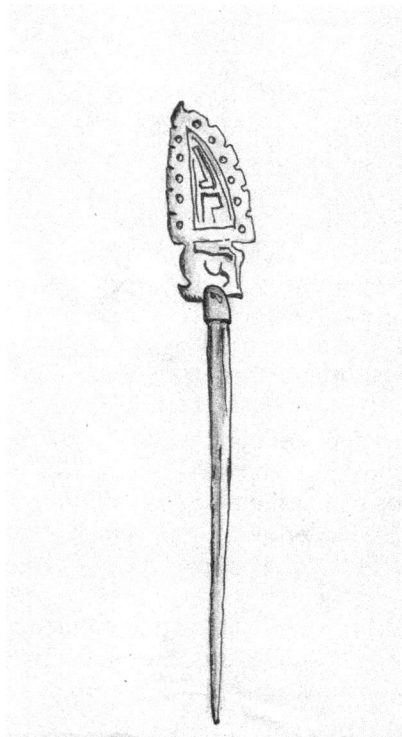

Figure 2.6. Shang Dynasty Bone Hairpin
Original drawing by Allen Y. Yu.

human sacrifices, usually children and women. These female human sacrifices seem to have been buried at the same time as the man. Sometimes a woman was decapitated prior to burial.[101] Cemeteries at Late Dawenkou sites have analogous human sacrifices, also mostly women and children.[102] The emergence of human sacrifice in various regions shows that as society entered the Bronze Age, social stratification intensified gender distinctions.

3

‿

Shang Dynasty

During the Early Bronze Age, society changed in myriad ways and became extremely unequal. People high and low inherited their status, and birth mattered more than age or gender in apprortioning one's overall position in society. Administrative institutions advanced to the point that a talented leader could form and maintain a large polity. In some places a small hereditary elite wielded immense authority over the mass of commoners. The most successful of these nascent states gradually expanded to become the Shang dynasty (ca. 1600–1046 BCE). The Shang exercised hegemony over much of the north China region, where they created the most sophisticated civilization ever seen in East Asia. Shang aristocrats constructed cities, waged war, invented writing, conducted elaborate religious rituals, and surrounded themselves with impressive luxury goods.

The origins of the Shang state remain shrouded in mystery.[1] Perhaps leaders expanded their realm by enticing others to participate in a superior political framework. More likely, however, they probably used the strategy employed by other archaic states and extended their borders primarily through conquest. Kinship bonds held the Shang polity together. Nobles served as clan elders, providing them with power and wealth. A noble lorded over a domain inhabited by clan members who worked, worshipped, and even went into battle together.

The Shang invented a complicated script that they used for religious and commemorative purposes. Kings communicated with their ancestors by scratching messages on bone and turtle shell. In addition, the nobility etched names and short statements on treasured bronze ritual vessels.

Some characters include a female component (*nü* 女). Most of these feminized terms are proper names that disappeared from the written language
after the end of the dynasty.[2] However, later scribes retained useful characters with a female component, and these became part of the standard
Chinese script. The orthography, etymology, and uses of ancient characters offer clues about early attitudes toward women. Modern characters
that contain a female radical, most of which date back to antiquity, consist
of four types. About a quarter are kinship terms. Many others denote
objects and activities closely associated with women, such as childbirth.
A third category conveys stereotypically female attributes such as beauty
and grace. A final set expresses negative concepts such as ugliness, adultery, jealousy, inferiority, and betrayal.[3]

As in other parts of the world, religious imagery conveyed society's
gender values. Ancient Chinese had little interest in goddess worship.

Figure 3.1.   Characteristic Shang Characters with a Female (*nü*) Component
Original drawing by Allen Y. Yu.

Some scholars have asserted that sacrifices held at an earthen alter (*she* 社) grew out the worship of a primal Earth Mother, but they lack any substantive evidence for this claim.[4] More promisingly, oracle inscriptions mention that the king of Shang sacrificed to two deities called Eastern Mother (Dongmu) and Western Mother (Ximu).[5] In spite of the parallel names, the Shang almost always worshipped these two goddesses separately and do not seem to have considered them a linked pair. Some specialists have suggested that Eastern Mother may have represented the sun (which rises in the east) and Western Mother the moon, although this interpretation remains pure speculation. Others have alleged that the Han dynasty goddess Xiwangmu (Queen Mother of the West) evolved out of the primal Ximu (Western Mother).[6] However, an immense gap of eight or nine centuries separates references to these two deities, so their similar names are likely a coincidence.

Like their male counterparts, noblewomen and royal consorts spent much of their time conducting a wide array of religious ceremonies.[7] Some rituals marked special occasions, such as sacrifices undertaken when an army marched off to war or rites held to ward off disaster. Women performed other rituals at regular intervals, including ceremonies to worship nature deities. Most ancestors and deities were either male or unsexed.[8]

In this age of nascent ideas and institutions, religion provided the most sophisticated body of thought. The Shang applied shamanism to politics. Kings claimed to be able to manipulate supernatural forces, making shamanism into an ideological tool that could bolster their prestige and garner support.[9] The chief shamans were male. Female shamans seem to have mostly specialized in rainmaking rites.[10] As usual, whenever a practice became useful, men took control.

Early Bronze Age society comprised a steep hierarchy, and women of each rank lived very differently.[11] The king and major aristocrats, who concurrently served as leaders of important clans, occupied the highest positions. Minor nobility made up the mid-level elite. Most people were commoners who lived near their extended kin in small rural communities ruled by clan leaders and nobles. At the very bottom of society, slaves and captives suffered a debased status.

Many slaves were female. The Shang often enslaved enemy women captured in war.[12] Foreign peoples also sent in female slaves to the king as tribute.[13] The Shang lacked a general term for slave. They called the lowliest people by various terms, and the nuances of these appellations remain unclear. The nobility treated slave women as chattel and exchanged them as gifts alongside luxury goods. For example, one inscription records a gift of "many women" together with strings of cowries, which the land-locked Shang considered rare and valuable.[14]

The diet, dwellings, tools, and basic lifestyle of the common people had changed little since the Neolithic period. Excavations of ordinary homes in Anyang, the last Shang capital, revealed extremely simple dwellings with subterranean foundations similar to Stone Age prototypes.[15] Shang commoners constructed their houses in a standard rectangular layout, with each having between one and five rooms. These simple dwellings had only the most rudimentary facilities, such as a dedicated space for storage and a spot for cooking.

As during the Neolithic, most people died relatively young. A man or woman who survived infancy might live into their thirties. The average male commoner residing in Anyang lived to about age thirty-three and women to twenty-nine.[16] Given this low life expectancy, most of a female commoner's close relatives would have been dead by the time she turned

Figure 3.2. Shang Script Documents Male Domination of Agriculture. The character *nan* 男 (left), meaning man, depicts a hoe and field. Husband (*fu* 夫, right) shows a hand holding the sort of stone axe used to clear virgin land.

twenty.[17] In contrast, the elite seems to have lived much longer, benefiting from a superior diet and an advantageous way of life.

A woman's appearance depended on her rank. While ordinary women probably dressed very simply, elaborate clothing marked the noble-woman's high station.[18] A jade figurine of a female aristocrat depicts her wearing a robe ornamented with heavy silk brocade panels that hang down in front. This impractical garb made it clear to everyone that, unlike most women, she did not perform domestic chores. Noble ladies wore their hair in elaborate coifs held together with numerous pins. The tombs of elite women contain immense numbers of hairpins carved from jade, ivory, and bone.

While women from elite families held an elevated status vis-à-vis ordinary people, it seems that the Shang considered women lower than men overall. Cemeteries contain very different numbers of male and female graves for people of every social stratum.[19] Regardless of a woman's social station, she was less likely to receive a formal burial than a male counterpart. At one cemetery for high-status people, burials of men exceed those of women by a ratio of two to one. And at a burial site for the mid-ranking elite, male remains outnumber female 1.55:1. The same disparity can be seen in the graves of ordinary people. At two cemeteries for commoners, men outnumber women by between 1.25:1 and 1.5:1. Presumably the discrepancy in the number of formal burials reflects attitudes toward the overall worth of people of each sex.

Although Neolithic peoples experimented with many different types of burials, the Shang standardized funeral customs. People interred in proximity tended to receive similar treatment.[20] Over time, elite funerals became increasingly elaborate. Late Shang burials consisted of three main types, which differed according to the rank of the deceased.[21] Large and medium-sized tombs often have one or more entrance ramps leading down to a chamber that contained the deceased, who was encased in one or two coffins. These tombs contain items symbolizing high status, such as bronze vessels, jade objects, and even human and animal sacrificial victims. Deceased members of the lower elite were interred inside a coffin, which was sometimes surrounded by an additional outer coffin. These burials usually have some simple funerary goods such as pottery vessels. A small number include bronze weapons, bronze ritual vessels, or one or two human sacrifices. During the Late Shang, commoners had an extremely simple burial. The deceased was wrapped in a woven mat and lowered into a pit. At most, deceased commoners might be accompanied by one or two pottery vessels.

Most people were buried singly.[22] Women were almost always buried face up, while men were buried either face up or face down.[23] Otherwise,

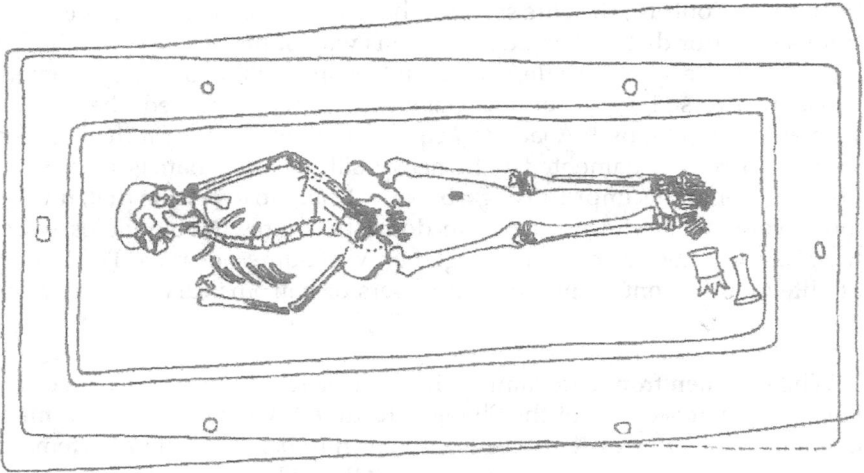

Figure 3.3.   Tomb M207, Individual Burial of a Woman
Yinxu Xiaomintun Kaogudui, Henan Anyang shi Xiaomintun Shangdai muzang 2003–2004 nian fajue jianbao, Kaogu 1 (2007): 35.

women were not buried differently from men of comparable status, but
were interred in a manner that reflected their social rank.[24] Female commoners either received no formal burial or else were placed in a simple
pit grave without a coffin. Mid-ranking women might be buried in a
coffin together with some pottery ritual vessels.[25] Noblewomen received
elaborate burials. A representative noble tomb houses the skeleton of a
woman between age fifty and fifty-five, which was originally enclosed in
a cloth-covered coffin.[26] Her burial goods included two pottery vessels, a
stone battle axe (symbolizing rank), and ornaments made of stone, shell,
and jade.

The highest status women had extremely grand tombs. One Late Shang
noblewoman, aged thirty-five to forty, was buried with ninety items
made from bronze, jade, shell, and bone, including an array of prestigious
bronze ritual vessels and weapons.[27] A large tomb in Jiangxi contains
encoffined skeletal remains, apparently female, together with 475 items
made of bronze, 754 of jade, as well as other prestige objects.[28] A shrine
constructed above the tomb provided a place for descendants to conduct
rituals in honor of the deceased.[29]

Joint spousal burial did not become standard until the Zhou dynasty.[30]
Although the Shang did not inter married couples together in the same
pit, they were often buried side-by-side in a pair of complementary
graves.[31] Usually they placed the man on the left side and the woman to
the right.[32] Spousal burial was common among ordinary people. These

humble paired graves suggest that although the elite practiced polygyny, commoners were monogamous. Men and women of the highest status were buried singly, usually at a distance from their spouse. In some cases, subsidiary burials of male and female dependents surround the tomb of an important man.[33] These satellite graves probably contain the remains of servants, relatives, or minor spouses. Most dependents were female, suggesting that numerous women waited on a man of importance.

The Shang continued to practice human sacrifice. Although some Neolithic peoples had occasionally killed children or low-ranking people to accompany the dead, this form of burial was never common. During the Shang dynasty, however, human sacrifice became a regular feature of important tombs and a standard way to denote the high status of the deceased.[34] Sacrificial victims did not always die together. Sometimes they were killed over time and gradually added to a major tomb.[35]

Some sacrificial victims were female.[36] For example, a pit at the site of an Early Shang capital at Zhengzhou contains four victims, including two girls aged between fifteen and seventeen.[37] And a pit near a major Late Shang tomb at Anyang contains the remains of three women together with the skeletons of horses.[38] The joint sacrifice of low-status women and horses implies that the elite considered them analogous chattel. Long after the deceased had been laid to rest, descendants sometimes killed a woman as a sacrificial offering to the spirit of an ancestor. An inscription on a bronze vessel records the sacrifice of two women to a group of ancestors.[39]

Unfortunately, archaeologists have not bothered to determine the sex of most sacrificial victims, so the gender ratio remains unclear. Although the Shang sometimes sacrificed women, it seems that they did not favor them for this rite. Many victims were young men. One typical tomb contains nine sacrificial victims, all mature men. Most likely they were enemy warriors captured during battle.[40] It seems that the Shang often sacrificed male prisoners of war and enslaved female captives.[41]

Some sacrificial pits contain large numbers of female victims. Two large pits in the royal cemetery district of Anyang contain the remains of more than thirteen hundred victims. The earlier pit contains mostly men, whereas women and children predominate in the later one.[42] However, this sort of mass burial of women was exceptional. In most large pit burials, male victims far outnumber women. One typical sacrificial pit contains 370 victims, consisting of 319 men and fifty-one women, a ratio of 6.3:1. In another pit grave with 1,178 sacrificial victims, the ratio of men to women is 9.7:1.[43]

In addition to evidence from mortuary archaeology, writings on bone, turtle shell, and bronze provide information about female lives. Inscriptional evidence reveals the complex system of names and titles used by

Shang women. Although a man had a relatively stable identity, an elite woman was called by various names and titles that were adjusted according to her stage of life and her relationship with the person addressing her.[44] Because links to blood and marital relatives underpinned a woman's identity, female names often employed kinship terms.

A female name sometimes consisted of a single character. Sometimes a woman was simply called by a given name such as Mei, Huang, or Xun.[45] About 80 percent of the characters used as women's names include a female radical.[46] Many of these characters did not ordinarily have the female component; scribes added it to feminize a character and make it more suitable for use as a woman's name.[47] More complex names consisted of a combination of two or more characters.[48] The initial character expressed an aspect of a woman's identity, such as her place of birth, clan marker, or a kinship term, followed by her given name. Sometimes writers inverted the order of the characters and put her personal name first.

The Shang called both female and male children *zi* 子. Inscriptions refer to a particular child by the formula *zi-x*, combining the general term for child with a specific name.[49] The use of the same term for boys and girls suggests that the Shang considered gender distinctions fairly unimport-

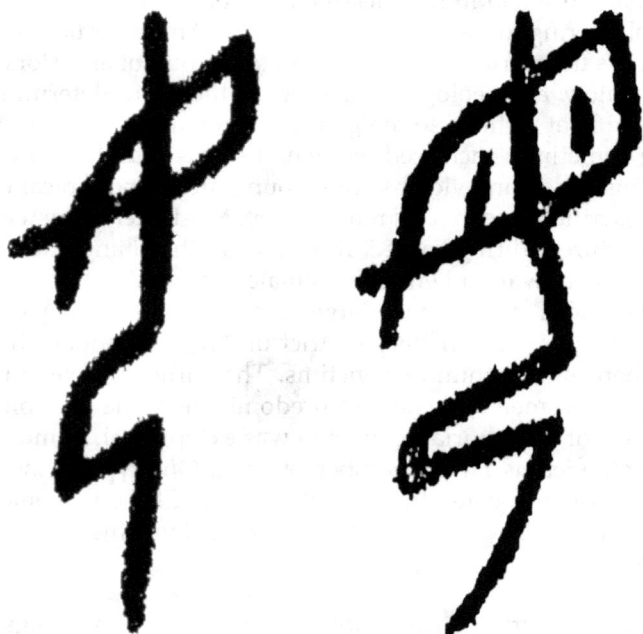

Figure 3.4. *Nü* 女 (left) Depicts a Kneeling Woman. *Mu* 母 (right) Is a Kneeling Woman with Accentuated Breasts.

ant during childhood. Several inscriptions inquire after the pregnancies of people called zi-x, showing that a woman could maintain the childish appellation zi into adulthood, even after men had abandoned it.[50] Perhaps the Shang thought that a name that included zi sounded diminutive and endearing.

Women were often called *nü* 女.[51] This graph appears independently, in conjunction with other characters, and also as a component in more complex characters. In later eras this term meant woman or daughter, but the Shang used it differently. *Nü* often appears on bronze vessels given by parents to a daughter or commissioned by a woman herself, so x-*nü* could refer to a wife.[52] Nevertheless, the term was usually associated with younger women. Scribes sometimes combined *nü* and *zi* to form *nüzi*, although the meaning of this compound remains unclear.[53]

Although the orthography of *nü* depicts a kneeling woman, this pose did not necessarily convey depressed status. In an era long before the invention of chairs, everyone sat on the floor, and kneeling figures often have positive connotations in Shang orthography.[54] Some female figures in ancient mythology were called *nü-x*, inverting the usual order of name and title. The use of this character in the name of the goddess Nü Wa suggests that *nü* carried neither diminutive nor pejorative connotations.[55] In sum, *nü* seems to have been an ambiguous term that could refer to a woman, girl, mother, female deity, or the spouses of deceased kings and nobles.[56]

The Shang also called women *mu* 母.[57] In later eras *mu* meant mother, but during the Shang dynasty a young woman could be a *mu* before marriage.[58] The characters *nü* and *mu* look very similar in oracle script, and initially their meanings were probably closely related.[59] Inscriptions often use *nü* and *mu* interchangeably, and scribes sometimes united them to create the compound *nümu*.[60] Many names contain either *nü* or *mu* together with another character, resulting in the appellation x-*nü* or x-*mu*. The initial character often identified a noblewoman's clan or natal domain.[61] Also, children often referred to their deceased mother as *mu*.[62]

Scribes also sometimes combined *mu* with the ambiguous term *hou* 后 to produce a name for a high-status woman, such as *hou mu* x or *hou* x *mu*.[63] During the Zhou dynasty *hou* meant queen and became incorporated into the system of titles, but at this stage it does not seem to have denoted a specific post or status. Instead it referred in general terms to a high-ranking person.[64] Perhaps *hou mu* meant "mother of the heir."

Although the closely related characters *nü* and *mu* appear in many inscriptions, the Shang most commonly called elite women *fu* (帚 or 婦).[65] In subsequent eras this character simply meant wife, but the Shang used it differently. Philologists spent decades debating the identity of people called *fu*. Given the importance of *fu*, experts initially assumed that some of them were men, but over time it became clear that all *fu* were female.⁶⁶ These women were important figures. Numerous divinations express concern for the wellbeing of *fu*. Kings inquired about matters such as sickness, whether she would encounter disaster, and her safety while traveling.⁶⁷ Other divinations sought information about a pregnancy. Inquiries frequently asked whether she should conduct a particular sacrificial ritual.

Several kinds of women held the title *fu*. The most prominent were married to the king.⁶⁸ A Shang king held his wife in high regard. Not only did she command respect as a royal consort, but she also had powerful kinsmen and her own domain.⁶⁹ Marriage cemented the bond between the king and his wife's clan, making her the intermediary between two powerful forces in Shang society. A royal consort came to the capital accompanied by an entourage from her natal clan, and sometimes these retainers became involved in affairs of state, further bolstering her position.

Not all *fu* were royal spouses, but all of them seem to have been married and enjoyed high status.⁷⁰ In a number of inscriptions, a king inquires whether he should love the children of a particular *fu* like his own.⁷¹ These women were clearly not his wives, so besides royal spouses, other elite women could be called *fu* as well. Some *fu* seem to have been a king's sister or the wife of his brother or son. Others belonged to prominent families or clans.⁷² And some were wives of high officials.⁷³ For example, one inscription refers to the "*fu* of Shi Ban," a prominent military officer. In this case, his wife seems to have been called by the honorific title *fu* due to her husband's rank.⁷⁴ The wives of Shang aristocrats and foreign nobles could also be called *fu*. About a quarter of *fu* women had a character referring to a foreign place in their name, and these women were probably the daughters of foreign leaders who intermarried with the Shang nobility.⁷⁵

Some *fu* undertook administrative or ritual duties, making them somewhat analogous to male officials.⁷⁶ Given the primitive state of the Shang bureaucratic system, officials usually had vague responsibilities and authority. The king often empowered a trusted person to temporarily serve as an official and carry out a particular mission on an ad hoc basis. A temporary official title would expire after the task had been completed. The informality of this emerging administrative system gave women opportunities to exercise authority. Inscriptions mention "many *chen*" (*duo chen* 多臣) in tandem with "many *fu*" (*duo fu* 多帚), suggesting that the two groups may have had analogous roles. In later eras, *chen* could refer to either an official or a debased bondservant, so the parallels between *fu* and *chen* do not clarify the status of these women. However, the highest ranking *fu* presented tribute, led armies, and conducted major rituals, demonstrating that *fu* status qualified some women to participate in major affairs of state.

Numerous bronze inscriptions consist of the lone character *fu*. Shang bronze inscriptions tend to be much shorter than those engraved during the Zhou dynasty, and a one-character inscription is not unusual. When used singly, this character might have had one of several meanings. In some one-character inscriptions, *fu* seems to refer to the person who commissioned the vessel. Longer inscriptions have identifying phrases such as "*Fu*-x made this wine vessel," so the lone character *fu* might be an abbreviation of this kind of statement. Alternatively, *fu* might refer to the woman who had been given the vessel by someone else. Or perhaps the single character *fu* might refer to the female ancestor who received the

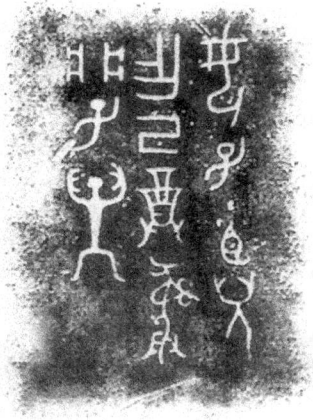

Figure 3.5. Shang Bronze Inscriptions Mentioning Women
Chen Yingjie, "Shangdai jinwen zhong zhi 'nüzi' mingci shuolue," Kaogu yu wenwu 4 (2010): 105.

sacrifices conducted using this vessel. A longer inscription reads "conduct the *bin* 賓 sacrifice for Fu Ding and Fu Xin," identifying the recipients of sacrifices made with that vessel. So in some cases, the lone character *fu* may have indicated the intended recipient of sacrifices in a highly abbreviated form.

More often, inscriptions combine *fu* with another character to form a name, such as Fu Dong, Fu Jian, or Fu Xuan. Many personal names contain an added female radical to feminize them. As a result, the famed Fu Hao 婦好 was actually probably named Fu Zi 婦子. Although the addition of a female radical changes the pronunciation of this character from *zi* to *hao* in Mandarin (and from **tsə* to **hû* in Old Chinese), ancient scribes might simply have considered *hao* an alternate way of writing *zi*.[77]

When *fu* appears in a two-character compound name, the other graph probably evoked a characteristic of a woman's husband or father—his clan, rank, profession, name, or place.[78] Sometimes a name combines *fu* together with as many as five other characters, each providing some information about a woman's husband. Because a wife's name stressed her husband's identity, she would have had an entirely different name before marriage.[79] And after she died, her descendants combined *fu* with one of the ten characters from the heavenly stem calendrical cycle (*tiangan*) to construct a posthumous name such as Fu Jia or Fu Ding.

Although the Shang system for constructing female names and terms of address might seem dauntingly complex, it makes sense when seen as a succession of names marking the phases of a woman's life.[80] Because an elite woman derived her social identity from shifting kinship ties and roles, she progressively assumed a series of names and titles. A young girl was called *zi* 子. She became *nü* 女 when older. After she married, her husband called her *fu* 帚, but she was *mu* 母 to her children and *gu* 姑 to her daughter-in-law.[81] Wives were also called *shuang* 爽, *shi* 奭, *qi* 妻, and *qie* 妾.[82] After she died her children worshipped her spirit as *mu* 母 whereas her grandchildren referred to her as *bi* 妣 (ancestress).

The intricate system of female names highlights the importance of marriage and family ties to a woman's selfhood and image. In this respect, men and women differed fundamentally. Although male identity was also tied to kinship, a man's basic position in society did not change when he married or started a family. He had a relatively stable status and identity. In contrast, when a woman wed she assumed a new set of kin, fundamentally altering her primary social ties and changing the way society viewed her.[83]

In later times the status of a son determined that of his mother, but during the Shang the opposite held true. A mother's background had a major impact on her children's social standing. Some oracle inscriptions identify a man as the son of a particular woman, implying that her status influenced his social identity.[84] Because a wife's background affected the social position of a couple's children, it was particularly important for a king or nobleman to marry the right spouse. Shang kings had no choice but to marry down to a woman of inferior background, but marrying too low would degrade their sons.[85] The eldest son of King Di Yi was born to a mother from a low-ranking family, disqualifying him from becoming heir. Instead a younger son, born to a mother from a more important family, inherited the throne.[86]

While commoners were monogamous, elite marriage practices are less clearcut and remain a subject of debate. Some scholars have argued that Shang nobles were also monogamous, others believe that they were polygynous, and a third opinion holds that they alternated between these two systems. Uncertainty over elite kinship stems from the nature of the written sources, which consist mostly of divinatory inscriptions addressed to royal ancestors. A man only conducted sacrifices to his birth mother and not to his father's other consorts, so if a royal consort never had sons or else her son did not become king, the surviving texts would probably not mention her. As a result of lacunae in the sources, the number of wives of each king remains uncertain.[87]

A woman could only have one husband. And in some periods, elite men may have been monogamous.[88] Yet several late Shang kings had more than one consort who received posthumous sacrifices, indicating that they were polygynous. For example, four wives of King Zu Ding gained admission into the royal ancestral cult.[89] Also, some kings simultaneously had two consorts, ranked as primary wife and minor spouse.[90] When viewed from the perspective of Bronze Age societies worldwide, Shang royal polygyny does not seem unusual. Leaders in many places took multiple spouses to symbolize sexual potency and confirm their special standing among men.[91]

Although a man might have had two or more spouses of different ranks, the Shang did not yet formally distinguish between wives and concubines. The terms *qi* 妻 and *qie* 妾, which later referred specifically to wife and concubine, respectively, both meant wife during the Shang era. Sometimes these two terms were used interchangeably to refer to the same woman, showing that *qie* as yet had no pejorative connotations.[92] Although the Zhou later distinguished between half-brothers born to a wife or concubines, the Shang sacrificial system as yet did not recognize this distinction. When King Wu Ding sacrificed to his father, his twelve brothers born to various mothers participated in the ritual with him.[93]

Although royal spouses lacked a hierarchy of titles, they nevertheless held higher or lower ranks. King Wu Ding had unions with a number of women, but only three were considered official consorts akin to queens, hence worthy of receiving posthumous sacrifices from royal descendants. Also, only a king's major consort would be buried in a large individual tomb lavishly appointed with prestigious burial goods.[94] Minor spouses were interred in a much simpler manner.

In later times the Zhou prohibited marriage with someone from the same clan, or even with the same surname. However, the characters *xing* 姓 and *shi* 氏, which the Zhou used to indicate descent from a remote common ancestor, do not appear in Shang inscriptions.[95] Although the descendants of the Shang kings took the surname Zi 子 after the Zhou conquest, this appellation does not appear in Shang sources. After being conquered, the Shang remnants probably took a surname so that they could participate in the alien Zhou kinship system.[96] Since surnames did not yet exist during the Shang dynasty, they could not possibly have practiced surname exogamy. During the Shang, the basic unit of kinship was *zu* 族, not *xing* 姓. *Zu* referred to a tightly knit clan bound together by descent from a common ancestor and communal ties such as shared economic interests, land use, religious rituals, and military duties.

The way that the Shang organized kinship relations meant that, judged by later Zhou standards, they practiced neither surname endogamy nor exogamy. These concepts simply had no relevance in a society that lacked surname-based kinship groupings. Sometimes it seems that the Shang kings married a relative.[97] In most cases, however, spouses were either unrelated or else shared a very tenuous tie.[98] The Shang nobility also frequently intermarried with the ruling clans of surrounding foreign peoples, who were initially completely unrelated by blood.

The Shang elite often used marriage as a tool of realpolitik. According to legend, political marriage dates back to the dawn of civilization.[99] Kings and high nobles married strategically to bring powerful kin groups together. By marrying several women, a polygynous Shang king could ally with multiple clans, increasing his network of core supporters. An intricate web of marriage ties helped the Shang overcome the limits of their embryonic administrative institutions and hold their polity together.[100]

The Shang also used marriage as a tool of foreign relations, enticing surrounding peoples to participate in their political system through intermarriage. The names of many elite women include characters associated with foreign places, showing that kings regularly intermarried with foreign nobility to integrate peripheral regions into the Shang state.[101] Most famously, after the Zhou people emerged as a powerful military force, the ruling lines of Shang and Zhou began to intermarry.[102]

Under the patrimonial system of government, the king ruled over the state like a father presiding over his family.[103] This system made little distinction between the king's family, royal court, and government, so kinship ties carried great significance. In consequence, a king's primary consort enjoyed immense power, prestige, and wealth. Even though Shang society was both patriarchal and patrilineal, a woman who married an important man could nevertheless exercise some political power.[104]

Shang royal consorts lacked a unique title equivalent to queen. Nevertheless, the king's spouses enjoyed status and power, so it seems appropriate to refer to them as such.[105] Mortuary archaeology has yielded considerable information about these women. Unlike the Late Shang kings, who were entombed in a royal cemetery, their consorts did not have a dedicated burial area and were laid to rest in various places around the capital. Ancient construction damaged one royal consort's tomb, showing that the Shang themselves had forgotten where some previous queens had been buried.[106] Looters emptied all of these tombs except one, but the remains that escaped destruction suggest that Shang queens had extremely lavish burials. A representative tomb covers ten square meters and originally contained an array of bronze vessels and other luxury goods as well as five sacrificial victims.[107]

Zhou and Han writers recorded ancient legends and snippets of Shang history that passed down the names of a few Shang queens. By combing this textual information with inscriptional evidence, specialists have gradually pieced together many names of the primary consorts of the Shang monarchs. The rival reconstructions of K.C. Chang and Jia Shiheng incorporate the findings of earlier scholars. Inscriptions recorded the posthumous appellations used in ancestral sacrifices, so the first character of a woman's name varied according to her relationship with the person conducting posthumous rites.[108] While a husband would call the deceased woman *fu* 帚, her son addressed her as *mu* 母 and her grandson as *bi* 妣. Four of the six consorts prior to King Tang (Da Yi) never received initiation into the sacrificial system, so their names have not been preserved.[109] The reconstructed lists begin with the consort of King Da Yi, also known as Tang. Because he was the first monarch to use the title king (*wang*), historians consider him the founder of the Shang dynasty.

In addition to a king's spouses, other women also attended him and carried out tasks on his behalf. A woman could even serve as a *chen* 臣, although it is not clear what she would do in this capacity.[110] In later eras the character *chen* could mean official, but also sometimes denoted a prisoner of war or slave, so these women were not necessarily performing important tasks. Also, women as well as men held a post called *bao* 保, whose duties remain unclear. In Shang script, the orthography of this character depicts a person carrying a baby on the back. Sometimes *bao* just meant protection, as when an ancestor's blessings shielded a person from harm.[111] Perhaps a *bao* served as nanny or teacher to royal children.[112]

Table 3.1. Shang Dynasty Kings and Their Principal Consorts

Kings	Consorts (K.C. Chang's Reconstruction)	Consorts (Jia Shiheng's Reconstruction)
Da Yi 大乙	Bi Bing 妣丙	Bi Bing 妣丙
Da Ding 大丁	Bi Wu 妣戊	Bi Wu 妣戊
Bu Bing 卜丙		
Da Jia 大甲	Bi Xin 妣辛	Bi Xin 妣辛
Da Geng 大庚	Bi Ren 妣壬	Bi Ren 妣壬
Xiao Jia 小甲		
Lü Ji 呂己 or Yong Ji 雍己		
Da Wu 大戊	Bi Ren 妣壬	Bi Ren 妣壬
Zhong Ding 仲丁	Bi Ji 妣己, Bi Gui 妣癸	Bi Ji 妣己, Bi Gui 妣癸
Bu Ren 卜壬		
Jian Jia 戔甲		
Zu Yi 祖乙	Bi Ji 妣己 (or Bi Geng 妣庚)	Bi Bing 妣丙
Zu Xin 祖辛	Bi Geng 妣庚, Bi Jia 妣甲	Bi Geng 妣庚, Bi Jia 妣甲
Qiang Jia 羌甲	Bi Geng 妣庚	Bi Geng 妣庚
Zu Ding 祖丁	Bi Geng 妣庚, Bi Xin 妣辛, Bi Ji 妣己, Bi Gui 妣癸	Bi Geng 妣庚, Bi Jia 妣甲, Bi Gui 妣癸, Bi Yi 妣乙
Nan Geng 南庚		
Hu Jia 虎甲 or Xiang Jia 象甲		
Pan Geng 盤庚		
Xiao Xin 小辛		
Xiao Yi 小乙	Bi Geng 妣庚	Bi Geng 妣庚
Wu Ding 武丁	Bi Xin 妣辛, Bi Gui 妣癸, Bi Wu 妣戊	Bi Xin 妣辛, Bi Gui 妣癸, Bi Wu 妣戊
Zu Ji 祖己		
Zu Geng 祖庚		
Zu Jia 祖甲	Bi Wu 妣戊	Bi Wu 妣戊, Bi Ji 妣己
Fu Xin 父辛		
Kang Ding 康丁	Bi Xin 妣辛	
Wu Yi 武乙	Bi Wu 妣戊	Bi Wu 妣戊
Wen Wu Ding 文武丁 or Wen Ding 文丁	Bi Gui 妣癸	
Fu Yi 父乙		
Di Xin 帝辛		

Alternatively, *bao* might have simply been a general honorific appelation conferred on important people rather than a specific office.

Even if a woman lacked an official title, she could still assist the king in various ways.[113] Most importantly, elite ladies frequently conducted some of the key sacrifices that legitimized the Shang state. Women also helped with routine royal affairs. Kings ordered women to come and go from the capital on official business and handle matters on their behalf. Some inscriptions specify that a woman was to carry out a particular duty, such as overseeing agricultural labor in a certain place. And sometimes a woman would aid the king on her own initiative, such as reporting an unusual occurance to the throne.[114]

The greatest royal consorts played important roles in Shang society. Fu Jing, known posthumously as Bi Wu, was the first of the three wives of King Wu Ding.[115] More than two hundred oracle inscriptions mention her. The prominent location of her tomb, in an unusually prestigious location near the cemetery of the kings, further attests to her importance.[116] Although looters ransacked Fu Jing's tomb, they left behind a huge bronze vessel far too heavy to carry away. This enormous square cauldron is the largest ritual vessel ever discovered at the Anyang site.[117] Archaeologists discovered forty-nine sacrificial victims inside the tomb and another twenty-two on the entrance ramp. The unusually large number of human sacrifices confirms that Fu Jing enjoyed an exceptionally high position in society, even for a queen.

Fu Jing played important roles in the administration of the Shang state.[118] Most dramatically, she led troops into battle several times, defeating an army from a place called Pang. Fu Jing also oversaw planting and harvests in the most central and important part of the Shang realm. One inscription mentions her supervising the planting of millet in the king's inner domain. Her high position brought great wealth, so Fu Jing had the prestigious duty of presenting tribute to her royal husband, such as turtle carapaces used in divination rites. On one occasion she presented thirty sets of turtle shells, another time she brought in forty, and once she submitted one hundred carapaces to the king. Due to Fu Jing's importance, King Wu Ding repeatedly divined to express his concern for her health, particularly when she was pregnant. After she died, subsequent generations sacrificed to her and sought her posthumous blessings.

In spite of Fu Jing's numerous achievements, her reputation has been dwarfed by that of Fu Hao, one of the most famous women in Chinese history.[119] When archaeologists discovered Fu Hao's tomb in 1976, they were stunned to find that looters had overlooked it. This is the only major tomb from the Late Shang capital of Anyang that was not plundered. The tomb of Fu Hao has yielded the richest trove of Shang dynasty artifacts ever recovered, and its excavation marks a milestone in world archaeology.

The name Fu Hao or Hao is inscribed on 109 items in the tomb, clearly identifying this as her burial site.[120] Excavation yielded astonishing riches, including 468 bronzes, 755 jades, sixty-three stone items, forty-seven semiprecious stones, 564 hairpins and other items carved from bone, three ivory vessels, sixty-one ceramic vessels, fifteen items made of shell, and 6,820 seashells.[121] Fu Hao had used some of these items herself, while others were made to accompany her in the afterlife.[122] The tomb contained sixteen human victims as well as the remains of six sacrificed dogs.[123] Originally a shrine building measuring 6.5 by 5 meters stood on top of the tomb, which her husband and progeny used to conduct sacrifices to her spirit. It likely had a roof but no walls and was supported by numerous columns arranged in two bays.[124]

Despite Fu Hao's current fame and the magnificence of her tomb, she was not King Wu Ding's most important consort.[125] Fu Jing's tomb is located near the royal cemetery, whereas Fu Hao was buried in a far less impressive location. Fu Jing's tomb has an entry ramp, whereas Fu Hao's has none. And Fu Jing was interred with far more human sacrifices. Also, despite the grandeur of Fu Hao's bronzes, this set of ritual vessels simply conformed to standard Shang mortuary conventions and did not represent an exceptional burial for someone of her status.[126] However dazzling her riches appear to modern eyes, Fu Hao surely considered Fu Jing her superior.

In addition to bronze ritual vessels inscribed with the name Fu Hao, numerous oracle inscriptions also mention this person. However, these divinatory records come from different eras, showing that more than one Shang royal consort was called Fu Hao.[127] The Shang did not use a large variety of names, so people from different eras often shared the same ap-

Figure 3.6. Detail of Houmu Wu Square Bronze Cauldron, from the Tomb of Fu Jing Rosemania.

pelation. The woman interred in this tomb seems to have been the spouse of King Wu Ding.

As was often the case with women's names, Hao 好 seems to be a feminized version of a simpler character. Scribes added the female radical *nü* to the name Zi 子 to create an appelation that looked suitably feminine.[128] In some inscriptions her name is simply written Fu Zi, proving that Fu Hao was a feminized version of her name. Researchers have put forward several theories about the meaning of Zi.[129] Some believe she originated from the Zi clan. Others theorize that Zi may have simply been a given name that identified her personally. Alternatively, it might refer to her natal state. According to this interpretation, she came from a marginal kingdom and married the king of Shang to cement a political alliance. Afterwards she used the name of the state of Zi as her moniker.

Although this tomb contains numerous bronze vessels inscribed Fu Hao or Hao, twenty-eight items bear other names. The largest, an immense square bronze cauldron weighing 235 kilos, is inscribed Mu Xin.[130] This is a posthumous name of the sort used in ancestral sacrifices. Oracle records also mention sacrifices to a female ancestor called Mu Xin, so it seems that Mu Xin was the posthumous name of Fu Hao. She was called Fu Hao while alive and Mu Xin after her death.[131]

This tomb also includes twenty-six objects inscribed with the name Hou Tu Mu, perhaps another name for Fu Hao.[132] These objects may have been cast as dowry vessels or else commissioned by Fu Hao herself. In the latter case, the character Tu (which died out with the Shang and lacks any equivalent in modern Chinese script) would have probably been her "style" (*zi*) or personal name. Nevertheless, some specialists doubt that the name Hou Tu Mu refers to Fu Hao and argue that these items originally belonged to someone else.[133] They believe that Fu Hao acquired these objects as war booty or received them as gifts. Her tomb contains other bronzes inscribed with various names, some of them clearly referring to people other than Fu Hao, so Hou Tu Mu might possibly have been a different person.[134]

Material and inscriptional evidence relating to Fu Hao preserves some of the most important historical data from the Shang dynasty. Her story not only reveals the achievements of a remarkable individual but illuminates the lives of elite women in Early Bronze Age society. Some writers have anachronistically romanticized Fu Hao into a heroic proto-feminist who battled the rise of patriarchy.[140] But to appreciate her life, people today must go beyond anachronistic ideological labels and understand her actions within the context of her age.

As a member of the aristocracy, Fu Hao controlled a domain that constituted the basis of her wealth and power. Although the location of this place remains unknown, her lands lay beyond the capital and outside the central royal region controlled by the king. Divinatory inscriptions repeatedly mention her coming and going as she traveled between her fief and the capital.[141] Other *fu* also had fiefs, and the king divined about rainfall and harvests on their lands.[142] Nor were *fu* ladies nobles in name only. Like male aristocrats, they actively ruled over the people residing on their domains, supervising agricultural work and other important matters.[143]

In such a simple economy, land and grain constituted the most important forms of property. Control of a domain's agricultural lands provided wealth that could be exchanged for numerous luxury goods, such as the immense cache of bronze and jade in Fu Hao's opulent tomb. These rare items were not meaningless extravagances. Prestige goods confirmed a woman's high status and exhibited her eminence to the world. The Shang obsession with luxury goods suggests that a woman could raise her status by displaying symbols of high rank.[144]

Fu Hao devoted much of her time to performing elaborate sacrifices to ancestors and deities. These rites had immense significance. With such simple institutions, the Shang relied heavily on religion and ritual to provide ideological support, bind the state together, and accomplish practical goals. Given the importance of ceremony to the maintenance of this system, the participation of Fu Hao in ritual activities positioned her at the center of the Shang oikoumene.

Like her counterpart Fu Jing, Fu Hao and members of her entourage acquired, prepared, and consecrated turtle bones and shells for the king to use in divination rituals.[145] About half of the presentations of turtle carapaces came from noblewomen.[146] Fu Hao also conducted important rituals herself, such as the worship of heaven, rites to ward off disaster, and sacrifices to nature deities.[147] *Fu* ladies performed a variety of rituals, such as rainmaking and shamanistic ceremonies.[148] However, most of their sacrifices consisted of offerings to appease the royal ancestors, intended to prevent them from harming the living. Several inscriptions mention Fu Hao sacrificing to both deceased kings and female ancestors.[149] One typical oracular query asks whether she should sacrifice pigs and sheep and conduct a ceremony to the deceased King Fu Yi.[150]

Because Fu Hao had a domain that provided income, like other nobles she rendered tribute to the king. The primitive Shang economy as yet lacked efficient transportation, currency, or regular commerce, so the presentation of tribute and circulation of gifts served as a pragmatic way to allocate resources. In addition to turtle carapaces, *fu* sent in other kinds of tribute to the center as well, showing them to have been well integrated into the exchange of luxury goods used to confirm and display high status.[151] Because women sometimes married into the royal line from important clans on the Shang's periphery, allied states may have sent in tribute to the king via their women who had married Shang nobles.[152]

The king did not keep most of the luxury goods that he received. Instead he dispersed them among the elite to reinforce his bonds with important nobles and inculcate loyalty in the recipients. Fu Hao received a portion of this royal largess. Some items in her tomb may originally have been tribute goods presented to the king, including bronze bells and a jade halberd sent in to the court by two foreign peoples on the margins of the Shang realm.[153] Given Fu Hao's importance, however, perhaps she had dealings with these foreigners and received these gifts from them directly. Whatever their provenance, displaying these sorts of exotic items would have elevated Fu Hao's standing at court.

More than two dozen objects in Fu Hao's tomb are inscribed with the names of other people. In addition to exchanging prestigious luxuries with her royal spouse, Fu Hao also participated in an extensive network of gift giving among the nobility.[154] The Shang elite circulated gifts to strengthen social relationships and reinforce hierarchies.[155] Given the importance of this system of exchange, it did not make sense to be stingy. Gift giving inculcated a sense of obligation in the recipient while bringing esteem to the giver.

Although Fu Hao participated in many important events in the capital, in retrospect her military activities seem most impressive. In this period, clans also served as military units, and the noble who ruled a clan's domain served as their senior officer during times of war. Because Fu Hao presided over an important domain, she led soldiers into battle. The prevailing view of warfare further encouraged female participation. The Shang regarded battles as conflicts among ancestral spirits as well as living people.[156] Given this belief, a woman's kinship affiliation qualified her to go to war on behalf of deceased progenitors. During subsequent dynasties, women were almost always barred from leading troops, so the intimate involvement of Shang women in military matters marks an exceptional episode in China's gender history.

Fu Hao led troops on several major expeditions, fighting against various foreign peoples.[157] She participated in almost every major military campaign of her era. One inscription even mentions Fu Hao leading an army of thirteen thousand soldiers, the largest force mentioned in Shang records.[158] The unusual size of this army makes it clear that Fu Hao did not just lead troops raised on her own lands, but commanded one of the greatest campaigns of the entire dynasty.

The impressive military equipage in Fu Hao's tomb confirms that she not only participated in war but also considered martial achievements an important aspect of her identity. Her tomb includes numerous weapons, including halberds, knives, and arrowheads.[159] Two huge bronze battleaxes, intricately decorated with fearsome animal motifs, are engraved with Fu Hao's name. Given their size and weight, these were probably symbolic ritual objects rather than actual weapons.

Fu Hao was not unique among Shang noblewomen in going to war.[160] Fu Jing also led armies against several enemies.[161] Although Fu Jing's tomb suffered extensive looting, robbers left behind 251 bone arrowheads.[162] Presumably the tomb originally contained far more impressive bronze weapons as well. Although it cannot be known whether women fought on the battlefield, female generals defended the borders, took military orders from the king, and relayed intelligence to the capital. Sometimes a *fu* and her husband guarded a border region together. Fu Jing and other women also went hunting, which the nobility considered analogous to war, as the two pursuits required many of the same skills.[163]

In spite of the impressive victories of Fu Hao and Fu Jing, the female role in warfare should not be exaggerated. The Shang frequently fought their enemies, and only a small percentage of records about war mention women. Moreover, men were also far more likely than women to be buried with weapons. During the Neolithic era, relatively few female graves contain weapons.[164] However, militarism constituted an extremely important aspect of Shang identity, and their martial culture encompassed women to some degree. In the Early Shang, both deceased men and women were interred with weapons.[165] Perhaps instruments of war indicated the high status of an individual woman or her clan. Alternatively, women buried with weapons may have been actively involved in war in some way. The association of women with warfare seems to have declined over the course of the dynasty. At a cemetery for the lower elite dating to the Late Shang, all of the 160 tombs with bronze weapons belonged to men.[166] Toward the end of the dynasty, with the exception of a few exceptionally powerful royal consorts and noblewomen, warfare seems to have become a male activity. Fu Hao and Fu Jing were probably some of the last Shang women to lead armies.

The solicitude of Fu Hao's husband further attests to her importance. Oracle inscriptions record King Wu Ding repeatedly inquiring after Fu Hao's health and safety. He asks if she will get well soon and whether she will come down with a toothache.[167] These inquiries reflect the Shang belief that illnesses and other misfortunes were caused by supernatural curses, likely from a disgruntled royal ancestor. When the king pleaded for the good will of his ancestors on Fu Hao's behalf, he performed what anthropologists refer to as a ritual of affliction to placate a malicious spirit and remove a curse.[168]

King Wu Ding divined more than twenty times regarding Fu Hao's pregnancy and childbirth, inquiring after her health and asking whether the baby would be born alive.[169] Not only were these rites a way to obtain information, but they were also believed to induce fertility and ensure a happy delivery.[170] The king also showed keen interest in the child's sex. He wanted to know whether the baby would be male, in which case the birth would be considered "auspicious." The wording of these divinations makes it clear that the Shang kings preferred sons to daughters.[171]

The mechanics of Shang governance accounts for the preference for sons. Given the need for an heir and the support that a son could provide his royal father, the monarch was eager to have male progeny. But even though kings preferred sons, they did not consider daughters useless. Because the Shang arranged political marriages to ally themselves with important clans, they married off daughters to key nobles and foreign leaders, thus building alliances and consolidating the realm.[172]

After returning from an extended campaign against Ba, Fu Hao fell ill and died. Afterward, King Wu Ding dreamed about her. The Shang believed that the dead continue to exist on the margins of the human world, so he considered this dream consequential and feared that it might portend harm.[173] Even after Fu Hao died and became an ancestor, she remained a powerful figure, and people believed that she could influence the living for good or ill. The king appeased her with regular sacrifices to ensure her blessings.[174]

To receive the proper obsequies, an ancestor needed an appropriate name. The first character of a posthumous name depended on who wrote it. For example, a son would call his mother *mu* 母 whereas a grandson and more remote descendants would write *bi* 妣.[175] So the deceased Fu Hao could be called either Mu Xin and Bi Xin, depending on who was referring to her. As for the second character, both kings and their spouses had one of the ten heavenly stems (*tiangan*) in their posthumous names.[176] The Shang calendar used stem characters as names of the ten days of the ancient week. Presumably the stem character in an ancestor's name marked the day of the week when descendants performed routine propitiatory sacrifices. Most deceased kings had stem characters from the first half of the cycle, showing that they received sacrifices in the earlier part of the week, which the Shang considered more auspicious. The names of most ancestresses included a stem character from the second half, relegating their rituals to a less prestigious period.[177] Because male and female ancestors tended to have different stem characters, a Shang king would sacrifice to his mother and father on different days. A king and his primary spouse never had the same stem character in their posthumous names. However, a king might share a character with minor spouses, presumably because they were relatively unimportant.[178] If a king had several consorts, it seems that the stem characters in their posthumous names were selected in sequence according to the order of death.[179]

Once a deceased royal consort had a posthumous name, she could receive regular sacrifices within the cultic system known as *zhouji* 周祭, which consisted of five cyclical ceremonies.[180] Not all members of the royal household acquired a place in the ruling line's ancestral cult. Usually, only if a woman's son became king would she be integrated into the calendar of official sacrifices, although multiple consorts of a few kings entered the sacrificial schedule for unknown reasons.[181] This stress on the patriline marks the beginnings of a shift toward the type of kinship system practiced by under the Zhou dynasty.[182] The Shang considered sacrifices to ancestresses important and maintained them even after their defeat and absorption by the Zhou. A bronze cast during the Western Zhou era has a Shang-style inscription stating that it was used for sacrifices to a deceased mother.[183]

After Fu Hao's death, she received regular sacrifices of the types typically conducted for important ancestors.[184] The Shang regarded these rituals as immensely significant. Only a king had the authority to sacrifice to the royal ancestors on behalf of the entire community, entreating their blessings and dispelling curses. The Shang emphasized the importance of these rituals to impress everyone with the power of their forebears. Because only the ruler could properly appease his ancestors, his subjects not only respected his temporal authority but also held him in awe for his ability to control the supernatural.[185]

The official sacrificial system consisted of numerous rituals conducted at various times and places. For example, the ancestress Bi Geng received fifteen kinds of sacrifices made at nine places.[186] During these rites, participants dedicated twenty-four sacrificial offerings to her, including pigs, cattle, sheep, dogs, weapons, and slaves. Some rites were routine. Others implored for blessings or were made in response to a dream, sickness, or even a bad mood.

Although ancestresses could affect the living for good or ill, the Shang did not consider them as important as male ancestors. Deceased men received five times as many divinatory inquiries as women. When a king wanted to implore for something particularly important, such as a good harvest, he sacrificed to a deceased king.[187] Although the most important female ancestors had their own shrine, some lacked a dedicated ritual space.[188] A woman might receive sacrifices in her husband's shrine, diminishing her to a subsidiary member of her husband's cult.[189] A similar discrepancy in attitudes toward male and female ancestors can be seen in the numbers of bronze ritual vessels dedicated to male and female ancestors. The Shang inscribed numerous bronzes with the name of the ancestor who would receive sacrifices using a particular vessel. Among a group of 2,655 inscribed bronze vessels, 93.29 percent were dedicated to male ancestors and only 6.71 percent to deceased women.[190] Descendants dedicated many other vessels to a deceased couple rather than an individual, making the wife an appendage of her husband's sacrificial cult.[191]

The Shang believed that an ancestress had the power to induce fertility, and many rituals directed to deceased women pleaded for progeny. These rites included prayers and the sacrifice of bulls, rams, and pigs.[192] The kings paid more attention to some ancestresses than others. Prior to the final phase of the dynasty, the throne usually passed successively between brothers before descending to the next generation. As a result, a king's aunts had often already been initiated into the ancestral cult during his lifetime. A king's close kinship link with these senior female relatives made it likely that he would pay particularly scrupulous ritual attention to them. Also, an ancestress who had given birth to a king enjoyed higher ritual status than those without royal progeny. The Shang simplified their sacrificial system toward the end of the dynasty, removing consorts who had not produced a royal heir from the ritual schedule.[193]

Fu Hao remained active even after death. The Shang believed that the deceased continued to perform religious sacrifices. An ancestor could sacrifice to a higher-ranking ancestor or someone further back in the past.[194] The Shang also thought that two ancestors could marry one another through a posthumous wedding ceremony.[195] Several oracle inscriptions ask whether the deceased Fu Hao should wed the god Di, or perhaps the great predynastic monarch Tang. As Fu Hao had been married to King Wu Ding in life, it seems that the Shang considered death akin to divorce. Fu Hao became untethered from her husband when she died, so she was free to marry a different man in the afterlife. A noblewoman's husband may have determined her social standing while she was alive, but she reclaimed a more independent personal identity in death.

4

~

Western Zhou Era

In 1046 BCE an army of Zhou soldiers and their allies defeated Shang forces and established a new dynasty. In contrast to the Shang, who developed out of the Neolithic Longshan peoples of north China, the remote ancestors of the Zhou seem to have been pastoralists who originally inhabited steppelands to the north or west of the Chinese heartland. Contacts with settled peoples spurred the Zhou to adopt agriculture, construct fixed settlements, and develop an increasingly complex state. Yet in spite of the considerable influence that Zhou received from Shang, their cultures continued to differ in important respects. Accordingly, the sudden overthrow of Shang by Zhou brought about a dramatic transformation of politics, kinship, religion, ritual, values, and thought, fundamentally affecting the lives of women.[1]

After the Zhou conquered Shang and united the two realms, they found themselves ruling an unprecedently large and diverse state. The new elite realized that they could not use their traditional methods to rule such a huge area, nor could they adapt the equally inadequate Shang system. The Zhou had no choice but to construct innovative institutions capable of holding together their large and fissile realm. Moreover, immediately after the establishment of the new dynasty, a series of rebellions threatened its existence, exposing its fundamental weaknesses. To stabilize the state, the Zhou founded an innovative system, granting fiefs and noble titles to relatives of the king and representatives of key clans. Shared rituals, the exchange of prestige goods, and intermarriage tied aristocrats to the king and also to one another. The resulting network of interlocking bonds not only restored order but also allowed the Zhou dynasty to endure for almost eight centuries.

Women found themselves facing changed circumstances. A poem comparing baby boys and girls would seem to bode ill for women in this new society.[2] The poet describes how a newborn son plays with a jade scepter, as befits the future lord of the household. In contrast, parents give their daughter a toy spindle whorl to symbolize her expected role in life—performing domestic chores in the home. According to this constricted vision of womanhood, after the girl grew up she would be expected to bear children, prepare meals, weave cloth, and stay out of trouble.

This abridged image of womanhood fails to convey the complexity of female life. The shift from Shang to Zhou saddled women with new burdens, but also brought them novel opportunities. To a large extent, the possibilities and responsibilities that a woman faced depended on her particular situation. Women enjoyed some privileges. Zhou authorities exempted female convicts from tattooing and mutilating punishments, treating them more gently than men.[3] Queens issued commands, handed out largess, and conducted imposing court ceremonies. And within the family, a mother could leverage the loyalty and affection of her children to bolster her status within the household. In other respects, however, women faced new restrictions.

Most information about women during the Western Zhou era (1046–771 BCE), the dynasty's initial phase, comes from two kinds of sources. Epigraphic texts record aspects of elite female life. Like the Shang, the Zhou continued to inscribe treasured bronze ritual vessels. While the Shang usually wrote very brief statements, often consisting of a single character, the Zhou composed much longer texts.[4] Western Zhou bronze inscriptions often commemorate an important event such as marriage, ancestral sacrifices, or the receipt of royal largess. Fortuitously, many inscriptions mention women. Not only did some inscriptions composed by men discuss a woman's activities, but female aristocrats also commissioned bronze vessels on their own behalf, leaving behind traces of events that they considered important.[5]

Poetry describes Zhou women from an extremely different perspective than bronze inscriptions. Some ancient poems began as the lyrics of folk songs, whereas others featured in ceremonies and performances held at noble courts across China.[6] Editors compiled hundreds of poems into a compendium eventually called the *Classic of Poetry* (*Shijing*). Due to their ritualistic nature, ancient poems often employ stock phrases to express conventional sentiments.[7] Yet in spite of the formulaic language, these texts convey many details of female life, ranging from the grand activities of queens to the experiences of poor women teetering on the edge of survival. Rather than offering a unitary vision of womanhood, ancient verses portray a wide array of female types, describing women in the throes of love as well as those dealing with terrible hardship.

Few of these poems can be dated with certainty. It seems that numerous authors composed them over a long period of time, from the eleventh century down to about 600 BCE. The ancients believed that women wrote some of these poems, although claims of female authorship remain contested and men probably wrote most of them.[8] Even after large numbers of poems began circulating in tandem, the contents of various manuscripts of collected poetry differed. Han dynasty scholars collated the standard Mao edition that readers today consider definitive, although originally it represented just one of several versions.[9]

The antiquity of these poems awed subsequent generations, and later readers assumed that such ancient writings must surely deal with weighty matters. Even though many poems began as naïve songs, exegetes reverently treated each poem as a profound statement about the fundamental nature of humanity. They often inserted anachronistic ideas into their interpretations or used these texts as hermeneutic tools to understand unrelated narratives.[10] Scholars attributed lofty moral sentiments to verses about quotidian matters. They even reread poems with blatant sexual content as statements regarding moral wisdom.[11] Readers today have to cut through centuries of this worshipful commentary to recover the original authorial intentions behind these ancient works.

Because the sources for Western Zhou history differ so much from Shang materials, they provide extremely different perspectives on women's lives. Whereas Shang divinatory texts describe what women did, Zhou inscriptions and poems often put forward moral standards and archetypes. For example, numerous poems explain ideal female appearance in detail. These clearly articulated criteria of beauty had an immense impact on the development of Chinese views of ideal womanhood. In later eras, when poets or artists portrayed a beautiful woman, they often followed the guidelines set down in these early poems.[12] Numerous other models and archetypes likewise influenced the ensuing development of gender discourse.

Sometimes a poem provides straightforward information about conventional beauty, inscribing social values on the female body and using it to communicate cultural meanings.[13] The most attractive woman is tall, fair, and slender. The poet often employs imagery from nature to obliquely convey comely appearance, declaring a woman to be as lovely as jade or flowers. Other poets take a Petrarchan approach, borrowing metaphors from nature to convey the beauty of each part of the body. An attractive woman has fingers like blades of grass, a neck like a tree grub, teeth like melon seeds, forehead like a cicada, and eyebrows like moth antenna.[14] These highly detailed lists conveyed a male poet's sense of control and ownership over the woman he describes.

Poets lavished attention on women's clothing and hair, employing a rich vocabulary to describe costume and ornaments.[15] They even had words for the various shades of dyed cloth. Given the distinctive ways that nobles and commoners dressed at the time, clothing and hair styles instantly conveyed a woman's social status. People considered luxurious accouterments such as silk clothing, ivory hairpins, and elaborate cosmetics important components of beauty.[16] Although few women could live up to these demanding ideals, these notions nevertheless set the standards that future generations strove to emulate. Henceforth for the length of imperial history, women judged their own body and behavior against the epitomes conveyed in ancient poetry.[17]

Poets also frequently commented on the female paragon's integrity. They believed that beauty encompasses character as much as physical perfection. Conventional female virtues included respect for elders, filial regard for parents, attentiveness to one's husband, helpfulness, loyalty, and industry.[18] The idea that virtue constitutes an intangible aspect of female beauty has remained a standard assumption down to modern times.

Poetry also conveys the model female personality. The ancient female ideal differs from the reclusive woman described in medieval poetry, confined to her boudoir and paralyzed with grief for an absent lover. Although gentle, the archetypal woman portrayed of ancient poetry could also be tenacious and brave when necessary.[19] The strong and self-assured Western Zhou woman seems far removed from the reclusive, obedient, self-sacrificing female stereotype of later eras. In this simple agricultural society, a forthright personality could be extremely useful, and people regarded vigor as attractive.

Bronze inscriptions offer detailed information about elite women's names and terms of address. Unlike the Shang system, a Zhou noblewoman lacked a fief of her own. She received an honorific title, corresponding to her husband's rank, only through marriage. The name of the king's spouse took the form *wang*-x, composed of the character *wang* 王 (king) together with another character identifying her individually. Likewise, a duke's wife was called *gong*-x, using her husband's title (*gong* 公) together with her own name.[20]

Beyond these simple titles for the highest-ranking women, the situation becomes much more complicated. When a noblewoman referred to herself, she used one of fifteen formulas to construct a name with between one and four characters. Moreover, each person addressed a woman in a manner appropriate to their relationship, often having to choose from among several possibilities. A father could use six kinds of appellations when speaking of a daughter, husbands called wives in eight different ways, and an official referring to the wife of his lord could select from among five formulas.[21]

The components of a woman's name identified her by conveying information about her particular identity. Some names included a kinship term. Like men, a woman's name could have one of the five characters that marked the order of her birth among her siblings (*bo* 伯, *meng* 孟, *zhong* 仲, *shu* 叔, *ji* 季).[22] Due to the Zhou custom of surname exogamy, a woman's name often included her natal surname (either *xing* 姓 or *shi* 氏), regardless of whether she was married.[23] Other nomenclature included her natal state, husband's state, or husband's name. A relative sometimes referred to a woman by an appropriate kinship term.

Although people sometimes called a woman by a single character, usually her natal surname, more often they combined two or more characters to produce a more informative appellation. For example, Jin Jiang was married to the lord of Jin and had a father surnamed Jiang, while Wang Bo Jiang was the eldest daughter (*bo* 伯) born to a family surnamed Jiang and married to a king (*wang*). Sometimes people added an honorific prefix to a name, such as *da* 大 (great) or *zi* 子 (a term connoting nobility). *Fu* 婦 remained a polite term of address for women, although the connotations were not as grand as before.[24] A king could refer to his wife by a term that identified her as his consort, such as *fei* 妃 or *liangnü* 良女.[25] And if a man had more than one wife, each of them might affix one of four characters (*da* 大, *xiao* 小, *zhang* 長, *shao* 少) to her name to distinguish her from his other spouses.[26]

A deceased woman received a posthumous name for use in ancestral rites. While the Shang generated a two-character name using a standard formula (kinship term plus stem day), the Zhou addressed deceased women by various designations ranging from one to four characters. Long posthumous names conveyed respect and perhaps appealed to people's aesthetic sense as well. A name might include characters designating title, kinship relation, status as an ancestor (such as *kao* 考), commendatory posthumous expressions (including *wen* 文, *hui* 惠, *gong* 恭, *mu* 穆, and *sheng* 聖), natal surname, and terms giving the specific identity of the deceased.[27]

As before, society constituted a steep pyramid. Little information remains about people of the lowest status. The Zhou enslaved some women captured in battle, and distant nobles and foreign peoples also presented female slaves to the palace as tribute. The Zhou often referred to a female slave simply as "woman" (*nü* 女).[28] Inscriptions and transmitted documents also mention a kind of female slave called *qie* 妾, some of whom were attached to the palace.[29] During the Shang dynasty *qie* meant wife, and later the term meant concubine, so the Western Zhou usage implies that men used these women sexually. As people began to clearly distinguish wives from concubines, they called concubines by a term that had become associated with slavery, emphasizing their low status.

In the Early Western Zhou, mourners still sacrificed human victims and placed their bodies in the tombs of the most important people. Unlike the Shang, who sometimes killed numerous people to accompany the deceased, the Zhou usually only sacrificed one or two victims. Different kinds of people suffered sacrifice, including men, women, and children, although mature women were a minority.[30] By the Late Western Zhou, the custom of human sacrifice went into decline and tombs dating to the end of this era rarely contain human victims.[31] Instead of killing people, mourners used figurines and luxury goods to convey the high station of the deceased.[32]

Slaves, captives, and other people of debased status probably made up only a small fraction of the population. During the Western Zhou, most people were commoners. As before, the average woman lived in a small rural settlement where she devoted her days to domestic chores and agricultural labor.[33] Women carried out a wide range of tasks around the home. In addition to childcare and routine domestic chores, they chopped firewood, fished, and foraged for wild plants. Because a married woman had to clothe her family, she spent much of her time on textile work, including picking mulberry leaves, raising silkworms, spinning, dyeing, weaving, and sewing.[34]

Some scholars theorize that women played an important role in the religion of the common people. In many cultures, shamans are female, and such was the case in China as well. Ancient documents refer to so-called lewd sacrifices that featured female shamans beating drums and dancing during ecstatic rituals.[35] Some female shamans may have masqueraded as drought demons or exposed themselves to the elements in ceremonies to invoke rain.[36] However, information about these practices is scanty and any discussion of Zhou female shamanism remains highly conjectural.

Myths regarding the female deity Xiwangmu (Queen Mother of the West), who later attracted fervent veneration, began to take shape in this era. Some scholars believe that myths surrounding this goddess initially developed out of tales describing a real woman who ruled over a tribe of the Qiang people located to the west of the Zhou heartland.[37] According to this theory, a charismatic female tribal leader became a vassal of the Zhou king, attracting wide attention. After her death, tales regarding this powerful woman became increasingly exaggerated, resulting in her eventual apotheosis as a deity.

Although the consorts of the Shang kings lacked a unique title, the wives of Zhou monarchs were addressed in distinctive ways and can definitely be considered queens.[38] Bronze inscriptions call royal consorts by the formula *wang*-x, combining the royal title *wang* 王 with the character of their natal surname. More generally, queens were also referred to as *wangfu* 王婦, *wangqi* 王妻, *jun* 君, *junshi* 君氏, and *tianjun* 天君. When a king had more than one spouse, his consorts were classified into different ranks. The primary wife was called *qi* 妻 while secondary wives had a title that distinguished them according to their degree of primacy (as *yuanfei* 元妃, *cifei* 次妃, and so on). People also sometimes called the king's primary spouse *hou* 后. However, some men such as court scribes and minor officials also held the title *hou*, so this term did not yet specifically mean queen.[39] The Eastern Zhou bureaucracy lacked male officials called *hou*, while royal spouses retained this title, so in the later phase of the dynasty *hou* referred solely to the queen.

Transmitted documents preserve a few names of Western Zhou queens, and bronze inscriptions provide most of the remainder, so it is possible to reconstruct a list of the primary Western Zhou royal consorts by combining these two types of sources.[40] Table 4.1 lists each Western Zhou king, his queen, and the source of her name. The dates for each king's reign follow the provisional estimates put forward by the Xia-Shang-Zhou Chronology Project.[41]

The elite did not yet expect royal women to remain sequestered from public gaze, so Western Zhou queens participated in important activities. Together with the officials under their command, Western Zhou queens aided their husbands in conducting affairs of state. In particular, they kept the government running when the king was away from the capital on official business. Due to the queen's importance, anyone desiring an audience had to be vetted by an appropriate official, and elaborate procedures regulated her interactions with others.[42] Restricting access to the queen made meeting her an honorable privilege.

Given the nascent state of the Western Zhou bureaucratic system, governance still relied heavily on ritual. Royalty, nobles, and officials often conducted a ceremony as a way of accomplishing something important. They considered some rites a female purview, and responsibility for some ritual duties descended from mother-in-law to daughter-in-law.[43] Ceremony provided a queen with her most important entrée into affairs of state.

Sometimes the queen attended major rites in the presence of the monarch. For example, an inscription apparently dating to the reign of King Kang describes his consort Wang Jiang participating in the *xiangyinjiu* wine drinking ritual, conducted to welcome major guests or else to convene a conclave for discussing important matters.[44] Queens also presided over court rituals in the king's absence. An inscription records that while an unnamed king was leading his troops in a war against Chu, his royal

Table 4.1. Western Zhou Kings and Queens

King	Reign	Queen(s)	Source
Wen	1099–1047	Tai Si 太似	*Shiji*
Wu	1046–1043	Yi Jiang 邑姜	*Shiji*
Cheng	1042–1021	Wang Si 王似	Bronze inscription
Kang	1020–996	Wang Jiang 王姜	Bronze inscription
Zhao	995–977	Wang Qi 王祁, Wang Yuan 王員, and/or Wang Ren 王任	Bronze inscriptions
Mu	976–922	Wang Jiang 王姜, Zu Jiang 俎姜, or Wang Zu Jiang 王俎姜	Bronze inscription
Gong	922–900	Wang Wei 王為 (?)	Bronze inscription—the identity of this woman is contested
Yi	899–892	Wang Bai Jiang 王白姜	Bronze inscription
Xiao	891–886	Wang Jing 王京 (?)	Bronze inscription—her identity is contested (Jing may have been a minor consort)
Yi	885–878	Wang Ji 王姞	Bronze inscription
Li	877–841	Shen Jiang 申姜	*Shijing*, bronze inscription
Xuan	827-782	Qi Jiang 齊姜	*Lienü zhuan*
You	781–771	Wang Shen 王申 (Shen Jiang 申姜), then Bao Si 褒姒	*Shiji*

consort, also named Wang Jiang, conducted a wine drinking ritual with a noble.[45] King Kang's wife Wang Jiang also handled ritual matters while he was away from the capital officiating at a ceremony elsewhere. She ordered the grand protector (*taibao*) to conduct a rite in accordance with the standard ritual schedule.[46]

On other occasions, queens conducted ceremonies outside the capital in one of the noble domains. King Kang's wife Wang Jiang traveled to perform a ceremony at an ancestral temple built by Duchess Yin Ji to honor her deceased husband Duke Mu.[47] Royal ladies also had a role in the performance of certain ancestral rites. Although the king himself conducted the most important of these sacrifices in the ancestral temple, highborn girls presided over minor rites. And before a princess married, she would go to the ancestral temple to report the impending union to previous generations of the royal line.[48]

Kings and queens also had a duty to hand out largess. As with many Bronze Age polities, the Western Zhou state had a redistributive economy.[49] The kings acquired resources and prestigious goods and then gave most of them away to the nobility to prove their generosity, buy support, and bind together key players in the political system. Queens participated in the redistribution of goods and regularly presented nobles with gifts of substantial value. For example, they commissioned precious bronze ritual vessels to hand out to important personages.[50]

Because the Western Zhou system relied so heavily on redistribution, the queen's control of key economic resources gave her a significant role in government. Most importantly, queens could hand out parcels of land to the nobility. An inscription documents Wang Jiang, wife of King Zhao, presenting a noble named Yu with three hundred *mu* of land as well as the grain harvested from an adjacent field.[51] Land grants underpinned the political order, so the right to allocate parcels of land attests to her power. As seen in this inscription, queens also controlled major quantities of grain, another fundamental measure of wealth in this agricultural society. An inscription records that on one occasion King Kang's wife Wang Jiang presented a noble with grain from certain fields, implying that she could allocate the harvests from various lands.[52]

Although a queen sometimes handed out substantial gifts of land or grain, most often she presented an aristocrat with symbolic tokens of her regard. These gifts included cowry shells, slaves, cloth, fur clothing, ornaments, silver, cattle, and an herb used to flavor alcohol.[53] Once, a queen presented a nobleman with three hundred fish.[54] Even if an item lacked much tangible value, the nobility nevertheless treasured it as an impressive token of royal favor. When a noble received a present from a queen, however small, he might cast a bronze vessel to commemorate the event, confident that his descendants would look back at this sign of the queen's esteem with pride. Significantly, the wording of some inscriptions shows that the recipient felt gratitude toward the queen herself and not the king. The nobility did not see the queen merely as the king's representative, but as a power in her own right.

Queens exercised a degree of authority over officials and nobles and sometimes ordered them to perform specific tasks. Inscriptions record a queen issuing instructions to an official of the royal household, craftsmen attached to the palace, the grand protector (*taibao*) official, slave overseers, and others.[55] According to later accounts, at the beginning of the dynasty Tai Si, the wife of King Wen, managed the inner quarters of the palace while the monarch handled affairs in the outside world.[56]

Western Zhou queens also maintained a marginal presence in warfare. Although classical texts give the impression that women had been completely banned from any involvement with war, inscriptional evidence nevertheless shows that queens accompanied their husbands on campaigns. Early in the dynasty, Wang Si, consort of King Cheng, went with her husband on a military expedition, and later queens followed her example.[57] The sight of a royal lady on the battlefield did not yet strike soldiers as strange or inappropriate. Even so, the Western Zhou marks a transitional period in women's relation with warfare. Although a woman could still travel with an army, the queen no longer led troops or had a formal military role.

During the Eastern Zhou, elite women became completely estranged from warfare. Women lost even symbolic links with war, and they no longer displayed weapons to convey high female status. Of the hundreds of bronze weapons and tools excavated from tombs in the state of Jin, for example, all except three were discovered beside men.[58] The tombs of male nobles also frequently include ornaments for horses and chariots, while these items were rarely buried with their wives, suggesting that the nobility had also excluded women from riding horses and chariots.[59] The Eastern Zhou nobility redefined female identity to exclude any association with martial pursuits. Henceforth people considered it extremely unseemly for a queen or noblewoman to even accompany a campaigning army.

Over time, royal women became closely associated with integrity, and writings began to portray queens as exceptionally virtuous. The belief that a queen should have impeccable morals emerged from Early Western Zhou political discourse about the mandate of heaven (*tianming*).[60] This ideology held that a king could reign as a legitimate monarch only with the blessing of heaven, which supported him as long as he hewed to exemplary moral standards. Having a virtuous woman close to the seat of power helped assure the king's legitimacy and the dynasty's continuation, so writers began to laud queens for their virtue.

Ancient court poetry includes hymns of praise describing the high ethical standards of the major female ancestors of the Zhou kings. Most importantly, poets heaped praise on the grandmother and mother of King Wen and the mother of King Wu, the two monarchs responsible for founding the dynasty.[61] These women received commendation not just for specific achievements but also for their exceptional character, elevating them into moral paragons. The ancients considered virtue heritable, so praising early queens as exceptionally good they implied that these virtues had been passed down to later generations of kings, bolstering royal pretensions to moral legitimacy. The Zhou nobility accepted this idealized view of early queens, and some inscriptions urged women to imitate ancient royal paragons such as the mother of King Wen.[62] The belief that the earliest queens possessed exceptional virtue became a mainstay of political ideology, helping to explain how the Zhou received the mandate of heaven, overpowered the Shang, and established a new dynasty.

The number of Zhou bronze inscriptions mentioning queens decreased over time. During the Late Western Zhou, queens became less active and engaged in few noteworthy activities. And as the Zhou monarchs declined in importance over the course of the dynasty, their consorts became less prominent as well. The informal nature of female power also accounts for the decreasing influence of queens over affairs of state. Women rarely participated in administrative institutions, so the rise of bureaucratic government robbed them of opportunities to exercise power.

Like queens, the wives of noblemen held a high position in society and exercised power within their husband's realm. Whereas some elite Shang women had their own domain, under the Zhou system all fiefs belonged to men. Moreover, a noblewoman lacked an independent title.[63] Bonds with a noble husband and aristocratic kinsmen accounted for her wealth, influence, and status. Although a noblewoman stood far above most people in Zhou society, she ranked below her husband.

The tomb of Lord Yu and his wife excavated at Baoji, Shaanxi, illustrates the relationship between a noble and his spouse. Lord Yu's tomb contains the remains of his favorite concubine Er, who had been sacrificed for the burial. A nearby tomb houses the body of his wife Jingji. The number of key ritual vessels customarily symbolized rank. Lord Yu was interred with forty bronze vessels and Jingji with nineteen, while Er had only ten. Of these, Yu's array included thirteen *ding* and *gui* vessels, the most ritually significant kinds, while Jingji had eleven and Er had nine. Lord Yu's vessels are more lavish and diverse than those belonging to the two women.[64] The carefully calibrated numbers of ritual vessels in these affiliated tombs, decreasing in odd numbers from husband to wife to concubine, symbolized their relative positions in the social hierarchy. In contrast to the bronzes, Jingji had only two jade animal pendants while Er had fifty-one. Although ritual regulations strictly stipulated the number and kind of bronze vessels, minor jade ornaments lacked ritual consequence, so the taste of the deceased dictated their number and variety.[65]

Archaeologists have conducted extensive excavations of the noble cemetery of Jin, a large and important state. Changes in the tombs of the wives of marquises between the tenth and eight centuries reflect a gradual realignment of relations between noble spouses. Although a noble wife always had a smaller tomb and fewer burial goods than her husband, the size of noblewomen's tombs steadily decreased.[66] Most importantly, over time the number of bronze ritual vessels in women's tombs declined. Only ritually insignificant burial goods, such as jade ornaments, continued to outnumber those of men.[67] As funeral rituals dictating the sizes and contents of tombs became standardized, the scale of female tombs diminished, graphically illustrating how the rise of the rites depressed elite female status.

Although a noblewoman ranked below her husband, she nonetheless commanded wealth and power. Female aristocrats had audiences with the king in the capital, and monarchs would sometimes visit a noble's wife while traveling.[68] Like their husbands, noblewomen sometimes received prestigious gifts from the king. However, while men received items associated with authority and wealth, such as weapons and land, women were usually given symbolic presents of trivial value such as clothing and cosmetics.[69]

A few inscriptions record a noblewoman ordering underlings to carry out a particular duty. In one instance, a woman named Duchess Ji (Gong Ji) ordered someone named Ci to manage a group of people. She subsequently rewarded Ci for his service, and he cast an engraved bronze vessel to record her largess.[70] Another inscription records how a woman named Duchess Si (Gong Si) presented someone named She with cowries.[71] However, these inscriptions are unusual. Overall, few engravings mention commands or gifts emanating from the wives of nobles. Either people did not consider the activities of noblewomen worth commemorating or else these women did not usually take an active role in administering their husbands' noble realms.

Three unusual inscriptions mention an important woman named Geng Ying who lived during the reign of King Kang. When read in tandem, they reveal her to have had particularly important interactions with the monarchy.[72] One of these documents describes how the king rewarded Geng Ying with a bronze cup, jade tablet, and cowries in recognition of her diligence and service. The second text states that the king visited her home and once again rewarded her with gifts, this time cinnabar and cowry shells. A third inscription explains that the queen gave Geng Ying cowries and silk. These laconic engravings do not mention why the king and queen repeatedly curried favor with this particular noblewoman. Geng Ying seems to have been unusually influential for some reason. Perhaps she came from an important clan and served as an intermediary between the monarch and her blood kin.[73] King Kang had to put down rebellions during his reign, so maybe he hoped that Geng Ying would convince her kinsmen to help him deal with military threats.

Geng Ying's importance highlights the utility of political marriage. Even before the dynasty was established, the Zhou had already begun to arrange marriages to manage their sensitive relationship with Shang.[74] After the founding of the Zhou dynasty, kings strategically married off their daughters to key nobles to gain allies.[75] Because the nobility had to marry their children to someone of similar noble background but a different surname, they usually took a bride from a different state. The combination of class endogamy and surname exogamy thus bound the aristocracy together in an elaborate network of overlapping kinship ties.[76]

It seems that a woman from an important noble line enjoyed particularly high status, as some women had unusually lavish tombs in contravention of ritual standards.[77] And burial goods with nomadic characteristics illustrate marriages between Chinese nobles and the ruling clans of various foreign peoples referred to in tandem by the blanket term Rongdi.[78] As the authority of the Zhou kings declined and the realm fragmented, giving rise to continual warfare, political marriage among the nobility assumed increasing importance.

Despite the general exclusion of women from the bureaucracy, one office remained open to them. As during the Shang, a woman could still become a *bao* 保 (protector). It remains unclear whether *bao* was a specific administrative position or merely an honorific title.[79] Both men and women served as *bao*. During the reign of King Cheng, male *bao* oversaw the actions of the youthful monarch. Female *bao* seem to have supervised the rearing and education of royal and noble children. Queens rewarded female *bao* for their service by presenting them with gifts.[80]

Ancestral sacrifices remained important, even as ritual practices diverged from those of the previous dynasty. The Zhou kings venerated all of their predecessors but held Jiang Yuan, their primal female ancestor, in especially high regard, commemorating her with elaborate ceremonies.[81] As the first mortal ancestor of the Zhou, she represented their genesis as a people, earning her pride of place in the state sacrificial cult. Moreover, because Jiang Yuan had married into the line of Zhou ancestors surnamed Ji, the union of Ji and Jiang also marked the origins of the custom of surname exogamy underpinning the Zhou kinship system.[82]

The Zhou elevated Jiang Yuan into a moral paragon to portray their origins as respectable, and poets exalted her as the epitome of virtue and an ideal mother. Nonetheless, modern readers might find it odd that the Zhou considered Jiang Yuan a maternal icon. She abandoned her son Hou Ji (the first male ancestor of the Zhou) at birth, exposing him to the elements with the intention of killing him. The belief system of the time accounts for behavior.[83] Because Jiang Yuan had conceived her child by supernatural means, after stepping on a god's footprint, she considered his birth strange and inauspicious. She assumed that raising a freakish child would bring disaster upon the entire household. However, after the abandoned child received divine protection, she took him back and raised him to become a great ruler. Her success in nurturing the culture hero who inaugurated the rise of the Zhou people proved her exemplary maternal qualities.

Just as representatives of the state sacrificed to Jiang Yuan as ancestress of the Zhou people, each line of the aristocracy venerated their own ancestors. Noblewomen sacrificed to the ancestors of their husband line, and a bride might even come in to her new home already equipped with ritual vessels dedicated to his ancestors.[84] In addition, people of both sexes sacrificed to female forebears. Zhou sacrifices to deceased noblewomen differed from Shang procedures. The posthumous title *fu* 婦 had disappeared, and progeny referred to deceased women by one of three kinship terms: *mu* 母 (mother), *bi* 妣 (ancestress), and *gu* 姑 (father's sister).[85] A noble son sometimes cast a bronze ritual vessel to be used specifically for sacrifices to his deceased mother and placed it in his father's ancestral temple.[86]

Two unusually detailed inscriptions on a square bronze cauldron unearthed at Luoyang describe the rituals used to worship male and female ancestors in the Early Western Zhou.[87] A man named Wo commissioned this vessel to offer sacrifices to his ancestor Father Ji (Fu Ji). Inscriptions record in detail the rituals held for Father Ji's funeral. Wo was likely a scion of Shang nobility, so some of these rites may have reflected anachronistic Shang practices.

As the observances commenced, first Wo sacrificed to two ancestral couples who predated Father Ji. The first pair was Ancestor Yi (Zu Yi) and Ancestress Yi (Bi Yi), and the second Ancestor Ji (Zu Ji) and Ancestress Gui (Bi Gui). Then he conducted a ceremony called *zudian* directed solely toward female ancestors, with two constituent sacrifices.[88] After that, mourners performed a series of rituals that prepared the deceased for burial. Notably, this inscription emphasizes the prominence of rituals for female ancestors in a nobleman's funeral. By integrating sacrifices to female ancestors into funeral rites for a man, mourners showed their respect for deceased women and recognized their importance within the patrilineal kinship system.

Although women received posthumous sacrifices, men had a much higher position in the ritual system, and the relative importance of female ancestors steadily declined over time.[89] During the Shang dynasty, 93.5 percent of ancestral sacrifices to women were directed toward an individual and only 6.5 percent were made to a woman as a member of a married couple. During the Western Zhou, the proportion of sacrifices to individual women declined to 65 percent, whereas 35 percent of female ancestors received veneration together with their husband. By the Eastern Zhou, only 16 percent of ancestresses received individual sacrifice whereas 84 percent shared their husband's rites. Likewise, the Zhou dedicated far fewer ritual items for use in sacrificing to deceased women than men. The nobility commissioned 93 percent of dedicated bronze ritual vessels for a male ancestor and only 7 percent for a female. And while the tombs of male aristocrats include bronze bells and chime stones used in ancestral rites, women's burials rarely contain these esteemed items.

Figure 4.1. Wo Inscription Describing a Funeral Ritual
Feng Shi, "Wo fangding mingwen yu Xi Zhou sangdianli," Kaogu xuebao 3 (2013): 186.

These shifts reveal that nobility gradually demoted female ancestors and incorporated them into their husband's ancestral cult.

While bronze inscriptions focus on the activities of royalty and the nobility, poetry yields insights into the activities of ordinary people. The lives of common women differed immensely from those of the aristocracy. They resided in small agricultural villages, worked hard, and lived in proximity to nature. In these simple rural settings, local custom and passage of the seasons regulated daily life. Women dominated the domestic sphere, which served as the center of production and consumption, making them an influential force within the family.[90]

Common ancestors provided the clan with a shared identity, binding together large groups of people and fostering cooperation. As with the nobility, ancestral sacrifices had a prominent place in the ritual calendar. Women participated in the ancestral rites, albeit in a subsidiary manner. While men officiated at the ceremonies, women assisted them by gathering flowers and preparing the necessary foods.[91] Poetry provides few clues as to how ordinary people regarded female ancestors, and it is not known if they sacrificed to deceased women.

Although commoners venerated ancestors and gods, they observed far fewer ceremonies than the nobility. While the elite prided themselves on adhering to elaborate decorum and performing stately rituals, simple village festivals featured feasting, singing, dancing, and games. On some occasions, villagers encouraged boys and girls from different villages to mingle, and some of this revelry had romantic or sexual overtones.[92] Each region seems to have had different festive customs.[93] In some places, on a specific day the boys and girls of neighboring villages would gather together. They participated in communal activities or played games, such as gathering flowers, searching for firewood, tossing plums back and forth, fishing, or competing in simple tests of skill. Or they might just sing and dance. The festival concluded with a feast.

A rural festival held in the state of Zheng, located in what is now Henan province, provides an example of these sorts of festivities. At the appointed time, young people of both sexes gathered at the junction of two rivers, with the boys one one side and girls on the other.[94] They gathered wild plants, sang antiphonal songs, and eventually crossed the river to meet with members of the opposite sex. For a woman to accept a flower from a suitor symbolized their betrothal. Because the clan held farmland in common, marriage among commoners as yet lacked much financial significance, so young villagers seem to have had considerable freedom in choosing a spouse. Ancient poems imply that the common people did not place much value on female chastity, and some festivals may even have involved premarital sex.[95]

Ancient poetry emphasizes the freedoms enjoyed by female common-ers. They could make many decisions about the direction of their life: whom to love, when to marry, and whether to elope. Unlike later eras, when Confucian propriety regulated female behavior, ancient village women enjoyed considerable autonomy and expressed their feelings un-reservedly.[96] About a third of the poems in the *Classic of Poetry* describe love or longing. One describes a woman smitten with a tall man whom she noticed while he was drumming and dancing. Although he promised not to forget her, she does not expect him to keep his word.[97] Other poems stress the lover's tormented uncertainty. When a man goes off to gather wild plants, his partner finds their brief separation unendurable.[98] One woman's intense longing for an absent lover keeps her from sleeping at night.[99] A handsome man who does not keep his promises leaves behind a string of young women pining for him.[100]

Poets frequently employed images evoking fertility or sex.[101] Various readers have identified water, peaches, fish, plants, and birds as symbol-izing woman's sexual nature or fecundity.[102] Some tropes that seem banal today appeared extremely suggestive to ancient readers. For example, be-cause women often went to pick mulberry leaves to feed their silkworms, men regarded mulberry groves as mysterious feminine spaces charged with sexual possibility. Due to the intimate association between women and mulberry, simply mentioning this humble plant evoked feminine sensuality.[103]

In subsequent centuries, when ideas about marriage and chastity had tightened, people reacted to the romantic and sexualized innuendo of ancient poems with frisson and embarrassment. Although pedants tried to explain away amorous encounters as metaphor and simile, some read-ers doubted their tortured explanations. Educated Chinese of every gen-eration had to confront the disturbing legacy of ancient romantic poems, revered for their antiquity yet suspect for their suggestive content. Due largely to this compelling ambiguity, the *Classic of Poetry* had an immense and persistent impact on ideas about women.

Although commoners sometimes eloped, a proper marriage was ar-ranged by parents with the aid of a matchmaker. Early Zhou sources do not record the average marriage age, but one poem describes a young woman worrying that she would become embarrassingly old before she could find a husband.[104] Given the low life expectancy, people surely married young. The elite used matchmakers out of necessity. Due to sur-name exogamy, they needed an agent to help them locate a noble bride in another state. Yet even among ordinary people, matchmakers played a symbolic role in publicly legitimizing the union. A poem sums up the importance of employing an intermediary to uphold propriety.[105]

> When we cut firewood, how do we do it?
> Without an axe it would not be possible.
> When one ties a wife, how is it done?
> Without a matchmaker he cannot get her.

Ideally fiancés finalized their betrothal in the spring and married in the autumn.[106] During their courtship, a couple might exchange small gifts.[107] The parents of bride and groom formalized the betrothal by agreeing to the marriage in the presence of a matchmaker. Then the groom's family presented the bride's side with symbolic betrothal gifts, probably items of trivial value. The marriage was finalized at the appropriate time of year.

Due to the wealth and power of the nobility, elite marriage was a matter of great consequence. Not only did marriage bind together two important families but it also facilitated an exchange of wealth between them. The groom presented a betrothal gift to the family of the bride, whereas a nobleman's daughter entered marriage with a dowry consisting of valuables such as bronze ritual vessels and slaves. However, her father did not dower her with land, the primary form of wealth.[108] Because a noblewoman did not own land in her own name, she depended on her father when young, and after getting married her husband supported her.[109] Because aristocratic weddings often took place between families in distant places, the arrangements involved considerable effort. Most arduously, the groom or his representative would have to travel to the fief of his new father-in-law to meet the bride and bring her to his home.[110]

In some respects, elite Zhou marriage customs differed substantially from later norms. Noblemen were polygynous and sometimes a groom even married two or more women at the same time. The Zhou referred to simultaneously marrying multiple women as *ying* 媵.[111] Numerous bronze inscriptions and transmitted texts mention *ying* marriage.[112] Although *ying* marriage was not the norm, the elite not infrequently entered into these sorts of unions, and this practice endured into the early Eastern Zhou era.[113]

Literally, *ying* means "to send."[114] When used in connection with marriage, *ying* referred to dowry sent along with a bride. However, in this steeply hierarchical society, people as well as objects could accompany a bride. Sometimes a wife entered her new household together with servants brought from home.[115] In other instances, a sister or niece accompanied the bride and became lesser spouses of the same husband. Minor spouses would not necessarily enter the husband's household at the same time as the bride. In some cases, a girl would wait until she was sufficiently mature and then join the bride as a minor spouse.[116] If the main wife died, one of the secondary spouses might be promoted to take her place.[117] It is not clear whether the Zhou regarded accompanying spouses as wives or concubines, but their status was likely closer to the latter.[118]

Two types of women could be an accompanying spouse. Some were members of the bride's family.[119] However, there was no reason for a nobleman to make his daughter a mere concubine when he could marry her off as a primary wife, so secondary consorts were often unrelated to the bride. Also, states ruled by clans of the same surname might send along one or more women, presumably of a lower background, to accompany the bride.[120] *Ying* thus allowed several states to simultaneously forge a common bond, making it an exceptionally expedient form of political marriage. Aristocrats who had a rare surname would have had difficulty finding a suitable woman to accompany the bride. In this case, they could either forgo *ying* marriage or else send along women of a different surname.[121]

Ying should be considered a custom rather than a system.[122] Although not uncommon, this sort of marriage was never the norm and some noble lines apparently never participated in group weddings. Accompanying concubinage had practical functions.[123] Most importantly, it forged a bond between two or more powerful clans, making it a useful political tool. *Ying* also stabilized the position of the wife by clarifying her status in relation to her husband's concubines. Yet in spite of its utility, *ying* went into decline during the Eastern Zhou.[124] Changing kinship norms and the decay of the traditional Zhou system made it less useful as a tool of foreign policy, so the nobility began to marry off their daughters in other ways.

In theory, nobles had to marry someone with a different surname. According to myth, this custom dated back to the beginnings of Zhou history. Later kings upheld surname exogamy, making it the most basic principle of Zhou marriage that underpinned the entire kinship system. Because the Zhou conceived of marriage as a union between clans, if two people of the same surname wed, it would seem as if the kinship group was marrying itself.[125] The Zhou justified this custom as civilized and ethical, and believed that it made spouses more fertile. It also helped preserve the virginity of unmarried women by keeping them from having sexual relations with related men. Moreover, identifying strongly with one's lineage strengthened solidarity among relatives.[126]

Of course surname exogamy only became possible after people began to use surnames. They initially used these collective tags to identify kin who allegedly shared a common ancestor. Although the orthography of surnames had not yet standardized during the Western Zhou, most contained a female radical.[127] Feminized surnames seem to have developed out of the Shang dynasty custom of adding a female radical to the characters in women's names. Because polygynous Zhou nobles used their mother's name to distinguish them from half-brothers born to other

mothers, these feminized appellations gradually developed into surnames. When the Zhou began to use surnames to identify large groups
of distant kin descended from a common ancestor, surname exogamy
became possible.[128] During the Western Zhou, the elite strictly adhered
to surname exogamy. However, as traditions frayed during the Eastern
Zhou, the old rules broke down and people of the same surname sometimes wed.[129]

Male commoners could only afford one wife. And even though a king
or nobleman could take more than one spouse, in practice even aristocrats were usually monogamous.[130] Although terminology distinguishing
wives from concubines had yet to become standard, Western Zhou nobles
had already begun to differentiate between them.[131] People often buried
wife and husband together, highlighting the growing importance of the
marital bond.[132] Although a concubine might be buried with her master
as a sacrifice or an expression of his affection, the treatment of deceased
concubines was never consistent.[133]

In spite of the importance of marriage, wives maintained extremely
strong ties to their natal kin. Over the course of Chinese history, the
relationship between married women and their blood relatives differed
in each era. During the Zhou dynasty, people believed that a woman
remained a member of her natal clan even after marriage. Many bronze
inscriptions attest to the strong connection between a married woman
and the family of her birth.[134] Due to the importance of blood ties, women
tended to regard their blood relatives as true family, making her in-laws
seem like strangers in comparison.[135] One poem has an unhappy woman
complaining that she has to treat her in-laws like family.[136]

> Far from big brothers, from little brothers
> I must call a stranger "Father," . . .
> Must call a stranger "Mother"

Whatever her rank, marriage fundamentally altered a woman's life.
Athough the Zhou believed that spouses should treat each other with
respect, not everyone lived up to this expectation. A bleak confessional
poem describes an unfaithful husband who had constantly criticized his
hardworking wife and treated her roughly. In her old age, she looks back
on her marriage and feels that he had deceived her, bringing her nothing
but misery.[137]

> First you took to finding fault with me,
> Then you became rough with me.
> My brothers disowned me;
> "Ho, ho," they laughed.
> And when I think calmly over it,

> I see that it was I who brought all this on myself.
> I swore to grow old along with you;
> I am old, and I have got nothing from you but trouble.

Although this unlucky woman found marriage a miserable trap, poets portrayed the typical marriage as a constructive relationship, and wives regarded the loss or lengthy absence of her husband as a terrible deprivation. Numerous poems describe a woman longing for a faraway spouse. When soldiers serve on a distant campaign, "sad are their wives, left all alone."[138] Poems lamenting separation not only show emotional attachment between spouses, but also highlight the economic dependence of women on men. The death of a husband or a failed marriage could immediately bring a wife terrible hardship.

Every married woman hoped to become a mother, an honored role that raised her position in the family and society. Although the tenets of filial piety had yet to be thoroughly codified, this principle already served as a pillar of the Zhou ethical system and informed the behavior of sons and daughters. Filial piety initially honored male ancestors and fathers, but during the Western Zhou the focus of filiality shifted and people began to stress the bond between mother and offspring. Sons often showed far more regard for mother than father.[139] An inscription by a man named Shi, a descendent of the Zhou kings and dukes of Lu, emphasizes his bond with his mother. He attributes his success to his mother's diligent nurturing and promises that he will never forget her kindness.[140] The bond between mother and child did not end when she died. Apotheosis into an ancestress lent a woman supernatural powers, so sons sought the blessings of their deceased mother. Posthumous maternal protection could even help a man defeat his enemies in battle.[141]

Not every marriage succeeded, and couples sometimes separated. Society as yet lacked systematic divorce. A woman rarely left her husband, and all surviving evidence mentions a man casting off his wife. The customs of the time cannot really be termed divorce, as a dissatisfied man would simply abandon his wife. He would either leave home or else order her out of his house. Poetry critiques society's double standard toward men and women. While a man could freely forsake his wife, an abandoned woman suffered terribly. Poems describe the callous husband who discards a loyal wife after his fortunes improve. One woman even suffered abandonment merely because her bored husband wanted a change of pace.[142] The discarded women described in poetry feel anger and pain mixed with nostalgia for married life.[143]

The Zhou never developed a full-blown ideology of female chastity. Even so, in a society where people inherited their status, the nobility wanted to keep their family's bloodline clear, so they valued the virginity of brides and fidelity of wives. Although village festivals allowed young commoners to court each other freely, the aristocracy held women to strict standards of sexual integrity. A reputation for laxity could ruin a noblewoman's reputation.[144]

> In the wilds there is a dead doe;
> With white rushes we cover her.
> There was a lady longing for the spring;
> A fair knight seduced her.
>
> In the wood there is a clump of oaks,
> And in the wilds a dead deer
> With white rushes well bound;
> there was a lady fair as jade.
>
> "Heigh, not so hasty, not so rough;
> Heigh, do not touch my handkerchief.
> Take care, or the dog will bark."

The poet compares the seducer to a hunter, while the woman who succumbs to his charms suffers a symbolic death comparable to slain prey. This unequal view of male and female sexual autonomy grew out of the values of the day. The nobility feared that a daughter might become pregnant by a low-ranking man. In that case she would have to marry down, disgracing her kinsmen and wasting the opportunity to intermarry with a good family.[145] Fear of mésalliance meant that nobles kept young men and women from freely mingling. However, these restrictions contradicted the romantic ideals of literature. One poem explores the conflict between the inevitability of an arranged marriage and a young woman's desire for romance. The poet describes how a man wants to climb over a wall to visit his unmarried beloved. Rather than give in to his pleas, she worries about what her parents and brother will say and begs him to stop pursuing her.[146]

Once married, a wife was ideally the "companion of her lord till death." Wifely loyalty demonstrated a woman's character and elevated her in the eyes of others. Poetry even describes fidelity as a key aspect of female beauty.[147] Even so, people did not expect a widow to forgo remarriage for the sake of integrity. A poem describes a wife whose husband had gone away on a military campaign. After he did not return home for three years, she took him for dead and remarried.[148] This poet portrays the woman's remarriage as a mundane necessity. Only in later centuries would nascent rhetoric about virginity and chastity harden into a demanding ethic of lifelong fidelity to one man.

5

~

Eastern Zhou Era

In 770 BCE, attacks by recalcitrant nobles in cooperation with pastoral peoples forced the Zhou king to abandon his ancestral homeland and flee eastward. This change of royal capitals initiated the Eastern Zhou era, which lasted until 256 BCE, when the ruler of Qin deposed the last king of Zhou. An interregnum of several decades followed the end of the Zhou dynasty. Then in 221 Emperor Qin Shihuang conquered the various noble states and unified China under the Qin dynasty, marking the end of the period that historians refer to as antiquity.

Although Eastern and Western Zhou share the same dynastic name, the two periods differ in fundamental ways. During the Eastern Zhou, the decay of the previous system unleashed unprecedented productivity and mobility, spurring society to become far more prosperous, complex, and diverse. Cities grew in population and importance, commerce and industry flourished, and a wide range of social groups and occupations emerged. Although the Zhou king remained on the throne, the great aristocrats dismissed him as a decayed cipher. Under the enfeebled monarchy, noble realms became independent states in all but name.

As aristocrats fought one another for supremacy, increasingly violent conflict forced them to become more competitive by reforming their governments, giving rise to sophisticated bureaucratic and legal systems. Thinkers from a variety of schools struggled to make sense of these dizzying changes, and they advocated contradictory visions of the ideal life and good society. The discussion of so many alternatives enlarged people's psychological space and gave them an expanded sense of possibility. These myriad changes had a huge impact on women's lives, altering their interactions with the political system, family, and community.

As society became more fluid, the conventions for naming women changed once again. The rites declared that a woman ought to be referred to by her surname (*xing* 姓 or *shi* 氏) together with a term that marked the order of her birth.[1] In addition, a woman also had a given name (*ming* 名). Although it seems to have been impolite to call a woman by this name to her face, people often used it in writing.[2] Some inscriptions construct a name using a two-character formula that combines a kinship term such as daughter (*nü* 女), wife (*fu* 婦), or mother (*mu* 母) together with a given name.[3] Female appellations took many other forms as well. For example, the *Strategies of the Warring States* (*Zhanguo ce*) names women in twenty-seven different ways. And because the language of the state of Chu differed from that spoken in the Central Plains, southerners addressed women according to their own conventions.[4]

The decay of the Zhou monarchy made queens into inconsequential figures. But even as the power and prestige of these royal ladies diminished, their titles became more consistent.[5] The primary wife of the Zhou king was called by terms equivalent to queen (*wanghou* 王后 or *hou* 后). People referred to the wife of a deceased king, or mother of the current king, as queen dowager (*taihou* 太后). And before a prince became king, his primary wife was called lady (*furen* 夫人).[6] Lower-ranking consorts had distinctive titles that identified each woman's relative status.[7] As for female aristocrats, their names usually continued to follow Western Zhou conventions. People sometimes referred to a deceased noblewoman by the posthumous honorific title *jun* 君.[8]

Large clans broke down and the nuclear family became the main unit of kinship, giving women more influence over matters within the home.[9] As the circle of core blood relatives contracted, people increasingly valued affinal ties. Moreover, Zhou aristocrats usually excluded younger sons from government, lest they become rivals to the reigning lord. As a result, rulers often relied on their in-laws for support. Elite marriage brought together not just spouses but also two kin groups, making the union of husband and wife an expedient political tool. A savvy ruler could use marriage to ally himself with useful kinsmen, thus bolstering his own power.

The Zhou nobility practiced strict class endogamy. Kings married daughters of the aristocracy, the ruling houses of various states married each other, and the Chinese nobility forged marital bonds with the leaders of foreign peoples.[10] A dense web of marital ties bound together the aristocrats of different states through kinship and mourning duties, obligating them to aid their noble kinsmen.[11] Due to the importance of political marriage, even as women retreated from public venues, they retained influence by representing their natal family in their husband's court.

Zhou nobles usually sought to wed a spouse with a different surname. The *Zuo Commentary* mentions seventy-four states ruled by men of twenty different surnames. The diversity of elite surnames allowed most nobles to find a suitable spouse while observing customary exogamy.[12] Some people seem to have considered receiving a wife more honorable than providing a bride to someone else, so noble families of unequal importance often ended up intermarrying for the sake of propriety.[13]

Most importantly, rulers used marriage to build useful alliances. As warfare intensified, aristocrats sought to build ties that could strengthen their position. Marrying a woman from the right family sometimes made the difference between survival and annihilation, so the nobility carefully arranged these unions to obtain maximum strategic benefit. For example, the dukes of Lu used marriage to ally themselves with the state of Ju to the east; Ji and Qi to the northeast; Xuju to the northwest; Song, Chen Hu, and Chu to the southwest; and Zeng, Tan, and Wu to the southeast.[14] Over time, marriage links bound the dukes of Lu to noble neighbors on all sides, bringing them a degree of security.

Marriage could even benefit large and powerful states, as demonstrated by the prominence of marital alliances in the foreign policy of Chu.[15] In the Early Eastern Zhou, the kings of Chu intermarried with the rulers of nearby small states, thereby surrounding themselves with satellites and buffer zones. As time went on and the ferocity of warfare intensified, Chu began to intermarry with families of the other major states to gain military allies. The Chu kings negotiated marriages with an unusually wide range of partners to construct an extensive network of advantageous ties.

Ruling families used political marriage in varied ways. Sometimes the ruling houses of two states intermarried for generations. The elites of Qin and Jin repeatedly married, as did the noble rulers of Jin and Qi.[16] Although recurring unions eventually resulted in cross-cousin marriage, this seems to have been an unintended consequence. Alternatively, the remnants of the Shang ruling house in the state of Song seem to have preserved some of the marital traditions of their ancestors.[17] Although the lords of Song sometimes married the nobility of other states, they often took their wives from among the daughters of their own high officials, even when these women had the same surname.

The development of the character *pin* 聘 illustrates the political significance of elite marriage. In the Early Eastern Zhou this term referred to a friendly embassy of inquiry from one state to another.[18] Because some embassies were sent to arrange a marriage, the meaning of *pin* gradually came to mean betrothal. Political marriage served as a major foundation of the aristocratic system. The Zhou nobility intermarried for centuries, so each of them was related to almost all of the others in some way. As a result, the Eastern Zhou states used kinship terminology in foreign relations.[19] The major nobles called one another uncle or nephew, whether or not they were actually related in this way.[20] They even addressed non-Chinese rulers by these fictive kinship terms.

Political marriage had mixed effects on elite women. While powerful men exchanged women as tokens, it also elevated noble wives into de facto ambassadors.[21] A noblewoman's liminal place in the kinship structure, positioned between husband and father, gave her a conflicted identity. While marriage theoretically made her a member of her husband's family, her influence derived from ties to blood relatives. Due to the importance of the natal bond, female aristocrats tended to remain close to the family of their birth. Sometimes a noble wife would travel long distances to visit her natal relatives, and she would return to her natal family permanently if widowed or divorced.[22]

When war or intrigue forced a woman to choose between supporting her husband's state or that of her father, her loyalty usually rested with the latter.[23] Even though a woman's sons were integral members of her husband's line, she nevertheless tended to favor the interests of her natal relatives. An incident that occurred in 594 BCE exposes female loyalties at the time.[24] A woman named Yong Ji was the daughter of Zhai Zhong, a powerful minister in the state of Zheng. After Yong Ji married Lord Li of Zheng, she found out that her husband intended to remove her father from office. Forced to choose between the two men closest to her, Yong Ji supported her father. As Yong Ji's mother said, if a woman has to side with either father or husband, "how can they be compared?" Yong Ji warned her father of the plot, and he killed Lord Li in self-defense.

Political marriage may have positioned Eastern Zhou noblewomen at the cynosure of government, yet compared to the empresses dowager of later dynasties they wielded very limited formal power. Under the imperial system established by the Qin and Han dynasties, an ambitious empresses dowager might exploit the dictates of filial piety to dominate her son. By demanding obedience from the emperor, a mother could make herself the ruler of China in all but name. Ambitious Han dynasty empresses dowager usually placed their fathers and brothers in key positions, allowing the emperor's distaff kin to monopolize power.[25] During the Zhou, however, due to the combination of surname exogamy and class endogamy, a major noble usually married a woman from another state. As a result, her consort kinsmen usually remained far away and could exert little direct influence on policy. Moreover, filial piety as yet lacked sufficient authority to override the common assumption that governance should be a male preserve.

In spite of restrictions on female power, unusual circumstances occasionally allowed a noblewoman to take control of a state. Most famously, Duke Ling of Wei (r. 534–493) lost interest in governing toward the end of his reign and handed over the reins of power to his wife Lady Nanzi.[26] Although Nanzi committed adultery, overall she seems to have been a competent leader. Historians portrayed both husband and wife in mixed terms, although as time went on the assessments of their actions became increasingly negative. Critics condemned Lord Ling as an alcoholic weakling who foolishly became obsessed with a male favorite and handed over too many duties to his wife. Not only did Ling lack cultivation and a sense of obligation, but his failure to uphold normative gender roles seemed unmanly.[27] As for Nanzi, however intelligent and resourceful she may have been, she had overstepped her allotted place by taking on male responsibilities. Moreover, her adultery reaffirmed the negative stereotype of the sexually dissolute women who craves power. Lord Ling and Lady Nanzi threw the state of Wei into chaos, making this episode a cautionary tale. Both ultimately suffered censure for sowing confusion by blatantly transgressing political and gender norms.

Women also dominated the state of Qin for a time. A weak monarchy and flawed bureaucratic system allowed consort kin to gain an unusual degree of influence over the government.[28] Queen Dowager Xuan of Qin (d. 265 BCE) temporarily managed affairs of state on behalf of a young king, making her the first women in Chinese history to rule as regent.[29] At the time people may have dismissed the significance of such an unusual event, yet this affair ultimately had an enormous impact on the course of China's political development. Because Qin unified China, the early imperial system developed out of that state's institutions. Due to the precedent set in Qin by Queen Dowager Xuan, mothers and consorts of the Han dynasty emperors believed that they had the right to intervene in affairs of state. So the immense powers of Han dynasty empresses dowager and their relatives can be traced back to formative events in the state of Qin.

Despite the eventual significance of the few episodes of overt female power, these were exceptional arrangements. In general, noblewomen had far less to do with affairs of state than before. Even the names of most Eastern Zhou queens and noble consorts have been lost.[30] Presumably they left behind so few traces because they kept a low profile and exercised little influence beyond the walls of inner palace. As society militarized and fierce battles became increasingly commonplace, men completely banned women from any participation in warfare, excluding them from the most important events of that chaotic age.[31] And as the mechanics of administration became increasingly bureaucratic, the prohibition on women serving in office further checked female power.

At this time the relations between elite wives and husbands became more intimate. Changing burial customs reveal how the intensifying marital bond affected female identity. Although some noblewomen were laid to rest in individual graves, the joint burial of spouses became common.[32] Yet even when wife and husband rested side by side, their tombs often differed significantly. Although male and female tombs in earlier eras often had the same contents, Eastern Zhou burial goods became increasingly gender-specific.[33] Artifacts recovered from the aristocratic cemetery of the state of Jin exemplify this trend. The tombs of male and female Jin aristocrats are similar in size but contain extremely different items.[34] Men's tombs have numerous objects related to ritual and war, such as bronze vessels and weapons. In contrast, female tombs lack prestigious ritual vessels and instead contain stone and jade ornaments.[35]

In spite of the steady diminution of women's roles in public life, they could still exercise certain powers. Noblewomen dealt with some matters themselves. An inscription from the Early Eastern Zhou records a woman named Jin Jiang (the wife of Marquis Wen of Jin) stating that she had inherited responsibility for managing the rear palace from her deceased mother-in-law.[36] Although palace matters might seem trivial compared to major affairs of state, she considers them vital to the proper functioning of the state. Jin Jiang asserts that by taking care of routine palace administration, she provides her husband with essential support and thus contributes to his success as a ruler.

Other than maintaining an orderly household, noblewomen also occasionally affected politics, albeit obliquely. They sometimes met with men from outside the family, particularly those younger or lower in status, to enlist their support.[37] Most often, however, a noblewoman influenced affairs of state by discussing these issues with her father, husband, or sons in a domestic context. Due to the patrimonial nature of Zhou politics, meetings often took place among family members in the inner palace, allowing women to participate in important discussions. As the formal powers of women retracted, they increasingly exercised power by convincing a kinsman to take a particular course of action.[38]

During the Eastern Zhou, women usually engaged in politics to further their own interests or those of their kin. Sometimes a noblewoman promoted the welfare of her natal family or state. Because she identified closely with the family of her birth, even after marriage, she did what she could to deploy her husband's resources in their favor. Moreover, mothers intervened in dynastic struggles to position a son as heir to the throne, thereby bolstering their own power.[39] Women also occasionally intervened in politics to seek benefits for a paramour or to cover up their own malfeasance or adultery.[40]

Polygyny also sometimes led women to become involved in affairs of state and succession struggles. The harems of important men contained numerous women, so a wife might fear usurpation by a favored concubine.[41] Because nobles chose a spouse for her bloodline and a concubine for her beauty and charm, harem beauties posed a real threat to the unloved wife. And the favored concubine also feared being targeted by either a jealous wife or a prettier harem rival.[42]

In addition to leveraging their kinship ties, noblewomen had other techniques at their disposal as well. Sometimes a woman professed expertise at divination and used her mastery of this mysterious practice to pursue her political ambitions.[43] Most people believed in the veracity of prophecies, so a female diviner could direct her prognostications to influence powerful men. Justifying a course of action as fated or auspicious might spur a man to action on a woman's behalf.

Women also used eloquent language to sway men to follow a particular course of action. Some educated women became proficient in reciting and quoting canonical poetry in formal settings.[44] The Zhou elite considered this rhetorical technique extremely challenging, and many male aristocrats could not quote poetry properly. Given the inherent difficulty of this type of oral discourse, if a noble lady could argue her point by cloaking it in the elegant language of ancient verse, she invariably impressed her audience. Sometimes a woman appeared at banquets and other male gatherings and argued for a course of action by quoting the odes. Talented women also used other rhetorical techniques, similar to those employed by men, to win over important listeners.[45] But even if a woman became impressively eloquent, she had few opportunities to use this skill in public. Men usually excluded women from their gatherings, making it difficult for a talented woman to address an influential audience outside her family circle.

Convention increasingly restricted the power of women, and their participation in politics began to elicit strong reactions. Because women pursued their goals from behind the scenes, undermining regular procedures and institutions, female power became synonymous with turmoil. Also, a noblewoman's interests sometimes ran contrary to those of her husband's state. Shocked by examples of disorder, ancient authors emphasized the destabilizing effects of female power and urged their readers to strictly exclude women from affairs of state.

Female wisdom encompassed a wide range of knowledge and skills. Given the importance of ritual in stabilizing and organizing society, familiarity with the minutiae of ceremony constituted an esteemed form of wisdom. Moralists believed that performing canonical rituals inculcates virtue and constructive feelings in the participants.[46] Although ritual experts were mostly male, some women gained respect for mastering and practicing ceremonies.[47] In particular, women had important roles in funerals and mourning. Performing these complex rites properly earned them respect.[48] Elite women also received extensive training in the solemn dances and other ceremonies imploring the blessings of the ancestors.[49]

Confucians considered all human beings, including women, capable of raising themselves up through moral self-cultivation. Some women held themselves to a particularly high standard of virtue, and ancient authors readily recognized female moral achievements. Mencius (Meng Ke, 372–289 BCE) admits that female awareness of ethical values could even potentially exceed that of men. He tells the story of a braggart who returned home every day after having stuffed himself with good food. The women in his household wondered how he could afford to eat so well, and he told them that he spent his evenings feasting with rich and important men. Knowing his shady character, his wife and concubine suspected him of deceiving them. One evening they discreetly followed him when he left the house. They discovered that he visited a cemetery every night and begged for leftovers from families offering food to their ancestors. Upon finding out the truth, his wife and concubine both cursed him for his shamelessness, and he burst into tears of shame.[50] This story reveals Mencius' views of the female capacity for virtue. Although a man had disgraced himself without qualms, the women of his household understood correct behavior and berated him for exceeding the bounds of decency.[51]

In a society organized around kinship, knowing how to fit into a husband's family comprised an important aspect of female wisdom.[52] Literature stressed the importance of upholding kinship norms. The *Classic of Poetry* never praises a woman for her talent or intellectual accomplishments, and poets describe female virtue in vague language. Instead, the female paragon of these poems is the woman who successfully performs her family duties. The wise woman knows how to behave as a proper wife, mother, and daughter-in-law, thereby contributing to the family's success.

A few ancient women gained notice for their knowledge of written texts. However, in an era long before the invention of paper and printing, few people had access to books. Given the limitations of written media, people of both sexes put great stress on oral argumentation. The educated person could quote canonical texts verbatim when speaking before an audience.[53] A woman who quoted ancient poetry at a diplomatic meeting or banquet thus earned a reputation not just for eloquence, but also for intelligence and erudition.[54]

Nevertheless, various authors expressed skepticism about female intellectual capacity and viewed women's statements with suspicion.[55] Some men even considered women inherently inferior to men. The *Analects* (*Lunyu*) contains a passage in which Confucius (551–479 BCE) famously complains that women are "difficult to nourish" (*nan yang*). One translation renders this line as "Women and little people are hard to deal with," implying that they are prone to complaints and insubordination.[56] "Difficult to nourish" seems to belittle female intellectual capacity, and comparing all women to morally inferior men clearly derides female character. Although Confucius held that everyone could improve, he believed that it was more difficult for women to achieve outstanding virtue.[57]

As the basic structure of society shifted, kinship norms altered in response. The rise of powerful states stimulated the development of regional cultures, and kinship customs in each place exhibited a degree of variation.[58] The people of Chu did not make much distinction between wife and concubine. In Jin, a man and woman of the same surname could marry without stigma. In Qi, a family's eldest daughter often declined to wed so that she could remain home and devote herself to the domestic religious cult. And Qin law treated wife and children as the husband's property.[59] Yet in spite of these regional disparities, people in various places respected certain common kinship norms, and these customs served as an important force of unity in a time of division and chaos.

Most importantly, the marital bond steadily increased in importance and intimacy. Deceased couples were interred together much more often than before, showing a belief that marriage had bound them together for eternity.[60] As the ritual canon grew in sophistication, specialists set down specific rules for weddings and married life.[61] Rather than seeing marriage as a pragmatic coupling undertaken simply for procreation or economic advantage, ritualists imbued it with profound significance. They declared that marriage expresses lofty values by distinguishing the sexes, fixing basic gendered roles essential to proper human relations, and expressing a couple's commitment to filial piety.[62] Marrying and bearing children saw to the continuation of the family line, allowing proper care for elders and maintenance of the ancestral sacrifices.[63] And a man needed a wife to assist him in sacrificing to his forebears, making marriage a prerequisite for properly carrying out domestic ritual obligations.[64] In light of the many justifications for marriage, Mencius declared, "For a man and a woman to live together is the greatest of human roles."[65] Due to the importance of this institution, a husband ought to treat his wife with courtesy and deal with her in accordance with the rites.[66]

Ritual was not the only means to regulate family matters. As bureaucracy grew in scope and effectiveness, administrators brought core social institutions under the purview of the state, often substituting law for custom and ritual.[67] As a result of this trend, government officials began to regulate marital relations.[68] In the state of Qin, which had the most sophisticated bureaucratic system, officials demanded that betrothed couples apply for permission to marry at a local government office. This rule helped prevent incest and child marriage, and allowed officials to keep the tax registers up to date.[69] As legal systems developed, officials even began to handle conflicts among family members.

Figure 5.1.　Zhou Hairstyles
Original drawings by Allen Y. Yu.

Although commoners took only one wife, the nobility still practiced polygyny. Architecture reveals the size and complexity of polygynous families. A ruler's dwelling was subdivided into a warren of discrete spaces,
segregating his women from one another.[70] In theory, the incest rules of
the ritual code forbade marriage between people with the same surname.
As before, however, some people ignored this ban.[71] Sometimes even close
relatives wed. *Bao* 報 referred to marriage between collateral relatives of
different generations, such as a nephew marrying his aunt.[72] And when
a man died, his son might marry one of his father's other wives (but of
course not his own mother), a custom known as *zheng* 烝 or levirate.[73]
Some historians have dismissed these "incestuous" marriages as a reflection of the period's chaos.[74] But this anachronistic critique judges ancient
practices according to later standards. More plausibly, men may have
assumed that because they acquired a wife by paying bridewealth to her
family, she had a status akin to property and could be inherited by her
husband's kinsman when he died.[75] And because marriages were used to
force alliances beyond the circle of immedite kin, it seems that people assumed that a wife had married the entire kin group, rather than just one
man, so a widow should be remarried to one of her deceased husband's
kinsmen.[76] Whatever the motivation, the emergence of levirate shows

that people assumed that a woman ought to remain a member of her husband's family for life.

During the Han dynasty, kinship customs altered dramatically, and both *bao* and *zheng* became obsolete. Writers began to look back upon ancient marriages between relatives with horror, condemning them as blatantly incestuous. People of later eras usually lacked much familiarity with Zhou customs, so when reading ancient texts they often misinterpreted the motives for unions between relatives. In the imperial era, readers often assumed that the unrestrained sexual desires of Zhou aristocrats drove them to commit incest.[77] Yet in fact, certain incest taboos were simply weaker in antiquity than in later eras, and people of the time accepted some kinds of marriage between relations without comment.

Elite women married young.[78] Noblewomen underwent the pinning ceremony at age fifteen, at which time they would change their hairstyle to signal the onset of adulthood.[79] Henceforth they were eligible to marry, and women usually wed within the next five years. Noble grooms were typically older than the bride, often by a decade or more. The average marriage age of commoners is unknown.

Parents of the groom marked a betrothal by presenting a ceremonial gift to the family of the bride.[80] According to the rites, without this gift the bride would be considered a concubine instead of a wife. In practice, however, brides who eloped were still considered wives.[81] In later eras, the betrothal gift grew into a major transfer of wealth between families, but in antiquity families exchanged humble items of symbolic significance.[82] Bridewealth might include fowl, cloth, and deer pelts.[83] Although the rites did not require a family to send their daughter off to her new home with a dowry, the Zhou nobility nevertheless dowered their daughters with bronze vessels and servants.[84] Because a woman could not own property in her own name, dowries did not include land.

The wedding ceremony marked the most important transition in a woman's life. Among the elite, betrothals and weddings required the performance of numerous ceremonies.[85] First a divination confirmed the auspiciousness of a potential match. Then either side could make preliminary inquiries about the possibility of marriage. After both families agreed to the union, they chose an auspicious day. Timing was crucial, as people believed that the choice of wedding day affected a bride's fertility.[86] The groom's side then formally requested betrothal. If accepted, his family sent over appropriate gifts and he reported the impending match to his ancestors. Then either the groom or a representative went to escort the bride to her new home together with a representative of her family. Certain items such as carriages and paired drinking cups symbolized the union.[87] The couple visited the man's ancestral temple together and reported their marriage to his forebears before consummating it. After three months, the groom returned the horse that had carried the bride to her family, attesting to the permanence of the marriage. Finally, a bride might eventually visit her natal family to inquire after her parents' health. However complicated these provisions, none could be omitted. Not only would an incomplete wedding cast the legitimacy of the union into doubt, but people believed that failing to perform the wedding correctly courted disaster for the people involved.[88]

A new wife found herself surrounded by strangers in an alien environment. People expected her to defer to her new mother-in-law, whose attitude largely determined her fate. Only if a woman served as an exemplary daughter-in-law would she be considered fit to eventually become a respectable mother-in-law herself.[89] To thrive in her new home, it was imperative for her to bear children, as assuming the role of mother brought status and power within her husband's family. Filial piety regulated the relationship between parents and children, and mothers exercised considerable authority over their offspring.[90] Although a mother had to nurture and teach her sons, in later life she could demand their respect and service. A mother had good reason to cultivate her sons and ensure their success. After her husband's death, a son's rank determined a woman's status, so she shared his achievements and failures.[91] The authority of mother over son helps account for female complicity in the patrilineal system. The patriarchal family offered benefits for a woman who assumed the role of mother, so they had good reason to uphold its values.[92] And a wife gained repute by serving as a loyal guardian of the family order, which she could turn to her own advantage as she bore children and gained seniority.

People had begun to clearly distinguish wife from concubine, and they considered it immoral to treat a concubine like a wife or promote her to wifely rank.[93] Elite men routinely took concubines for sexual pleasure, procreation, and to display status. Institutionalizing concubinage had practical benefits, as clarifying the status of these women reduced competition for noble title and power among a man's children.[94] By automatically making the oldest son of the legitimate wife the father's heir, other sons had no grounds to compete with him. Degrading the status of minor consorts and their sons thus helped reduce conflict and stabilized society. Whenever a major noble tried to override this fundamental rule, chaos ensued.

Women became concubines in different ways.[95] Sometimes parents sent off their daughter to be the concubine of an important man because they considered this her best opportunity. In other cases, a man purchased a concubine from her family. And a servant might be promoted to concubine if she began to share her master's bed. Although concubines were not wives, a man could not take a concubine with the same surname, as their sexual relationship would constitute incest. The entry of a concubine into a household did not require any ceremony, although some men conducted abbreviated wedding rituals to welcome a concubine from a good family.[96] While a wife referred to her spouse as husband (*fu* 夫), a concubine was supposed to call him master (*jun* 君) and his wife mistress (*nüjun* 女君). If a nobleman had multiple concubines, they held different ranks within the harem.

All of a man's sons considered themselves brothers, but the sons of concubines had lower status. Not only did the oldest son of the legitimate wife have seniority among his brothers, but a wife's other sons also ranked above those born to concubines, regardless of their relative ages.[97] Brothers had different inheritance rights depending on their mother's status. Most importantly, the son of a concubine could not be enfeoffed with noble title.[98] After a concubine died, her children would conduct sacrifices to her spirit. However, her grandchildren were supposed to discontinue these commemorative rites due to her lowly standing in the family.

Zhou records also mention the presence of female entertainers in the households of the king and other important men.[99] Some rulers kept large numbers of performers, and they exchanged these women with other aristocrats alongside other gifts. Attitudes toward female entertainers varied according to region.[100] Men in the state of Zhao appreciated female talent and beauty, and they held attractive entertainers in high regard. In Yan, however, female entertainers had a degraded status. Occasionally female musicians were sacrificed to accompany a nobleman to the grave.[101]

Although human sacrifice had gone into decline, some tombs still contained victims, often women attached to the deceased in life.[102] Male tombs with multiple female sacrificial victims show that a large retinue of women surrounded the powerful man. Archaeologists excavating tombs from the state of Qi have discovered numerous female human sacrifices, believed to have been concubines, servants, slaves, and entertainers.[103] And the lavishly appointed tomb of the Marquis Yi of Zeng, dated to 433 BCE or later, includes the remains of thirteen women.[104] The custom of killing retainers to accompany the deceased tapered off gradually, enduring the longest in culturally marginal regions beyond the Central Plains, in the states of Qin, Chu, and Nanyue. The Han dynasty elite abandoned human sacrifice.[105]

Although the Zhou elite valued virginity in brides, they did not stress marital fidelity as much as people in later eras.[106] Women frequently remarried, and this seems to have been the typical expectation for young widows.[107] Extramarital affairs were considered embarrassing if made public, and parents would not recognize a child born of such a union. Nevertheless, Eastern Zhou records contain many instances of adultery, and people often reacted to these dalliances with nonchalance.[108] Even though ritualists had begun to advocate physical separation of men and women, actual practices remained relatively relaxed. Women could leave the home freely, and the sexes mingled at festive occasions.[109]

While there is almost no information about divorce among commoners, the elite regarded the dissolution of marriage as unremarkable. Couples divorced for a variety of reasons, ranging from incompatibility to political expediency.[110] In most places, divorce customs were still very informal.[111] A husband simply expelled his wife from the house, and she returned to the family of her birth. Husbands initiated all of the divorces mentioned in ancient records, so it seems that a wife did not dare to break up her marriage. The lack of female-initiated divorce probably stemmed from the unequal property system of the time. Since a woman could not own land in her own name, she lacked the resources to live on her own, leaving her financially unable to leave her spouse.[112]

As the administrative system developed in effectiveness and scope, formal divorce procedures began to emerge. Authorities in Qin, who relied heavily on bureaucracy and law to regulate society, set down systematic provisions for divorce. A man could divorce his wife through a legalistic process.[113] The Qin state freely allowed male-initiated divorce under the sole condition that a husband register his repudiation of the marriage at a local government office. Under Qin law, a woman lacked the right to divorce, so a wife who left her husband was considered to have absconded.[114] If government agents apprehended a runaway wife, she could be subject to punishment.

Evolving ethical discourse influenced ideas about marital fidelity. The concept of loyalty (*zhong*) was still relatively new, as the term did not even exist during the Western Zhou.[115] And loyalty referred only to allegiance to the state, not an individual. Devotion to another person, known as *xin*, implied a degree of reciprocity, so this sort of bond could be easily broken. In the case of marriage, once *xin* had been abrogated, a husband could dissolve the union without any qualms.

Zhou authors usually only condemned adultery when making a point about more significant themes. The *Zuo Commentary* often emphasizes a ruler's sexual dissolution to illustrate his lack of commitment to ritual norms. According to contemporary beliefs, failure to abide by the ritual canon courted disaster. A man who violated the rites in pursuit of sexual pleasure would likely come to a violent end or else produce offspring doomed to die young.[116] Historiography portrays extramarital sexual relations among the ruling class as inherently destabilizing and describes nobles who plunged their state into chaos by breaking kinship and administrative conventions for the sake of love.[117]

Even though sexual ethics remained relatively lax in comparison with the early imperial era, and people divorced and remarried without

Figure 5.2. Backside of a Bronze Mirror
Daderot.

stigma, the first glimmers of chastity rhetoric began to appear.[118] Initially, promotion of chastity seems to have been a reaction to the threats posed by unrestrained female behavior. Early advocates apparently regarded it as a way to stabilize society in an age of intensifying chaos by strengthening the marital bond.[119] With this pragmatic goal in mind, authors began to record a few stories about chastity, such as a widow who rejects remarriage or a woman forced to remarry who then refuses to speak to her new husband.[120]

In spite of this nascent praise for lifelong fidelity, early sources did not emphasize it. The general disregard for chastity had roots in the kinship system of the time. As part of the marriage ceremony, a bride visited her husband's ancestral temple and formally transferred allegiance to her husband's ancestors.[121] But even though she theoretically joined her husband's family, blood kin remained her primary attachment. Because remarriage did not affect a woman's primary kinship bond, most people did not see it as a problem.[122]

After death, a woman's progeny revered her as ancestor, fully integrating her into her husband's line of descent.[123] Despite a woman's enduring ties to natal kin, she was buried with her husband, and her children inducted her into his ancestral cult. The state of Lu continued to practice the traditional *zhaomu* system that arranged sacrificial tablets in the ancestral temple into two rows.[124] Although they placed a man's plaque in the row opposite his children, they put that of a woman in the same row as her sons and daughters. This positioning emphasized how a woman's reproductive role justified membership in her husband's ancestral line. Inscriptions on ritual bronzes show that an ancestress received sacrifices in four different ways. Her progeny honored her individually as both mother and forebear. They also venerated her together with her husband as both parents and an ancestral couple.[125]

During antiquity, large religious institutions had yet to emerge. For women, the loosely structured nature of Zhou religious life presented opportunities to assume spiritual leadership. As in other regions of the world, as religion became more developed, men progressively excluded women from core rituals and administration.[126] The lack of standardization and systematization that characterized Eastern Zhou religion still allowed women to participate in primary religious activities.

The religion of the common people centered on shamanism. By the Han dynasty, it seems that men dominated these religious practices, and the generic term for shaman (*wu*) usually referred to a man unless otherwise specified.[127] But during the Zhou, women still took on prominent shamanistic roles. Female shamans conducted sacrifices to various spirits and carried out rituals to keep inauspicious happenings at bay.[128] Some women interpreted omens to divine the future. Unlike men, who used turtle shells and yarrow stalks for divination, women usually predicted future events by interpreting dreams.[129] In the state of Qi, unmarried women practiced shamanism at home, making it the mainstay of the domestic cult.[130]

Female shamans also participated in public ceremonies. Some seem to have been involved in the rainmaking rites held during summer droughts.[131] Female shamans also venerated important ancestors in raucous spectacles. A bronze inscription from the state of Cai in the Early Eastern Zhou describes ancestral sacrifices that involved drinking and ecstatic dancing. During these rites, women sought the aid of powerful ancestors by performing a swaying dance while assuming a particular facial expression that evoked the saintly behavior of King Wen's mother.[132]

Shamans took part in several other kinds of ceremonies as well, gaining access to the supernatural by dancing, singing, and weeping. Women also conducted rites to ensure fertility and ease childbirth. They directed their fertility sacrifices to a deity known as the Supreme Matchmaker (Gaomei).[133] However, the elite expressed growing skepticism about the abilities of all shamans, male and female. As the reputation of shamanism declined, women gradually lost an important means to participate in religious life.[134]

Gods far outnumbered goddesses in the ancient pantheon, and male deities tended to be more important. Although many ancient gods lacked a specific gender, over time increasing numbers of deities became explicitly male. Most ancient goddesses had unarticulated forms and personalities, and were usually associated with natural spots such as rivers and mountains.[135] Over time, the number of these minor local goddesses declined.[136] A few ancient deities had an overtly sexual identity, and worshippers sometimes approached them almost as lovers.[137]

Nü Wa (also pronounced Nü Gua) stands out as the only major ancient goddess with a highly developed identity and mythology. Some texts connected her with the creation of the world. They describe remote antiquity as a time when the body parts of mythical beings contained the natural elements of the universe. Divine bodies and their constituent elements underwent a series of transformations that eventually resulted in the creation of the present world. This goddess was said to have undergone several of these key alterations.[138] As Nü Wa emerged as the sole important female deity, unrelated stories became appended to her core myths. Nü Wa repaired the shattered heavens after a catastrophic battle between two violent gods. She resided with other gods on a faraway mountain. And she was married to the paternal deity Fu Xi.[139] According to one account, she even created humanity.[140] During the early imperial era, although the image of Nü Wa frequently appeared in religious iconography, she declined in importance and held a diminished role in the Han dynasty pantheon.[141]

During the Eastern Zhou era, ideology became extremely sophisticated, allowing the most powerful forces in society to justify self-interested behavior as just and even altruistic. However, assertions regarding gender were often ambiguous, and thinkers put forward varied and contradictory ideas. The need to interpret classical writings about relations between the sexes sparked debates about the proper behavior of women that lasted until the end of the imperial era.[142]

Discourse about women increasingly positioned ideas within larger intellectual frameworks, making gender concepts components of comprehensive systems of thought. When people discussed theoretical matters, they often had pragmatic goals. Cruel warfare and rapid change had disoriented the populace. In reaction, incisive thinkers sought to stabilize society by promoting useful beliefs. Given the conflicts dividing society, they interpreted ritual, ethics, and cosmology to foster concord.[143] As part of this project, women's rightful place in the harmonious society became a topic of discussion.

To achieve social harmony, people had to respect the metaphysical unity believed to underlie the structure of the cosmos.[144] This way of thinking did not regard the harmonious society as an arbitrary social construct, but considered it a reflection of the natural order. Significantly, this vision of universal harmony did not imply sameness or equality. Just as the elements of nature differ in importance, so society should consist of people related to one another in clearly defined hierarchies. By adhering to the constraints appropriate to their roles, people could interact smoothly. Readers today will regard these assertions as transparently self-serving rationalizations for the strong to dominate the weak. In antiquity, however, thinkers portrayed hierarchical harmony as benefiting everyone. Complementarity and mutual support supposedly provided space for each person to flourish.[145]

The rise of harmony as an ideological ideal spurred a reexamination of the bond between spouses. In the name of marital harmony, a wife was expected to accept a position below her husband.[146] To thrive, she had to somehow turn this unequal situation to her advantage. Rather than fighting this inequity, wives tended to embrace their subordinate role and use it strategically to win prestige by promoting family harmony.[147]

The ideology of filial piety counterbalanced the submission of wife to husband. In remote antiquity the term *xiao*, which later referred to filiality, originally referred to a sacrificial ritual conducted to feed an ancestor, as people were believed to require food and drink even after death.[148] During the Western Zhou period, people made *xiao* offerings to deceased family members, remote blood relatives, in-laws, and even friends. The meaning of *xiao* altered over time, as people began to show their respect for the deceased by adhering to the principles they had followed in life. Eventually *xiao* became filial piety—a moral obligation to defer to living family elders. Confucian thinkers steadily elevated filiality in importance, declaring it the foundation of an ethical life and the wellspring of subsidiary virtues.[149] In addition, like the inequality of husband and wife, the obedience of child to parent also fostered harmony.

The rising importance of filial piety empowered women within the family. Significantly, Zhou thinkers did not make much distinction between obedience to father or mother. Because childbirth involved considerable danger and pain, offspring owed their mother lifelong devotion in recompense.[150] Thinkers often discussed a child's devotion to both parents.[151] They even compared the relationship between parent and child with that of ruler and minister.[152] So while the demands of harmony subjugated wife to husband, filial piety elevated a mother far above her children, placing them under lifelong obligation to respect, support, and obey her.[153] Although a son might remonstrate with an errant mother, under most circumstances he felt obligated to obey her.[154] The importance of filial piety to the history of Chinese women cannot be overstated. In the centuries to follow, the duty of children to serve and obey their mothers shaped family dynamics and even court politics.

The rise of elaborate forms of discourse, both verbal and written, further influenced women's lives by providing new and carefully argued justifications for patriarchy. In this respect, China conformed to trends seen throughout the world. All ancient civilizations gradually reconfigured gender relations by inventing patriarchal ideologies that depressed female status.[155] Chinese society had always recognized differences between the sexes. However, thinkers now used sophisticated bodies of thought to interpret difference as hierarchy, thus validating patriarchy in persuasive new ways.

Division of labor by sex had been a standard practice since the Stone Age. Gendered division of labor initially served as a pragmatic custom that raised a community's productivity by promoting specialization. But Eastern Zhou thinkers used this association of work with sex to justify vastly different gendered social roles. They seized on this primal practice as a foundation for the harmonious and moral society and imbued stereotypical male and female work roles with moral significance.[156] To make gendered work roles into an ideology, Zhou writers discuss male and female labor in deliberately simplistic terms. Although the average person carried out many different tasks each day, writers took the production of grain as symbolic of male work and textile making as the core female pursuit.[157] Although they further contrasted agriculture with other kinds of men's work (such as commerce and craft), cloth making remained the sole kind of normative female labor.[158] Male and female tasks were no longer just practical activities but expressed a person's innate gendered essence.[159] A woman who spent her time diligently weaving cloth proved herself a proper woman, hence a good person. Adherence to gendered work roles had become a way to publicly display virtue.

The valorization of gendered work roles became the basis of a far more comprehensive form of gender separation, as the belief that men and women should inhabit different work spheres expanded to cover every realm of life. Ritual experts classified social space into two regions closely associated with each sex, contrasting the feminine inner (*nei*) with masculine outer (*wai*) realm.[160] A woman could demonstrate her devotion to

Figure 5.3. Stylized Depiction of a Chu Woman

virtue by remaining within feminized spaces, conducting activities appropriate to that realm, and avoiding casual interaction with men. Advocates of separating the sexes warned that if women and men mingled freely, disaster would surely result.[161] While the gendering of social space and physical separation of the sexes affected men, it had a far greater impact on women. Female participation in public activities came to seem inappropriate and even immoral.[162] An emphasis on segregating the sexes also devalued women by seeing them primarily in physical terms as a body inhabiting gendered space.

Ritual texts sometimes describe the rules of gender separation in extreme terms, demanding that even wife and husband go to great lengths to remain physically apart lest they undermine the gendered division of space.[163]

> The men should not speak of what belongs to the inside (of the house), nor the women of what belongs to the outside. Except at sacrifices and funeral rites, they should not hand vessels to one another. In all other cases when they have occasion to give and receive anything, the woman should receive it in a basket. If she has no basket, they should both sit down, and the other put the thing on the ground and she will then take it up. Outside or inside, they should not go to the same well, nor to the same bathing-house. They should not share the same mat in lying down; they should not ask or borrow anything from other another; they should not wear similar upper or lower garments.

Strict adherence to these draconian admonitions would have made a married couple almost as distant as two strangers, even as they resided together in the same house. Most likely, few people followed such stringent guidelines to the letter. Nevertheless, the rise of such extreme discourse about separating the sexes had fateful consequences, as it became the standard template for gender relations.

Even in the Zhou, some people began to judge a woman's moral integrity based on her avoidance of men, male activities, and masculine spaces. She could win plaudits for remaining hidden in the inner recesses of the home, avoiding public places, and ignoring matters beyond the domestic sphere.[164] A woman who entered the exterior world of male affairs and exposed herself to the gaze of strangers began to appear selfish, as she failed to consider how her unseemly behavior would redound on her family's reputation. Writers even warned that women who usurped male roles and invaded masculine venues courted disaster for themselves and the men around them.[165]

Although these dictates initially had little effect on women's behavior, over time the ritual canon assumed increasing respectability and readers began to regard it as almost akin to holy writ. As the prestige of ritual texts rose, the distinction between the inner and outer worlds allocated to each sex became increasingly rigid.[166] Mencius even pondered whether it was proper for a man to touch his sister-in-law's hand to save her from drowning.[167] Although he concluded that the proper course would be to save a female relative from death, later thinkers such as the controversial Cheng Yi (1033–1107) eventually came to the opposite conclusion. Over time, some extremists came to value separation of the sexes more than life itself.

Even though women and men each had their own realm, these two spaces had unequal importance. Male monopolization of the most important places further restricted the opportunities available to women. And as separation elided into hierarchy, some people took the idea even further by asserting that a woman must obey the men around her. Before marriage, a daughter deferred to her father's wishes. And as husband and wife constituted a harmonious hierarchy, the good wife obeyed her spouse.[168] But what about a widow? Without a man to control her and act on her behalf, she might potentially invade male spaces and violate the norms of gender separation. To solve this problem, some thinkers tried to override the dictates of filial piety and placed the widowed mother under her son's control. Putting women under the successive authority of the three closest men in her life became known as the "three obediences" (*sancong*). According to this model, a woman ought to submit to her father and then her husband. After his death, she should obey her son.[169] Although it seems that few people in antiquity ever took this injunction seriously, the insertion of the three obediences into the heart of gender rhetoric nevertheless provided an additional boost to patriarchy and became a mainstay of gender rhetoric in later centuries.

Intangible cosmological concepts justified the separation and inequality of male and female in highly abstract terms. Some Eastern Zhou thinkers began to conceptualize the world through metaphysical models. They described the cosmos as a complex system consisting of invisible components whose interactions account for changes in the visible worlds of nature and humanity.[170] As these models integrated gender concepts, they imposed cosmological abstractions on the human world to organize relations between the sexes. The bifurcation of reality into yin and yang, which became associated with female and male, projected gender relations into the innermost workings of the cosmos. Likewise, the *Classic of Changes* (*Yijing*) promoted male-associated *qian* and female *kun*, abstract symbols consisting of broken and unbroken lines, to the forefront of an even more intricate metaphysical system. Juxtaposing the abstracted concepts of masculine heaven (*tian*) and feminine earth (*di*) further interjected gender into cosmology. By viewing the fundamental framework of the universe in terms of gendered hierarchical pairs (with *qian* taking pre-

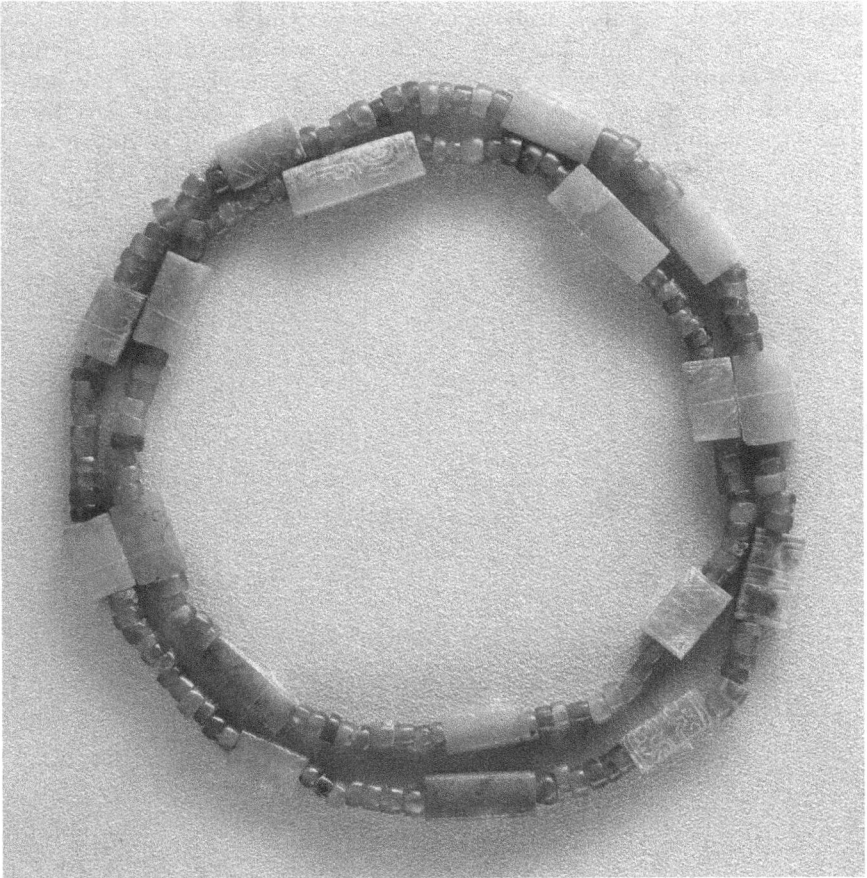

Figure 5.4. Bracelet of Semi-Precious Stones
Wulakuake

cedence over *kun,* yang over yin, and heaven over earth), early thinkers created sophisticated ideologies that subsequent generations employed to legitimize patriarchy and bar women from participating in key activities.

In spite of the emergence of highly articulated patriarchal thought and rhetoric, ideas about gender remained contested.[171] Ancient writings did not treat matters related to women systematically or at length. Instead, thinkers from various schools issued fragmentary statements outlining diverse views. In general, they remained aware of the indefinite complications of daily life and hesitated to issue blanket rules for female behavior. As a result, ancient writings about women often seem perplexingly inconsistent. While one passage describes a wise woman who prudently uses her talents, another declares women inherently foolish or demands that they remain confined to the home. However vague and contradictory classical writings regarding gender may have been, people of later eras took them as authoritative. Long after the end of the Zhou dynasty, these diverse and fragmentary ideas remained the starting point for discussions about the legitimate roles of women in society.

Epilogue

The Myth of the Evil Woman

In the Late Eastern Zhou era, thinkers constructed comprehensive intellectual systems, bringing a wide range of topics under discussion. As the scope of intellectual discourse expanded, they pondered female social roles, examining issues such as the proper relationship between spouses, the bond between mother and son, normative work roles, and gendered space. Most ambitiously, they tried to understand how women fit into the standard political ideology that legitimized rulers and explained the rise and fall of dynasties.

Some prominent Eastern Zhou writers denigrated female participation in government and demanded that rulers strictly exclude women from affairs of state. Because history provided the precedents used to legitimize political activities and policies, they also tried to remove accounts of powerful women from the orthodox narrative of bygone events. To do so, they had to explain away the positive examples of female administration preserved in historical records.

Most problematically, one of the ten main officials of the revered King Wu, conqueror of Shang and founder of the Zhou dynasty, was a woman. Surviving records refer to her as Wen Mu and Yi Jiang, probably alternate names for the same person.[1] As women's roles in public life receded, some thinkers began to belittle Wen Mu. They claimed that she had not really served as a minister but merely received an honorary official title for marrying into with the royal line. Confucius flatly denied that Wen Mu had been an official.[2] Yet in spite of these attempts to rewrite history, Wen Mu's precedent resonated down the centuries. Later writers often raised her name when discussing female participation in politics.[3]

Some thinkers appealed to standard political ideology to rationalize the exclusion of women from government. During the early Western Zhou, the authors of *Classic of Documents* (*Shangshu*) sought to explain and justify the overthrow of the Shang dynasty by Zhou troops. Because this state had endured for untold centuries, even its conquerors considered the destruction of Shang almost incomprehensible. The finest minds of the age sought to account for the fall of Shang and legitimize the new Zhou dynasty. The resulting model, known as the mandate of heaven (*tianming*), positioned the rise and fall of Shang within a comprehensive moral and cosmological framework that explained the rise and fall of dynasties.

According to the mandate of heaven account, the early Shang kings had been wise and good, and heaven endorsed them so that they could bring order to the world. Over time, however, the morals of Shang decayed, tempting the wrath of heaven. Ultimately the last king of the dynasty behaved so outrageously that he lost the mandate. Thereupon heaven shifted its blessings to the rulers of Zhou, who had shown themselves virtuous and competent. With heaven's support, Zhou then defeated Shang and became masters of the known world.

So how did women fit into this grand scheme? Western Zhou writings initially ignored women, concentrating entirely on male rulers and officials. Yet as thinkers began to appreciate the impact that a high-placed woman could have on major events, they tried to understand the place of female power in dynastic change. Some amended the mandate of heaven theory to bring women into the paradigm. They argued that female conduct represents a significant moral force that can help determine whether or not a ruling house retains supernatural sanction.

Ancient poetry conveys this viewpoint. As poets praised exemplary wives and mothers, they implied that a good woman could morally transform the people around her.[4] Ordinarily, female moral influence did not extend beyond the family. But when a queen or royal concubine affected powerful men in her circle, her influence could be noteworthy. In recognition of the potential political impact of women's virtue, female conduct became a major poetic theme. Of the 160 poems in the *Guofeng* (*Airs of the States*) section of the *Classic of Poetry*, sixty-six deal with female virtue or proper relations between the sexes.[5] The mothers of the early Zhou kings became idealized into saintly paragons of female propriety. They gained credit for attracting heaven's blessings, thus helping to found the dynasty. Writers even euhemerized early queens into fertility goddesses.[6]

As female propriety became linked to political success, people emphasized how a virtuous woman's influence might strengthen the state. One bronze inscription describes a woman named Jin Jiang, wife of Marquis

Wen of Jin. She conducted herself properly, maintained an atmosphere of virtuous decorum, and diligently assisted her husband.[7] In doing so, she helped him achieve his goals and strengthen the state. According to this inscription, success or failure depended on more than just the ruler. His spouse could also affect the quality of governance.

Although poetic accounts of female influence emphasized virtue, a woman could also harm those around her. The philosopher Xunzi (Xun Kuang, c. 310–235) famously argued that human nature is basically evil. This pessimistic viewpoint implied that if a woman lacked sufficient moral cultivation to overcome her inherently bad nature, she could easily commit misdeeds and tempt others to do likewise. As political theorists pondered the potential impact of female actions, they realized that an irresponsible or depraved woman might sway a powerful man to behave immorally. A highly placed wicked woman could even potentially bring down a state. As thinkers realized that female behavior could have a major impact, for good or ill, it became a subject of political and ethical discourse.

In pondering female iniquity, thinkers asked a very basic question: Why do some women violate the standards of propriety? In other words, moralists wanted to understand why a woman would commit evil acts if she had the option of being good. Of course, some people have base character or are simply ignorant of ethics. But in many cases, extreme emotions led a woman astray and motivate her to do something bad. Numerous narratives in the *Zuo Commentary* (*Zuo zhuan*) illustrate how unrestrained feelings could inspire both women and men to violate the rites and veer toward iniquity.[8] The *Zuo Commentary* describes in detail how lust could lead to licentiousness and chaos, sometimes even bringing down a ruler. The male and female characters in these sexualized narratives tend to differ. The women are much more prone to emotional extremes, with devastating consequences to themselves and the men around them. Moralists concluded that women as well as men must be taught moral and ritual norms, as these controls would help women suppress strong emotions that might lead them astray.[9]

The fundamental nature of female power also elicited concern. Ancient writers worried about the potentially corrosive influence of high-placed women on good government. As bureaucracy grew in sophistication to become the main tool of administration, women found themselves excluded from the mechanics of government. While the informality of Western Zhou administration had allowed women opportunities to participate in important matters and attend major gatherings, Eastern Zhou noblewomen could only exercise power indirectly by manipulating powerful men. For a woman to participate in politics, she would have to undermine the legitimate institutions of government. Any expression of female power thus implicitly threatened the stability of the state.

Women influenced politics in various ways. A talented woman might sway the opinions of important men by quoting poetry at a banquet. More often, however, authors describe how a woman flaunted her beauty or charm to win the attentions of a powerful man, then manipulated him to affect affairs of state. The *Zuo Commentary* contends that this sort of subversion usually had disastrous consequences.[10] A beautiful wife or concubine who might use her body to undermine proper government came to seem inherently dangerous.[11] As this line of thought gained currency, the female body assumed negative moral and political implications.

Ancient authorities criticized female participation in politics in other ways as well.[12] Female involvement in government violated separation of the sexes, which mandated that women and men carry out different tasks. The political goals that women tended to pursue also proved to be inherently destabilizing. Some high-ranking ladies intervened in court politics to have their son recognized as heir apparent, even if this meant altering the standard order of succession.[13] Other women concocted elaborate plots to dispose of an heir apparent and secure the right of succession for their own offspring, plunging a state into confusion or outright civil war. In addition, the thinker Han Fei (ca. 280–233) complained that doting mothers tended to spoil their children, making them morally degenerate and further degrading the quality of administration.[14]

By the fourth century BCE, it had become common to compare the roles of minister and consort, as they had an analogous relationship with their lord.[15] A ruler can favor both an official and a palace lady. They might share some common virtues, such as a lack of jealousy and tolerance for rivals. Likewise, either a depraved minister or consort could lead a ruler astray. The emergence of this unlikely comparison between male and female roles at court accounts for the oddly sexualized imagery of the long poem *Lisao* from the state of Chu, which describes the relationship between ruler and official in extravagantly romantic terms. While this unexpected language often baffles modern readers, the ancients were accustomed to thinking of the palace lady as a metaphor for an official. This comparison further underscored the erotic aspect of female power.

During the Eastern Zhou era, a master narrative gradually emerged to explain the fundamental nature of female power. Writers pieced together stories about evil women who misused their charms to lead a powerful man astray, thus bringing down a dynasty. Eventually this negative imagery about destructive women became the standard way that men thought about female power, exerting an immense impact on Chinese politics and gender relations.

The archetype of the evil woman had enigmatic beginnings. A line from the *Classic of Poetry* attributes the destruction of the capital of the Western Zhou to someone named Bao Si.[16]

> Majestic was the capital of Zhou,
> But Lady Bao Si destroyed it.

Although the poet gives Bao Si a major role in the downfall of the Western Zhou, he does not explain how or why she destroyed the dynasty. Yet in spite of the ambiguity, this brief passage had an enormous impact, as it implanted the seeds of the evil woman stereotype in political discourse.

The particulars of the Bao Si story emerged over time. *Conversations of the States (Guoyu)*, most likely written in the fifth century BCE, quotes the Jin court historian Shi Su telling her story in detail. Shi relates that a large black reptile, which emerged from a mysterious box full of poisonous dragon saliva, impregnated a young girl. This unnatural union produced a daughter. Her mother, unwilling to raise a child spawned in such a weird manner, abandoned her. A compassionate couple then rescued her and took her to a place called Bao, where she eventually entered the household of a man called Bao Ju. [17]

> Bao Ju, a man of Bao, had a lawsuit; he thus sent her to the king. The king received her and fell in love with her; he established her queen and she bore [for the king] Prince Bo Fu. Heaven created it a long time ago and its poison is great! [Heaven] will let [her] wait until [the king] fully abused virtue and then she will add to it [more crimes]. When the poison is fully developed, death is also imminent.

After Bao Si bore a son, she demanded that her smitten lover King You (r. 781–771 BCE) forsake his wife, Queen Shen, and the legitimate heir apparent, also called Shen, so that her own offspring could inherit the throne. Her machinations succeeded, and King You sent away the heir in disgrace. In revenge, the deposed heir apparent allied with the Western Rong peoples, defeated the Zhou army, demolished the capital, killed King You, and forced the new king and his retainers to flee their homeland and establish a new capital to the east.

This version of the Bao Si story takes an enigmatic reference in ancient poetry as a starting point and adds sufficient detail to turn it into a coherent narrative. Shi Su constructs the story in a way that elucidates Bao Si's motivations. Due to her freakish birth, she had an inherently evil nature, which accounts for her destructive behavior. In the poetic version, Bao Si was the sole perpetrator, but Shi Su emphasizes that the misguided King

Figure E.1. Bao Si
Wang Hui Wang (1736–1795) 翔.

You of Zhou bore primary responsibility for his own downfall. Nevertheless, Bao Si led the king astray, fomented chaos, and supplemented his crimes, making her complicit in his ruin.

During the Han dynasty, the historian Sima Qian (135?–86 BCE) added more particulars to the Bao Si story and injected it into his magisterial account of the fall of the Western Zhou featured in *Memoirs of the Historian* (*Shiji*). Subsequently the polymath Liu Xiang (77–6 BCE) retold the story of Bao Si in even greater detail in *Biographies of Women* (*Lienü zhuan*), a work that uses vignettes from the lives of model women to demonstrate the principles of female ethics.[18] In these extended Han dynasty versions, Bao Si is no longer even human. Instead she has become the incarnation of an evil spirit that had existed since the Xia dynasty. This malevolent creature entranced King You with her beauty and convinced him to engage in follies that ensured his ultimate self-destruction. The Han dynasty account of the Bao Si myth became extremely popular, and subsequent generations of readers enjoyed this supernatural morality tale. The utility of the Bao Si story, which added a moral dimension to a major historical event, explains why it became the standard account of the fall the Western Zhou, in spite of the exaggerated tone.

Aside from the entertainment value of this compelling legend, the Bao Si myth had other rhetorical functions as well.[19] King You's misplaced trust in such a blatantly evil woman reveals him as irresponsible and foolish, giving the historian reason to censure the self-destructive monarch.[20] According to the mandate of heaven theory, the final ruler of an epoch had to be evil enough to forfeit supernatural blessing. Shifting a large portion of the blame to a woman conveniently allowed historians to continue holding up the Zhou as a model dynasty while accounting for its devastation.

Over time, some skeptics questioned the veracity of this simplistic tale of good and evil.[21] In reality, the destruction of King You seems to have been far more prosaic. A factional power struggle involving both domestic and foreign powers ultimately resulted in his assassination and the collapse of his realm. Nevertheless, most readers preferred myth to reality because the fictitious version carries such a clear-cut meaning.

The archetype of the evil woman not only made a good story, but it also confirmed the orthodox view of history, demonstrating how a woman could lead a ruler to lose the sanction of heaven. Both aesthetically pleasing and edifying, historians applied this topos to explain the fall of every dynasty. Proponents of the mandate of heaven theory believed that the mother or wife of a dynasty's first ruler was always a paragon of virtue who helped attract heaven's benediction for the new government. Likewise, a consort of the dynasty's final king had to be sufficiently bad to justify the mandate's loss. Historians gradually concocted other evil

women analogous to Bao Si and inserted them into the standard historical narrative, claiming that a woman shared culpability for the fall of each
previous dynasty.

Most famously, Zhou and Han writers fabricated an evil woman called
Daji to help account for the collapse of the Shang dynasty.[22] As with the
Bao Si myth, Daji also had nebulous beginnings. The Western Zhou *Classic of Documents* contains a brief passage that blames King Zhou of Shang,
the dynasty's last monarch, for following a woman's advice.[23]

> The king said: "The ancients had a saying, 'The hen does not crow at dawn.
> At dawn the hen is exhausted at home.' Now the king of Shang has accepted
> a woman's words and put them to use."

Notably, this passage does not mention any woman by name. Nor is she
even identified as evil. Here the king of Shang's mistake is taking any
female advice, as the author presumably considers all women inherently
foolish. Nevertheless, by associating female influence with the end of
Shang, this revered work gave later writers grounds for alleging that a
woman had a hand in the dynasty's collapse.

The *Mozi*, compiled gradually over the course of the Eastern Zhou, developed this theme further. The Mohist school taught that the human and
natural realms are closely interconnected, analogous to the integral parts
of a single organism. This link is so intimate that the impropriety of an
important person can disrupt the workings of the natural world. Due to
the organismic nature of the cosmos, aberrations in the natural order can
presage the loss of heaven's mandate. The *Mozi* mentions two ill omens
related to women that warned of the impending fall of Shang: "female demons came out in the night" and "there were women who became men"
(or perhaps "there were women who acted as men").[24] Although this text
still does not identify a specific evil woman, it associates a strange and
malevolent female presence with the fall of Shang.[25]

The third century BCE thinker Xunzi had an enormous impact on
thinking about the influence of women on politics. Apparently influenced
by the myth of Bao Ji, Xunzi created a parallel female figure to explain
the end of the Shang dynasty.[26] In doing so, he took the previous inchoate
images of a woman involved in the fall of Shang and attributed them to
a concrete individual. Xunzi assigned her a name, calling her Daji, and
presented her to his readers as an important historical figure. According
to Xunzi's retelling of the fall of Shang, the evil Daji led King Zhou astray
and thus helped bring down the Shang.

In addition to Daji, Xunzi also describes a parallel evil female character
called Moxi, whom he identified as the consort of Jie, final ruler of the Xia
dynasty. Like Bao Si and Daji, Moxi also coaxed a powerful man to behave

Figure E.2. Daji as Portrayed in an Eighteenth-Century French Engraving

immorally, thereby causing him to lose the mandate of heaven and suffer destruction. Xunzi specifically accuses these women of convincing a man to act "chaotically" (*luan*), a term that held great significance for his contemporaries living amid the anarchy of the Warring States era.

The characters Daji and Moxi do not appear in any transmitted text prior to Xunzi. Moreover, their names differ from the sort used by Shang and Western Zhou women. The name Daji is a homonym for the phrase "grieved for herself" (*daji* 怛己), and Moxi can read as meaning "final happiness." Both names seem to have been fabrications intended to emphasize their dangerous allure and accentuate their culpability. Given these strange names and unprecedented narratives, it seems likely that Xunzi or some earlier Eastern Zhou writer fabricated these two characters. Although previous writers had hinted at a female role in political decline, Xunzi went further than before in emphasizing the role of evil women in dynastic collapse and providing specific names and stories to back up this point of view.

By giving women such a prominent place in the workings of the mandate of heaven, Xunzi significantly revised the standard political ideology. Western Zhou thinkers had blamed a decadent ruler for a dynasty's fall. Xunzi inserted an evil woman at the side of each final monarch and saddled them with a major share of the blame. While these women did not exercise power in their own right, they nevertheless wreaked havoc by convincing a foolish man to behave irresponsibly, thereby driving the dynasty toward destruction.

During the Western Han, a pivotal era when the standard conventions of Chinese historiography coalesced, Xunzi's vision of dynastic collapse became integrated into comprehensive narratives about the past.[27] When Sima Qian described the rise and fall of the ancient dynasties in *Memoirs of the Historian*, he implanted a good woman at the beginning of each dynasty and an evil woman at the end to illustrate the mechanics of the mandate of heaven. Sima embellished the stories of Bao Si, Daji, and Moxi, creating a detailed and compelling narrative for each and incorporating them into the orthodox narrative of antiquity. Sima Qian's modified version of the mandate of heaven theory, which depicted both female virtue and misconduct as significant historical forces, had immense influence on future generations and became the standard interpretation of the dynastic cycle.

Toward the end of the Western Han, the erudite scholar Liu Xiang gave an additional boost to the evil woman myth. He included biographies of destructive consorts in his compilation *Biographies of Women*, the most influential book about Chinese women ever written, reinforcing the belief that female malfeasance can help bring down a dynasty. Through the efforts of these widely read Western Han authors, the myth of the evil

Figure E.3. A Woodblock Print of Moxi, from an Illustrated Edition of Liu Xiang's *Biographies of Women* (Lienü zhuan)

woman entered the mainstream of Chinese discourse about politics and gender. After the end of the Han, which had been destabilized for centuries by powerful empresses and their kinsmen, powerful men repeatedly referred to the myth of the evil woman to demand the complete exclusion of empresses and concubines from administration.[28] The impact of these narratives endured to the end of the imperial era.

The assumption that women exert a morally corrosive influence cast suspicion on a ruler who enthusiastically enjoyed female companionship. People assumed that if a ruler spent too much time in the women's quarters of the palace, he might be tempted to ignore pressing matters and waste his time with frivolities, degrading the quality of administration. In the wake of the evil woman myth, an author merely had to mention that a ruler had allowed a woman to become involved with an important matter and the reader would immediately judge him irresponsible.[29]

Over time, writers increasingly portrayed influential women as highly sexual, thus accounting for how they affected politics. As a corollary, they saw frequent contact with women as inherently dissipating to a man. In contrast to male power, which draws from a number of strengths, the ancients assumed that a woman usually gains authority over others by manipulating her body. The myth of Bao Si and other depraved ancient characters implicitly asserted that female "power" (*de*) expresses unrestrained sexuality.[30] A ruler had to take care not to succumb to the allure of female beauty, lest a woman induce him to act improperly. Even musical performances had to be serious and oriented around men rather than an excuse for exhibiting female bodies.[31]

Ancient China was not unique in constructing rhetoric that justified excluding women from important matters.[32] In archaic states throughout the ancient world, men dominated emerging political systems and usually prohibited women from directly wielding power. When a woman had a hand in politics, in most instances she either exerted influence indirectly through male intermediaries or else she commandeered the patriarchal system. To combat female power, early civilizations tended to classify women as either respectable or licentious. The reputable woman was attached to a family or a comparable institution that could restrain her behavior. Those who escaped these restraints appeared shameless. Although these institutions enforced patriarchy, women who submitted to them nevertheless gained certain benefits. A woman who acted independently ran the risk of losing male protection and being victimized. And a disgraced woman who refused to behave decently would find it difficult to have a good and stable life. As with Bao Si and Daji, people in cultures around the world told stories about female malfeasance. These narratives warned men that women could destabilize patriarchal institutions and cautioned women to maintain an air of respectability.

During the Late Eastern Zhou, justifications for limiting female autonomy became increasingly sophisticated and detailed, constricting the bounds of proper female life. Of course, reality never completely conformed to ideals. During the Han dynasty, a long succession of empresses dowager used filial piety as an excuse to dominate weak emperors and run the government. And the Tang monarch Wu Zetian even managed to rule as an "emperor" in her own name. Nevertheless, custom, law, literature, and education absorbed these early ideas about gender, thereby translating rhetoric into social norms. Ancient gender concepts thus became the starting point for subsequent discussions of the proper roles for women and men. Over the next two millennia, people of both sexes endeavored to work out the implications of these formative ideas about powerful women.

Glossary

Anyang	安陽
Banpo	半坡
bao (title)	保
bao (form of marriage)	報
Bao (people)	褒
Bao Ju	褒姁
Bao Si	褒姒
Baoji	寶雞
Beishouling	北首嶺
bi	妣
Bi Geng	妣庚
Bi Gui	妣癸
Bi Wu	妣戊
Bi Xin	妣辛
Bi Yi	妣乙
bin	賓
binji	賓祭
bo	伯
Bo Fu	伯服
Cai	蔡
Cao Cao	曹操
Cao Pi	曹丕

Chang, K.C.	張光直
chen	臣
Chen Dongyuan	陳東原
Cheng (king)	成
Cheng Yi	程頤
chenqie	臣妾
Chu	楚
Chuci	楚辭
Chunqiu	春秋
Ci	次
cifei	次妃
cong	琮
da	大
Da Yi	大乙
Dadianzi	大甸子
Daji	妲己
daji ("grieved for herself")	怛己
Dawenkou	大汶口
Daxi	大溪
de	德
Di (god)	帝
di (earth)	地
Di Yi	帝乙
ding	鼎
Dong Yi	東夷
Dongmu	東母
duo chen	多臣
duo fu	多婦
duo nü	多女
Er	兒
erfei	二妃
Erlitou	二里頭
fei	妃
fu (father)	父
fu (a female title)	帚，婦
fu (an official position)	服
fu (husband)	夫
Fu Ding	婦丁
Fu Dong	婦冬

Fu Hao	婦好
Fu Ji	父己
Fu Jia	婦甲
Fu Jian	婦姦
Fu Jing	婦井, 婦妌
Fu Xi	伏羲
Fu Xin	婦辛
Fu Xuan	婦旋
Fu Yi	父乙
Fu Zi	婦子
furen	夫人
Gaomei	高媒
Geng Ying	庚嬴
gong (duke)	公
gong (honorific for deceased)	恭
Gong Ji	公姞
Gong Si	公姒
gou	姤
gu	姑
gui (bronze vessel)	簋
gui (leaving or returning home, marriage)	歸
Guifang	鬼方
Guo	虢
Guo Moruo	郭沫若
Guofeng	國風
Guoyu	國語
Hao	好
Han Fei	韓非
Hongshan	紅山
hou	后
Hou Ji	后稷
Houmu Wu	后母戊
Huang	媓
hui	惠
ji (term for birth order)	季
Ji (surname)	姬
ji (hairpin)	笄
jia (auspicious)	嘉
jia (family)	家

jia (to marry)	嫁
Jia Shiheng	賈士蘅
Jiang	姜
Jiang Qing	江青
Jiang Yuan	姜嫄
Jiangshi ren	姜氏人
Jiangzhai	姜寨
Jie	桀
Jin	晉
Jin Jiang	晉姜
Jingji	井季
Jingjie	旌介
jiuji	酒祭
jun	君
junshi	君氏
Kang (king)	康
kao	考
Keshengzhuang	客省莊
kuji	哭祭
kun	坤
Laoguantai	老官台
Li	厲
li chenqie	隸臣妾
liang	俍
liangnü	良女
Liangzhu	良渚
liaoji	燎祭
Lienü zhuan	列女傳
lihun	離婚
Liji	禮記
Ling	靈
Lisao	離騷
Liu Xiang	劉向
Longshan	龍山
Lu	魯
luan	亂
Lunyu	論語
Majiabin	馬家濱
Majiahong	馬家洪

Majiayao	馬家窯
Mao	毛
Mei	媚
meng	孟
Meng Ke	孟軻
ming	名
Mosuo	摩梭
Moxi	末喜, 妹喜
Mozi	墨子
mu (mother)	母
mu (an official position)	牧
mu (posthumous name, name of a duke)	穆
mu (unit of area)	畝
Mu Xin	母辛
nan	男
nan yang	難養
Nanyue	南越
Nanzi	南子
nei	內
Niuheliang	牛河梁
nü	女
Nü Gua	女媧
Nü Wa	女媧
nüjun	女君
nümu	女母
nüzi	女子
Pang	龐
Peiligang	裴李崗
Ping	平
qi (abandonment)	棄
qi (wife)	妻
Qi (state)	齊
qian	乾
Qiang	羌
qie	妾
Qijia	齊家
Qin	秦
Qin Shihuang	秦始皇
qu (take)	取

qu (to marry)	娶
ru	汝
Rong	戎
Rongdi	戎狄
saiji	奈祭
sancong	三從
Sanlihe	三里河
Shangshu	尚書
shao	少
she	社
She	奢
Shen	申
sheng	聖
shi (kinship term)	氏
shi (preparing for divination)	示
shi (wife)	奭
Shi Ban	師般
Shi Su	史蘇
Shiji	史記
Shijia	史家
Shijing	詩經
shu	叔
shuzi	庶子
shuang	爽
si	司
Si Tu Mu	司𡥉母
Sima Qian	司馬遷
Simu Wu	司母戊
Song	宋
tai furen	太夫人
Tai Si	太似
taibao	太保
taihou	太后
Tang (king)	湯
Tang (predynastic ruler)	唐
taowang	逃亡
Taosi	陶寺
tian	天
tiangan	天干

tianjun	天君
tianming	天命
wai	外
wang	王
Wang Bo Jiang	王伯姜
Wang Jiang	王姜
Wang Si	王似
wangfu	王婦
wanghou	王后
wangqi	王妻
Wei (state)	衛
Wei (dynasty)	魏
wen	文
Wen	文
Wen Mu	文母
Wo	我
Wu (king)	武
wu (shaman)	巫
wuer	巫兒
Wu Ding	武丁
Wu Zetian	武則天
xiao (lesser)	小
xiao (filial piety)	孝
Ximu	西母
xin	信
xing	姓
Xiwangcun	西王村
Xiwangmu	西王母
xiangyinjiu	鄉飲酒
xiuqi	休妻
Xuan	宣
Xun	姰
Xun Kuang	荀況
Xunzi	荀子
Yan (ruler)	炎
Yan (state)	燕
yang	陽
Yangshao	仰韶
Yanshi	偃師

yi (give)	詒, 貽
Yi (people)	夷
Yi (marquis)	乙
Yi Jiang	邑姜
Yijing	易經
yin (licentiousness)	淫
yin (cosmological principle)	陰
Yin Ji	尹姞
ying	媵
yinsi	淫祀
Yong Ji	雍姬
You (king)	幽
youji	侑祭
yu (sacrifice to deity)	禦
yu (sacrifice to prevent harm)	御
yu (birth of son)	余
Yu (noble)	旟
Yu (noble)	弓魚
yuanfei	元妃
Yuanjunmiao	元君廟
yueji	礿祭, 禴祭
yun	孕
Zeng	曾
Zhai Zhong	祭仲
zhang	長
Zhanguo	戰國
Zhanguo ce	戰國策
Zhao (state)	趙
Zhao (king)	昭
Zhao Yi	趙翼
zhaomu	昭穆
Zheng (state)	鄭
zheng (marriage form)	烝
Zhengzhou	鄭州
zhong (term for birth order)	仲
zhong (loyalty)	忠
zhongbiao hun	中表婚
Zhou (king)	紂
zhouji	周祭

zhuan	專
zi (child)	子
zi (style name)	字
zongfa	宗法
zu	族
Zu Ding	祖丁
Zu Ji	祖己
Zu Yi	祖乙
zudian	祖奠
Zuo zhuan	左傳

Notes

INTRODUCTION

1. Michael Nylan, "Afterword." In *Chang'an 26 BCE: An Augustan Age in China*, ed. Michael Nylan and Griet Vankeerberghen (Seattle: University of Washington Press, 2015), 506–07.

2. For detailed discussions of how the rise of the state exacerbated gender hierarchy see June Nash, "The Aztecs and the Ideology of Male Dominance," *Signs* 4 (1978): 349–62.

3. Deniz Kandiyoti, "Bargaining with Patriarchy," *Gender and Society* 2, no. 3 (1988): 274–90.

4. Sherry B. Ortner, "Gender Hegemonies," *Cultural Critique* 14 (1989-1990): 36–38.

5. For a discussion of gendered dual prestige systems, see Patricia L. Crown and Suzanne K. Fish, "Gender and Status in the Hohokam Pre-Classic to Classic Transition," *American Anthropologist* 98, no. 4 (1996): 804, 812.

6. Margaret W. Conkey and Janet D. Spector, "Archaeology and the Study of Gender," in *Advances in Archaeological Method and Theory, Volume 7*, ed. Michael B. Schiffer (Orlando: Academic Press, 1984), 2, 4, 6–7, 12; Ruth D. Whitehouse, "Gender Archaeology and Archaeology of Women: Do We Need Both?" in *Archaeology and Women: Ancient and Modern Issues*, ed. Sue Hamilton, Ruth D. Whitehouse, and Katherine I. Wright (Walnut Creek, CA: Left Coast Press, 2007), 29–30. For an overview of issues in the archaeology of gender, see Margaret W. Conkey and Joan M. Gero, "Gender and Feminism in Archaeology," *Annual Review of Anthropology* 26 (1997): 411–37.

7. Joan M. Gero, "Genderlithics: Women's Roles in Stone Tool Production," in *Engendering Archaeology: Women and Prehistory*, ed. Joan M. Gero and Margaret W. Conkey (Oxford: Basil Blackwell, 1991), 163–93.

8. Conkey and Spector, "Archaeology and the Study of Gender," 13.

9. Kent Flannery and Joyce Marcus, *The Creation of Inequality: How Our Prehistoric Ancestors Set the Stage for Monarchy, Slavery, and Empire* (Cambridge, MA: Harvard University Press, 2012), 35–36.

10. Richard W. Guisso, "Thunder Over the Lake: The Five Classics and Perceptions of Woman in Early China," in *Women in China: Current Directions in Historical Scholarship,* ed. Richard Guisso (Youngstown, NY: Philo Press, 1981), 48.

11. Tianlong Jiao, "Gender Studies in Chinese Neolithic Archaeology," in *Gender and the Archaeology of Death,* ed. Bettina Arnold and Nancy L. Wicker (Walnut Creek: Rowman & Littlefield, 2001), 58–59; Sarah Milledge Nelson, "Ideology, Power, and Gender: Emergent Complex Society in Northeastern China," in *In Pursuit of Gender: Worldwide Archaeological Approaches,* ed. Sarah Milledge Nelson and Myriam Rosen-Ayalon (Walnut Creek, CA: AltaMira Press, 2002), 74–76. The site report is Liaoning Sheng Wenwu Kaogu Yanjiusuo, "Liaoning Niuheliang Hongshan wenwu 'nüshen miao' yu jishi zhongqun fajue jianbao," *Wenwu* 8 (1986): 1–17. Bret Hinsch, "Prehistoric Images of Women from the North China Region: The Origins of Chinese Goddess Worship?" *Journal of Chinese Religions* 32 (2004): 71–78, argues that the Niuheliang site has no relation to the origins of Chinese goddess worship.

12. David N. Keightley, "At the Beginning: The Status of Women in Neolithic and Shang China," *Nan Nü* 1, no. 1 (1999): 26; Nelson, "Ideology, Power, and Gender," 78. For a discussion of the relation of Hongshan to other Neolithic cultures, see Katheryn M. Linduff, Robert D. Drennan, and Gideon Shelach, "Early Complex Societies in NE China: The Chifeng International Collaborative Archaeological Research Project," *Journal of Field Archaeology* 29, nos. 1/2 (2002-2004): 45–73.

CHAPTER 1

1. Here I use the term myth as analogous to ideology. Ben Halpern, "'Myth' and 'Ideology' in Modern Usage," *History and Theory* 1, no. 2 (1961): 129–49.

2. Wei Shou, *Weishu* (Beijing: Zhonghua, 1974), 101: 2241.

3. Jennifer W. Jay, "Imagining Matriarchy: 'Kingdoms of Women' in Tang China," *Journal of the American Oriental Society* 116, no. 2 (1996): 220–29.

4. Ann Taylor Allen, "Feminism, Social Science, and the Meanings of Modernity: The Debate on the Origin of the Family in Europe and the United States, 1860–1914," *The American Historical Review* 104, no. 4 (1999): 1089–91.

5. Johann Jacob Bachofen, *An English Translation of Bachofen's Mutterrecht (Mother Right) (1861): A Study of the Religious and Juridical Aspects of Gynecocracy in the Ancient World,* trans. David Partenheimer (Lewistown, NY: Edwin Mellen Press, 2003).

6. Lewis Henry Morgan, *Ancient Society or Researches in the Lines of Human Progress from Savagery through Barbarism to Civilization,* ed. Eleanor Burke Leacock (Glouster, MA: Peter Smith, 1974).

7. Frederick Engels, *The Origin of the Family, Private Property, and the State* (New York: Pathfinder, 1972). Karl Wittfogel, "The Society of Prehistoric China,"

Zeitschrift für Sozialwissenschaften 8 (1939): 138–86, describes how the views of Engels became integrated into Marxist narratives of Chinese history.

8. Wu Fei, "Jinshi renlun pipan yu muxi lun wenti," *Zhongguo zhexue shi* 4 (2014): 116–20.

9. Chen Dongyuan, *Zhongguo funü shenghuo shi* (Shanghai: Shangwu yinshuguan, 1937), 21.

10. P. Tolstoy, "Morgan and Soviet Anthropological Thought," *American Anthropologist* 54, no. 1 (1952): 8–17; Carolyn Fluehr-Lobban, "A Marxist Reappraisal of the Matriarchate," *Current Anthropology* 20, no. 2 (1979): 341–59.

11. Guo Moruo, "Shangceng jianzhu de shehui zuzhi," in *Guo Moruo quanji: lishi bian* (Beijing: Renmin Wenxue 1982), vol. 1, 230–34. For a detailed description of the orthodox Chinese Marxist version of prehistoric matrilinealism and matriarchy, see Li Genpan, Huang Chongyue, and Lu Xun, *Zhongguo yuanshi shehui jingji yanjiu* (Beijing: Zhongguo shehui kexue, 1987), 321–56.

12. Yao Dazhong, *Huanghe wenming zhi guang* (Taipei: Sanmin, 1981), 95; Luo Hongzeng, *Jianming Zhongguo gudai shi* (Beijing: Qiushi, 1986), 8; Jian Bozan, *Xian Qin shi* (Beijing: Daxue, 1990), 111; Han Longfu and Qiu Zhiyong, "Lun muquan shehui de xingcheng he yiyi," *Wuling xuekan* 5 (1995): 55–59.

13. Wang Zhen, "Luelun Yangshao wenhua de qunhun he duiouhun," *Kaogu* 7 (1962): 14; Zhao Wenyi, "Cong Banpo Jiangzhai yizhi yu minzuxue ziliao kan muxi shizu gongshe," in *Minzuxue yanjiu*, vol. 6, ed. Minzuxue yanjiuhui (Beijing: Minzu, 1985), 25; Gao Guangren, "Shandong diqu shiqian wenhua gailun," in *Shandong shiqian wenhua lunwenji*, ed. Shandong sheng jilu kaogu congkan bianjibu (Ji'nan: Shandong renmin, 1986), 40–55; Liang Anhe, "Xian Qin shiqi de zhongnong sixiang ji qi cuoshi," *Gujin nongye* 3 (1998): 31; Qiao Xinhua and Yang Guoyong, "Xian Qin funü juese bianqian de yuanyin," *Shanxi Daxue xuebao* 8 (2002): 20–23; Wang Guofu, "Cong Dadiwan yi, erqi wenhua yicun kan woguo gudai muxi shizu shehui," *Tianshui Shifan Xueyuan xuebao* 22, no. 6 (2002): 35.

14. Wu Ruzuo, "Cong muzang fajue lai kan Yangshao wenhua de shehui xingzhi," *Kaogu* 12 (1961): 691; Jian, *Xian Qin shi*, 111; Han and Qiu, "Lun muquan shehui de xingcheng he yiyi," 56. Although most hunting and gathering societies lack large kinship units, Australian aborigines developed clans within non-agricultural societies. In China, the clan probably emerged after the invention of agriculture, although larger kinship units may have started to develop even earlier. Flannery and Marcus, *The Creation of Inequality*, 15–16.

15. R.H. Barnes, "Introduction," in *Joseph Kohler, On the Prehistory of Marriage: Totemism, Group Marriage, Mother Right*, trans. R.H. Barnes and Ruth Barnes (Chicago: University of Chicago Press, 1975), 23–29.

16. Timothy Earle, *Bronze Age Economics: The Beginnings of Political Economies* (Boulder, CO: Westview Press, 2002), 14.

17. Alice Schlegel, *Male Dominance and Female Autonomy: Domestic Authority in Matrilineal Societies* (New Haven: HRAF Press, 1972), 1–2; Henrietta L. Moore, *Feminism and Anthropology* (Cambridge: Polity, 1988), 60.

18. Robert H. Lowie, *Primitive Society* (New York: Boni and Liveright, 1920), 189–91; G.P. Murdock, *Social Structure* (New York: Macmillan, 1949), 184–89; Robin Fox, *Kinship and Marriage: An Anthropological Perspective* (Cambridge: Cambridge University Press, 1967), 113; Kathleen Gough, "An Anthropologist Looks at

Engels," in *Woman in a Man-Made World*, ed. Nona Glazer-Malbin and Helen Youngelson Waehrer (Chicago: Rand McNally, 1972), 156–68; Joan Bamberger, "The Myth of Matriarchy: Why Men Rule in Primitive Society," in *Woman, Culture, and Society*, ed. Michelle Zimbalist Rosaldo and Louise Lamphere (Stanford: Stanford University Press, 1974), 263–80; Nanneke Redclift, "Rights in Women: Kinship, Culture and Materialism," in *Engels Revisited: New Feminist Essays*, ed. Janet Sayers, Mary Evans, and Nanneke Redclift (London: Tavistock, 1987), 113–44.

19. Fox, *Kinship and Marriage*, 104, 115, 120–21.

20. Lionel Tiger, *Men in Groups* (New York: Random House, 1969); Steven Goldberg, *The Inevitability of Patriarchy* (New York: William Morrow, 1973); Richard Pearson, "Social Complexity in Chinese Coastal Neolithic Sites," *Science* 213, no. 4512 (1981): 1078–86; Ortner, "Gender Hegemonies," 35–36. Seymour Parker and Hilda Parker, "The Myth of Male Superiority: Rise and Demise," *American Anthropologist* 81, no. 2 (1979): 291–92, dissent from prevailing views about the ubiquity of patriarchy.

21. Allen, "Feminism, Social Science, and the Meanings of Modernity," 1099–106.

22. Sarah Milledge Nelson, *Gender in Archaeology: Analyzing Power and Prestige*, second edition (Walnut Creek, CA: AltaMira Press, 2004), 92–94.

23. Alison Booth, "The Mother of All Cultures: Camille Paglia and Feminist Mythologies," *The Kenyon Review*, New Series 21, no. 1 (1999): 30; Cynthia Eller, *The Myth of Matriarchal Prehistory: Why an Invented Past Won't Give Women a Future* (Boston: Beacon Press, 2000); Camille Paglia, "Erich Neumann: Theorist of the Great Mother," *Arion* 13, no. 3 (2006): 9; Cynthia Eller, *Gentlemen and Amazons: The Myth of Matriarchal Prehistory* (Berkeley: University of California Press, 2011); Cynthia Eller, "Matriarchy and the Volk," *Journal of the American Academy of Religion* 81, no. 1 (2013): 213.

24. Richard Pearson, "Chinese Neolithic Burial Patterns: Problems of Method and Interpretation," *Early China* 13 (1988): 1–45; Keightley, "At the Beginning," 47–53; Elisabeth A. Bacus, "Gender in East and Southeast Asian Archaeology," in *Worlds of Gender: The Archaeology of Women's Lives Around the Globe*, ed. Sarah Milledge Nelson (Lanham, MD: AltaMira Press, 2007), 41–42; Gideon Selach, "Marxist and Post-Marxist Paradigms for the Neolithic," in *Gender and Chinese Archaeology*, ed. Katheryn M. Linduff and Yan Sun (Walnut Creek, CA: Altamira Press, 2004), 11–12.

25. Tolstoy, "Morgan and Soviet Anthropological Thought," 8–17; Nelson Graburn, "On Marxism and the Matriarchate," *Current Anthropology* 20, no. 3 (1979), 608–09.

26. Gu Yan, "Chiang Ch'ing's Wolfish Ambition in Publicizing 'Matriarchal Society,'" *Chinese Studies in History* 12, no. 3 (1979): 75–79.

27. Wang Ningsheng, "Yangshao Burial Customs and Social Organization: A Comment on the Theory of Yangshao Matrilineal Society and Its Methodology," *Early China* 11–12 (1985–1987): 6–32; Wang Ningsheng, "Yangshao wenhua zangsu he shehui zuzhi de yanjiu - dui Yangshao muxi shehui shuo ji qi fangfalun de shangquan," *Wenwu* 371 (1987): 36–43; Selach, "Marxist and Post-Marxist Paradigms for the Neolithic," 17–18; Wu Fei, "Muquan shenhua 'zhi mu bu zhi fu' de xifang puxi (shang)," *Shehui* 34, no. 2 (2014): 33–59; Wu Fei, "Fumu yu ziran: 'zhi

mu bu zhi fu' de xifang puxi (xia)," *Shehui* 34, no. 3 (2014): 1–36. Xu Shenzhan, "'Yangshao' shiqi yi jinru fuxi shizu shehui," *Kaogu* 5 (1962): 256–61, limits his critique to specific methodological problems. Xia Zhiqian, "Was There Ever a Matriarchy?" *Chinese Sociology and and Anthropology* 25, no. 4 (1993): 12, tries to salvage the concept of matriarchy by redefining the term so vaguely that it becomes virtually meaningless.

28. For some representative examples see Sun Zuchu, "Banpo wenhua zai yanjiu," *Kaogu xuebao* 4 (1998): 419–46; Ding Huiyu, "Luelun Daxi wenhua muzang fanying de shehui xingtai," *Sanxia luntan* 1 (2014): 19–23; Wu Ruowen, "Shouci pojie Banpo renmian yuwen zhi mi," *Wenshi yuekan* 12 (2013): 22–23.

29. Wang Qiwei, "Cong 'pinji zhi chen' xianxiang kan Shangdai funü de shehui diwei," *Yindu xuekan* 1 (2000): 22–26; Yuan Yuan, "Cong jiaguwen zhong de jige zi kan Shangdai nüxing," *Xiandai yuwen* 6 (2011): 147–48; Lu Xiaona, "Shangdai nüjie Fu Hao yu nüxing duikang yishi," *Yuwen jiaoxue tongxun* 7 (2013): 94–96.

30. Liu Pu, *Qinghai caitao wenshi* (Xining: Qinghai Renmin, 1989), 2, 7, represents an early example of the practice of interpreting the symbolism of images on Neolithic ceramics as either patrilineal or matrilineal. Many subsequent works use a similar methodology. For example, He Xingliang, "Banpo yuwen shi tuteng biaozhi haishi nüyin xiangzheng," *Zhongyuan wenwu* 3 (1996): 63–69, 118. Others discuss similar imagery in early literature. Chang Bin, "Cong Shijing kan shanggu xianmin de shengzhi congbai," *Guizhou minzu xueyuan xuebao* 2 (2000): 19. This methodology differs considerably from the ways that specialists elsewhere analyze symbolism on archeological artifacts. See John E. Robb, "The Archaeology of Symbols," *Annual Review of Anthropology* 27 (1998): 329–46.

31. Yang Kuan, *Xi Zhou shi* (Taipei: Taiwan Shangwu, 1999), 37; Sun Litao, "'Fu Xi' minghao kaoxi," *Qinghai shehui kexue* 2 (2014): 105–11; Liu Yi, Zhou Wenjie, and Cao Jingzhuang, "Yandi Yandi ling shiji zhi yanjiu," *Hunan shehui kexue* 2 (2014): 250–55.

32. Yang, *Xi Zhou shi*, 24.

33. Sheng Ying, "Lun Zhongguo shanggu nüshen," *Zhongguo wenhua yanjiu* 4 (2012): 130–41; Zhao Gaiping, "Huozhou shengmu miao bihua yu Nü Wa chongbai," *Shanxi dang'an* 4 (2014): 16; Liang Lei, "Lun Nü Wa yu Xiwangmu xingxiang ji yanbian," *Shaanxi Qingnian Qiye Xueyuan xuebao* 1 (2014): 70–74.

34. He Zhoude, "Hulu xingqiwu yu shengyu chongbai," *Kaogu yu wenwu* 3 (1996): 47–52.

35. Wang Yao, "Muquanzhi shiqi nüxing wenhua jieshuo—yi qinshu chengwei yanjiu wei zhongxin," *Yueyang Zhiye Jishu Xueyuan xuebao* 27, no. 2 (2012): 41–45; Bao Ximing, "Cong jiaguwen, jinwen 'xing' de yigou kan gudai hunyin xingtai de yanjin," *Anyang Shifan Xueyuan xuebao* 4 (2012): 89–91. Xu Yingying, "Tan Zhongguo gudai funü zhenjieguan de xingcheng yu bianqian," *Xue lilun* 32 (2012): 186–89, attributes the rise of chastity to the decline of matrilinealism and rise of patrilinealism.

36. Guo, "Shangceng jianzhu de shehui zuzhi," 222, is the most influential proponent of this view.

37. Descent: Xie Weiyang, *Zhoudai jiating xingtai* (Beijing: Zhongguo shehui kexue chubanshe, 1990), 21–26. Marriage: Wang Jiaxin, "Cong jiaguwen zixing kaocha Yin Shang shehui de hunsang xiguan," *Lishui Xueyuan xuebao* 36, no. 1

(2014): 48–51. Endogamy: Li Longhai, "Cong Shangzu de hunyin yange ji sheng-huo fangshi kan Shangdai de jicheng zhidu," *Yindu xuekan* 3 (2001): 18.

38. Influential classic studies that have served as models for subsequent archaeological methodology include Wu, "Cong muzang fajue lai kan Yangshao wenhua de shehui xingzhi"; Shi Tao, "Huanghe shangyou de fuxi shizu she-hui—Qijia wenhua shehui jingji xingtai de tansuo," *Kaogu* 1 (1961): 3–11; Chen Guoqiang, "Luelun Dawenkou muzang de shehui xingzhi—yu Tang Lan tongzhi shangque," in *Dawenkou wenhua taolun wenji*, ed. Shandong Daxue Lishixi Kaogu Jiaoyanshi (Ji'nan: Jilu Sushe, 1979), 101–04. W.L. Allen and J.B. Richardson, "The Reconstruction of Kinship from Archaeological Data: The Concepts, the Methods, and the Feasibility," *American Antiquity* 36, no. 1 (1971): 41–53, rejects these sorts of methods, arguing to the contrary that kinship customs usually cannot be determined from the examination of burial patterns and other archaeological data.

39. Fu Shaonan, "Cong *Shuowen jiezi* nüzi bu tanxi Zhongguo gudai funü wen-hua," *Yuyan jianshe* 9 (2014): 73–74; Jiang Huapeng, "Zhong Ri nüxing xingshi zhidu bijiao yanjiu," *Haixia kexue* 9 (2014): 77–79; Guo Ting, "*Shuowen jiezi*, nübu hanzi, yu shanggu hunyu wenhua," *Mingzuo xinshang* 9 (2015): 150–51. Edwin G. Pulleyblank, "Ji and Jiang: The Role of Exogamic Clans in the Organization of the Zhou Polity," *Early China* 25 (2000): 4, refutes this reading of surnames. And the assiduous Qing dynasty scholar Zhao Yi (1727–1814) compiled a long list of men in ancient times whose given names included a female radical in one of the characters, showing that a female-looking character did not necessary have feminine connotations. Zhao Yi, *Gaiyu congkan* (Shanghai: Shangwu, 1957), 923. Not only does orthography not necessarily preserve traces of much earlier prehistoric social institutions, but many characters eventually written with a female component originally lacked a gendered element. For example, see Shirakawa Shizuka, *Setsubun shingi* (Kobe: Hakutsuru Bijutsukan, 1969–74), 2387–489.

40. Liu Weiwei, "Daoxue zunchong nüxing yuanyuan tanxi," *Qinghai shehui kexue* 5 (2012): 13–17; Yu Qiangjun, "Daojia zhexue de nüxing qizhi jiqi dangdai jiazhi," *Shandong Nüzi Xueyuan xuebao* 115 (2014): 50–53.

41. Xie Chenxing, "Cong *Chu ci Tianwen* kan Xia minzu fuquanzhi zhansheng muquanzhi," *Zhongguo chengshi jingji* 2 (2012): 300, 302.

42. Ma Wei, "Qianxi Zhongguo gudai nüxing shehui diwei bianqian," *Lanzhou Jiaoyu Xueyuan xuebao* 28, no. 4 (2012): 23–24.

43. Liu Houqin, "Handai muxi yishi yanjiu," *Xianyang Shifan Xueyuan xuebao* 29, no. 3 (2014): 27–31.

44. Xu Haijing and Hou Shujuan, "Bei chao shangceng nüzi de hunlianguan," *Baicheng Shifan Xueyuan xuebao* 28, no. 6 (2014): 97–99, 112.

45. Eileen Rose Walsh, "From Nü Guo to Nü'er Guo: Negotiating Desire in the Land of the Mosuo," *Modern China* 31, no. 4 (2005): 448–86.

CHAPTER 2

1. Hillard S. Kaplan, Paul L. Hooper, and Michael Gurven, "The Evolutionary and Ecological Roots of Human Social Organization," *Philosophical Transactions of*

the Royal Society: Biological Sciences 364, no. 1533 (2009): 3289–99. Glynn Isaac, "The Food-Sharing Behavior of Protohuman Hominids," *Scientific American* 238 (1978): 90–108, believes that division of labor by sex dates back to at least the Middle Paleolithic, long before the emergence of biologically modern humans.

2. For example, among the Tasmanian aborigines, the men hunted kangaroos with javelins while women used rope loops to catch opossums, and also foraged for abalones and bird eggs. Flannery and Marcus, *The Creation of Inequality*, 47–48.

3. Nicole M. Waguespack, "The Organization of Male and Female Labor in Foraging Societies: Implications for Early Paleoindian Archaeology," *American Anthropologist* 107, no. 4 (2005): 666–76.

4. Parker and Parker, "The Myth of Male Superiority," 300; Hillard Kaplan, Kim Hill, A. Magdalena Hurtado, and Jane Lancaster, "The Embodied Capital Theory of Human Evolution," in *Reproductive Ecology and Human Evolution*, ed. Peter T. Ellison (Hawthorne, NY: Aldine de Gruyter, 2001), 293–317.

5. Zhang Hongyan, "Weishui liuyu Laoguantai wenhua fenqi yu leixing yanjiu," *Kaogu xuebao* 2 (2007): 173.

6. James G. Flanagan, "Hierarchy in Simple Egalitarian' Societies," *Annual Review of Anthropology* 18 (1989): 249–50; Julia A. Hendon, "Archaeological Approaches to the Organization of Domestic Labor: Household Practice and Domestic Relations," *Annual Review of Anthropology* 25 (1996): 46.

7. Yan Sun and Hongyu Yang, "Gender Ideology and Mortuary Practice in Northwestern China," in *Gender and Chinese Archaeology*, ed. Katheryn M. Linduff and Yan Sun (Walnut Creek, CA: Altamira Press, 2004), 38–40.

8. Zhang Changan and Yao Zhiguo, "Shilun Peiligang wenhua shiqi de shehui jieduan," *Zhongyuan wenwu* 2 (1996): 39–46.

9. A body that was not formally buried could have been disposed of in various ways. For example, it may have been exposed in the wild and eaten by predators, cremated, or been consigned to a river or marsh. Gwendolyn Leick, *Mesopotamia: The Invention of the City* (London: Penguin Books, 2001), 13.

10. Judith Brown, "Note on the Division of Labor by Sex," *American Anthropologist* 72 (1970): 1075–76.

11. George P. Murdock and Caterina Provost, "Factors in the Division of Labor by Sex: A Cross-Cultural Analysis," *Ethnology* 12, no. 2 (1973): 211.

12. Elman R. Service, *Primitive Social Organization: An Evolutionary Perspective* (New York: Random House, 1962), 44; Murdock and Provost, "Factors in the Division of Labor by Sex," 203; Sarah Milledge Nelson, "Ancient Queens: An Introduction," in *Ancient Queens: Archaeological Explorations*, ed. Sarah Milledge Nelson (Walnut Creek, CA: AltaMira Press, 2003), 3.

13. Wang Xiao, "Peiligang wenhua zangsu qianyi," *Zhongyuan wenwu* 1 (1996): 78, 80; Zhang and Yao, "Shilun Peiligang wenhua shiqi de shehui jieduan," 43–44; Keightley, "At the Beginning," 19–20. The orthography of Shang characters preserved the ideal of gendered division of labor. The earliest form of the character for father (*fu* 父) depicts a person using an axe, which was used to clear trees to make land suitable for cultivation. The character for man (*nan* 男) illustrates a digging stick and a field. Xu Jinxiong, *Wenzi xiaojiang* (Taipei: Taiwan shangwu, 2014), 92–95, 101–02.

14. For a detailed discussion of the idea that reciprocal exchange between the sexes constitutes the basis of sustenence, see Diane Lyons and A. Catherine D'Andrea, "Griddles, Ovens, and Agricultural Origins: An Ethnoarchaeological Study of Bread Baking in Highland Ethiopia," *American Anthropologist* 105, no. 3 (2003): 517.

15. Irene Good, "Archaeological Textiles: A Review of Current Research," *Annual Review of Anthropology* 30 (2001): 209. Textiles are not inherently associated with one sex or the other; the gendered meaning of textiles differs between cultures. For example, the Classic Maya associated weaving with high social station. Both elite women and men wove cloth. In contrast, the Aztecs associated weaving with women and used it to symbolize female identity. Elizabeth M. Brumfiel, "Cloth, Gender, Continuity, and Change: Fabricating Unity in Anthropology," *American Anthropologist* 108, no. 4 (2006): 866. Ancient Chinese recognized the high degree of skill necessary to make cloth. The original orthography of the character *zhuan* 專, which later meant "specialize," depicts a hand engaged in weaving. Xu, *Wenzi xiaojiang*, 110–13.

16. Sun Zuchu, "Lun zhongyuan xin shiqi shidai zhongqi wenhua," *Wenwu jikan* 4 (1996): 52, 56.

17. Scholars previously assumed that the emergence of agriculture increased the birth rate. A sedentary lifestyle presumably facilitated pregnancy, and farmers would welcome children as additional labor. However, the rate of population increase in early civilizations was not as high as has often been assumed. Women often tried to limit family size by nursing children longer to avoid frequent pregnancy. Bruce G. Trigger, *Understanding Early Civilizations: A Comparative Study* (Cambridge: Cambridge University Press, 2003), 397.

18. Wang Jianhua, "Henan Yangshao shidai renkou guimo ji xiangguan wenti de chubu yanjiu," *Huaxia kaogu* 4 (2010): 49–57.

19. Sun Lei and Wu Zhejiang, "Shengchi Duzhong yizhi Yangshao wenhua wanqi rengu yanjiu," *Huaxia kaogu* 3 (2010): 9.

20. Zhu Xiaoding, Lin Liugen, and Zhu Hong, "Jiangsu Pizhou Liangwangcheng yizhi Dawenkou wenhua mudi chutu rengu yanjiu," *Dongnan wenhua* 4 (2013): 63.

21. Zhu, Lin, and Zhu, "Jiangsu Pizhou Liangwangcheng yizhi Dawenkou wenhua mudi chutu rengu yanjiu," 54–55; Han Jianye, "Dawenkou mudi fenxi," *Zhongyuan wenwu* 2 (1994): 54–55; He Deliang and Niu Ruihong, "Zaozhuang Jianxin Dawenkou wenhua muzang fenxi," *Zhongyuan wenwu* 4 (1996): 27.

22. Marie Elaine Danforth, "Nutrition and Politics in Prehistory," *Annual Review of Anthropology* 28 (1999): 15.

23. Guo Min, "Shiqian xianmin de toushi xisu," *Zhongyuan wenwu* 2 (2007): 25–31; Gong Wen, "Yangshao wenhua zhuishi shulun," *Zhongyuan wenwu* 5 (2014): 24–32.

24. Liu Hui, "Ye shuo Dawenkou wenhua baya xiguan de yuanyin," *Minsu yanjiu* 4 (1996): 26–27; Liu Xianzhang, "Dawenkou zangsu de zongjiao neihan," *Taishan Xiangzhen Qiye Zhigong Daxue xuebao* 3 (2001): 14; Wang Zheng, "Dawenkou wenhua 'wo ya' zangsu yu baya gusu de wushu wenhua neihan," *Yishu kaogu* 1 (2008): 69, 90–95.

25. A pottery head with two long lines painted under each eye might represent body painting. Li Yongkui, Zhang Xiaopo, and Zhang Xian, "Linxia shi faxian Machang leixing renxiang caotao," *Kaogu yu wenwu* 3 (2003): 96.

26. Sun, "Banpo wenhua zai yanjiu," 435.

27. Ding, "Luelun Daxi wenhua muzang fanying de shehui xingtai," 19–20.

28. Changzhou Shi Bowuguan, "Changzhou Weidun xinshiqi shidai yizhi disanci fajue jianbao," *Shiqian yanjiu* 2 (1984): 68–69.

29. Shandong Sheng Bowuguan, "Tantan Dawenkou wenhua," *Wenwu* 4 (1978): 65; He and Niu, "Zaozhuang Jianxin Dawenkou wenhua muzang fenxi," 30; He Deliang, "Lun Zaozhuang Jianxin Dawenkou wenhua yicun," *Huaxia kaogu* 4 (1998): 52; Wang Guangming, "Shilun Dawenkou wenhua de hezangmu," *Wenwu chunqiu* 1 (2005): 5, 7; Ma Yan, "Anhui Weichisi Dawenkou wenhua tukengmu suizangpin suo fanying de shehui xianxiang," *Sichuan wenwu* 5 (2005): 28.

30. Wang Huajie, "Guanyu Chuodun yizhi Majiahong wenhua muzang: zangshi xingbie guanxi de tuice," *Changjiang wenhua luncong* (2007): 19.

31. Irene Silverblatt, *Moon, Sun, and Witches: Gender Ideologies and Class in Inca and Colonial Peru* (Princeton: Princeton University Press, 1987), 5, 20, demonstrates how a society can be structured around parallel gendered realms, each considered respectable and necessary.

32. Wang, "Cong Dadiwan yi, er qi wenhua yicun kan woguo muxi shizu shehui," 35. An analysis of bone chemistry from remains at the Pueblo Bonito site in North America found that men consumed more meat and cultivated foods whereas women ate more foraged foods. As a result, women had a lower level of nutrition and suffered from lower quality of health and higher mortality rate. If women in Neolithic China had responsibility for gathering wild foods, their diet might also have differed from that of men. Danforth, "Nutrition and Politics in Prehistory," 15.

33. Sun Lei, "Henan Shengchi Duzhong yizhi Yangshao wanqi rengu de zhigu yanjiu," *Jiangnan kaogu* 5 (2014): 93–94.

34. Wang Fen, "Mudi kongjian jiegou yu shehui guanxi de guanlianxing sikao - yi Dawenkou shiqi mudi wei li," *Dongfang kaogu* 9 (2012): 123.

35. Yu Fuwei, Li Yuee, and Jia Caixia, "Luoyang Yangshao he Longshan wenhua shiqi muzang yanjiu," *Luoyang Ligong Xueyuan xuebao* 3 (2007): 56.

36. For descriptions of some representative graves, see Nanjing Bowuyuan, Xuzhou Bowuguan and Pizhou Bowuguan, "Jiangsu Pizhou Liangwangcheng yizhi Dawenkou wenhua yicun fajue jianbao," *Dongnan wenhua* 4 (2013): 29–30, 32–35.

37. Yan Wenming, *Yangshao wenhua yanjiu* (Beijing: Wenwu, 1989), 260.

38. He Deliang and Sun Po, "Shilun Lunan Subei diqu de Dawenkou wenhua," *Dongnan wenwu* 3 (1997): 24, 28.

39. Jiao, "Gender Studies in Chinese Neolithic Archaeology," 55. Dawenkou culture is conventionally divided into four periods. The number of joint mixed-sex Dawenkou burials increased from 7 percent in phase I to 50 percent in phase IV. Wang, "Shilun Dawenkou wenhua de hezangmu," 4.

40. Jiao, "Gender Studies in Chinese Neolithic Archaeology," 56.

41. Liu Li, "Ancestor Worship: An Archaeological Investigation of Ritual Activities in Neolithic North China," *Journal of East Asian Archaeology* 2, nos. 1–2 (2000): 137–38.

42. Qiang Gao and Yun Kuen Lee, "A Biological Perspective on Yangshao Kinship," *Journal of Anthropological Archaeology* 12, no. 3 (1993): 289; Liu, "Ancestor Worship," 140–42; Gong Qiming, "Cong kaogu ziliao kan Yangshao wenhua de shehui zuzhi he shehui fazhan jieduan," *Zhongyuan wenwu* 5 (2001): 32.

43. Keightley, "At the Beginning," 11–12.

44. Jiao, "Gender Studies in Chinese Neolithic Archaeology," 56.

45. Sarah Milledge Nelson, *Shamanism and the Origin of States: Spirit, Power, and Gender in East Asia* (Walnut Creek, CA: Left Coast Press, 2008), 124–25.

46. This sitation would not have been unique. For an analogue from Northern Mesopotamia, see Flannery and Marcus, *The Creation of Inequality*, 260, 265.

47. Donald M. Wolfe, "Power and Authority in the Family," in *Studies in Social Power*, ed. Donald Cartwright (Ann Arbor: University of Michigan Institute for Social Research, 1959), 99–117.

48. Gendered roles can either be seen as complementary or hierarchical. Christine S. VanPool and Todd L. VanPool, "Gender in Middle Range Societies: A Case Study in Casas Grandes Iconography," *American Antiquity* 71, no. 1 (2006): 55.

49. For example, among the Siuai people of the Solomon Islands, women raise the pigs that men use to advance their status. So a husband appropriates the fruits of his wife's labor to empower himself. Flannery and Marcus, *The Creation of Inequality*, 116.

50. Flanagan, "Hierarchy in Simple 'Egalitarian' Societies," 254.

51. He Deliang and Niu Ruihong, "Dawenkou Yilongshan wenhua quzhi zangsu tanxi," *Liaohai wenwu xuekan* 1 (1996), 79–84.

52. Jiao, "Gender Studies in Chinese Neolithic Archaeology," 55.

53. Wang, "Guanyu Chuodun yizhi Majiahong wenhua muzang: zangshi xingbie guanxi de tuice," 19–20.

54. Gao and Lee, "A Biological Perspective on Yangshao Kinship," 292; Liu, "Ancestor Worship," 142.

55. Luo Kun, "Shilun Shangdai Yindu renkou de ziran goucheng - jian tan ruhe liyong kaogu ziliao yanjiu lishi," *Kaogu* 4 (1995): 346–47.

56. Liu, "Ancestor Worship," 142–43.

57. Ma, "Anhui Weichisi Dawenkou wenhua tukengmu suizangpin suo fanying de shehui xianxiang," 25. Also He, "Lun Zaozhuang Jianxin Dawenkou wenhua yicun," 52; Zhu Naicheng, "Xin Zhongguo diyibu xin shiqi shidai mudi fajue zhuankan de tedian ji qi xueshu yingxiang – chongdu 'Dawenkou' you gan," *Nanfang wenwu* 3 (2011): 1–7.

58. Sun, "Banpo wenhua zai yanjiu," 435, 437.

59. For a discussion of how excluding women from ceremonies bolsters male power, see Diane Bolger, "Figurines, Fertility, and the Emergence of Complex Society in Prehistoric Cyprus," *Current Anthropology* 37, no. 2 (1996): 371.

60. Luan Fengshi, "Shilun Yangshao shiqi zhongqi de shehui fenceng," *Dongfang kaogu* 9 (2012): 44–56.

61. For a cogent overview, see Wang Zhenzhong, "Zhongxin juluo xingtai, yuanshi zongyi yu qiubang shehui de zhenghe yanjiu," *Zhongyuan wenhua yanjiu* 4 (2014): 5–14.

62. Timothy K. Earle, "Specialization and the Production of Wealth: Hawaiian Chiefdoms and the Inka Empire," in *Specialization, Exchange, and Complex Societies,*

ed. Elizabeth M. Brumfiel and Timothy K. Earle (Cambridge: Cambridge University Press, 1987), 89; Peter Peregrine, "Some Political Aspects of Craft Specialization," *World Archaeology* 23, no. 1 (1991): 2.

63. For a discussion of how the exclusion of women from prestigious activies and their related material culture depressed female status, see Lisa J. LeCount, "Like Water for Chocolate: Feasting and Political Ritual Among the Late Classic Maya at Xunantunich, Belize," *American Anthropologist* 103, no. 4 (2001): 947. Joy McCorriston, "The Fiber Revolution: Textile Extensification, Alienation, and Social Stratification in Ancient Mesopotamia," *Current Anthropology* 38, no. 4 (1997): 517–18, describes how male control of productive capacity heightens gender inequity.

64. Jui-man Wu, "The Late Neolithic Cemetery at Dadianzi, Inner Mongolia Autonomous Region," in *Gender and Chinese Archaeology*, ed. Katheryn M. Linduff and Yan Sun (Walnut Creek, CA: Altamira Press, 2004), 62–63, 67, 70; Xu Zhaofeng, "Xiajiadian xiaceng wenhua leixing bianxi - jiyu Erlitou wenhua leixing de duibi yanjiu," *Dongbei shidi* 2 (2010): 11; Yan Xiang, "Cong Majiayao wenhua de zangsu tan wanwu you ling guan," *Hebei Qingnian Guanli Ganbu Xueyuan xuebao* 3 (2010): 58.

65. Zhang Xuechen, "Longshan shidai Rizhao diqu yinshi wenhua lice," *Huaxia kaogu* 3 (2011): 81–87, 108; Song Yanpo, Jia Jiali and He Deliang,"Shandong Tengzhou Zhuanglixi Longshan wenhua yizhi chutu dongwu yicun fenxi," *Dongfang kaogu* 9 (2012): 609–26; Jin Guiyun, "Longshan wenhua jumin shiwu jiegou yanjiu," *Wenshizhe* 2 (2013): 99–111.

66. For example, in Papua New Guinea, raising pigs is often a female task. Monica Minnegal and Peter D. Dwyer, "Women, Pigs, God and Evolution: Social and Economic Change among Kubo People of Papua New Guinea," *Oceania* 68, no. 1 (1997): 47–60.

67. Pang Yaoxian and Pang Ping, "Majiayao wowen caitaoweng yongtu lice - jian tan wengguan zangsu de jige wenti," *Sichou zhi lu* 8 (2010): 14; Yan, "Cong Majiayao wenhua de zangsu tan wanwu you ling guan," 58. Data from other regions of the world show mixed evidence for the diets of men and women in chiefdom societies. While the sexes had an equivalent diet in some societies, in others women had an inferior diet and worse health. Danforth, "Nutrition and Politics in Prehistory," 15.

68. Chen Tiemei, "Zhongguo xin shiqi shidai chengnianren gu xing bi yichang de wenti," *Kaogu xuebao* 4 (1990): 511, 513; Keightley, "At the Beginning," 62.

69. Keightley, "At the Beginning," 7–9.

70. Shanxi sheng Linfen Xingshu Wenhuaju, "Shanxi Linfen Xiajin cun Taosi wenhua mudi fajue baogao," *Kaogu xuebao* 4 (1999): 462; Han Dao, "Cong Taosi yizhi kan Zhongguo Longshan shidai wangquan de xingcheng," *Lishi gouchen* 3 (2014): 177.

71. Keightley, "At the Beginning," 27; Gansu Sheng Wenwu Kaogu Yanjiusuo and Xibei Daxue Sichou zhi Lu Wenhua Yichan Baohu yu Kaogu Yanjiu Zhongxin, "Gansu Lintan Mogou mudi Qijia wenhua muzang 2009 nian fajue jianbao," *Wenwu* 6 (2014): 12–13, 16–17.

72. Zhongguo Kexueyuan Kaogu Yanjiusuo Gansu gongzuodui, "Gansu Yongjing Qinweijia Qijia wenhua mudi," *Kaogu xuebao* 2 (1975): 65; Yi Hua, "Cong Qijia dao Erlitou: Xia wenhua tansuo," *Xueshu yuekan* 12 (2014): 140.

73. Liu Li, "Shandong Longshan wenhua muzang xingtai yanjiu: Longshan shiqi shehui fenhua, yili huodong, ji jiaohuan guanxi de kaoguxue fenxi," *Wenwu jikan* 2 (1999): 40, 42.

74. Shang Minjie, "Dui shiqian shiqi chengnian nannü hezang mu de chubu tantao," *Zhongguoshi yanjiu* 3 (1991): 50, 52–53. Many joint graves contain two people of the same sex. Xia Zhiqian, "Tantan tongxing maizang xisu," *Shiqian yanjiu* 4 (1984): 98–103.

75. Liang Xingpeng, "Shilun Keshengzhuang erqi wenhua," *Kaogu xuebao* 4 (1994): 401.

76. Pang and Pang, "Majiayao wowen caitaoweng yongtu lice," 16.

77. Gao Wei, Gao Tianlin, and Zhang Daihai, "Guanyu Taosi mudi de jige wenti," *Kaogu* 6 (1983): 533.

78. Qian Yaopeng, Zhou Jing, Mao Ruilin, and Xie Yan, "Gansu Lintan Mogo Qijia wenhua mudi fajue de shouhuo yu yiyi - 2008 niandu quanguo shida kaogu faxian zhi yi," *Xibei Daxue xuebao* 5 (2009): 9.

79. Harriet Zurndorfer, "Polygamy and Masculinity in China: Past and Present," in *Changing Chinese Masculinities: From Imperial Pillars of State to Global Real Men*, ed. Kam Louie (Hong Kong: Hong Kong University Press, 2016), 17.

80. Wang Lei, "Shilun Longshan wenhua shidai de renxun he renji," *Dongnan wenhua* 4 (1999): 25–26.

81. Jia Zhiqiang and Mu Wenjun, "Taosi leixing shehui xingzhi de kaoguxue fenxi," *Xinzhou Shifan Xueyuan xuebao* 27, no. 3 (2011): 127–28.

82. Liu, "Ancestor Worship," 129, 153; D. Howard Smith, "Chinese Religion in the Shang Dynasty," *Numen* 8, no. 2 (1961): 145–46.

83. Liu, "Ancestor Worship," 145–51.

84. Zhejiang Sheng Wenwu Kaogu Yanjiusuo and Zhejiang Hangzhou Shi Yukeng Qu Wenguanhui, "Zhejiang Yukeng Xingqiao Houtoushan Liangzhu wenhua mudi fajue jianbao," *Nanfang wenwu* 3 (2008): 48; Zhang Zhongpei, "Liangzhu wenhua mudi yu qi biaoshu de wenming shehui," *Kaogu xuebao* 4 (2012): 408.

85. Wu, "The Late Neolithic Cemetery at Dadianzi, Inner Mongolia Autonomous Region," 68–69.

86. Zhang Chi, "Shijiahe juluo xingsheng shiqi zangyi zhong de xin guannian," *Kaogu* 8 (2014): 68–80.

87. Keightley, "At the Beginning," 21–24.

88. Zhengzhou Shi Wenwu Gongzuodui and Zhengzhou Shi Dahecun Yizhi Bowuguan, "Zhengzhou Dahecun yizhi 1983, 1987 nian fajue baogao," *Kaogu xuebao* 1 (1996): 111.

89. Corinne Debaine-Francfort, *Du Néolithique à l'âge du bronze en Chine du nord-ouest: La Culture de Qijia et ses Connexions* (Paris: Éditions Recherche sur les Civilisations, 1995), 263.

90. Shanxi Sheng Linfen Xingshu Wenhuaju, "Shanxi Linfen Xiajincun Taosi wenhua mudi fajue baogao," 459–86.

91. Zhang Zhixin, "Suzhou de Liangzhu yicun ji gudai," *Suzhou Daxue xuebao* 1 (1997): 112, 115.

92. Wu, "The Late Neolithic Cemetery at Dadianzi, Inner Mongolia Autonomous Region," 59, 62, 82, 85–86.

93. Trigger, *Understanding Early Civilizations*, 88–89, 484–85. The Asante of West Africa conducted human sacrifices up into historic times, so their version of the practice is particularly well understood. When an Asante king was dying, he would choose women to accompany him to the grave. Other women might be subsequently chosen as well. After his death, these women dressed in celebratory clothing and fine gold ornaments, got drunk on palm wine, and were strangled. The Asante considered it an honor to serve as a sacrificial victim. In addition, however, they also sacrificed condemned criminals and captives taken in war. Flannery and Marcus, *The Creation of Inequality*, 445.

94. John M. Ingham, "Human Sacrifice at Tenochtitlan," *Comparative Studies in Society and History* 26, no. 3 (1984): 379.

95. Wang Kelin, "Taosi wanqi Longshan wenhua yu Xia wenhua - lun Huaxia wenming de xingcheng (xia)," *Wenwu shijie* 6 (2001): 25.

96. Ai Guangkuo, "Henan Erlitou wenhua muzang de jige wenti," *Kaogu* 12 (1996): 64.

97. Wu, "The Late Neolithic Cemetery at Dadianzi, Inner Mongolia Autonomous Region," 61.

98. Graves M24 and M27 from Xiwangcun culture, a transition point between Yangshao and Longshan, each contain the remains of a woman buried with a bone dagger. Archaeologists speculate that these women were killed with the daggers interred in their graves, likely because they had committed some kind of transgressive act that the community could not tolerate. Zhang Tianen, "Qianlun Xiwangcun leixing jige wenti," *Kaogu yu wenwu* 2 (1994): 70–81. Not all human sacrifices in Neolithic China may have been involuntary. In some cultures, it was considered an honor or duty to be sacrificed during the funeral of an important person. Flannery and Marcus, *The Creation of Inequality*, 221.

99. Zhao Ye, "Liangzhu wenwu renxun renji xianxiang shixi," *Nanfang wenwu* 1 (2001): 33. For a similar example, see Shanghai shi Wenwu Baoguan Weiyuanhui, "Fuquanshan yizhi disanci fajue de zhongyao xianxiang," *Dongnan wenhua* 3 (1987): 51.

100. Zhao, "Liangzhu wenwu renxun renji xianxiang shixi," 34–35.

101. Jiao, "Gender Studies in Chinese Neolithic Archaeology," 57; Debaine-Francfort, *Du Néolithique à l'âge du bronze en Chine du nord-ouest*, 221–22, 264; Mao Ruilin, "Huanghe shangyou de zaoqi qingtong wenming: Lintan Mogou yizhi Qijia wenhua mudi," *Dazhong kaogu* 3 (2013): 46.

102. He and Sun, "Shilun Lunan Subei diqu de Dawenkou wenhua," 25; Jia, "Longshan shiqi de gucheng yu muzang," 42.

CHAPTER 3

1. For a detailed exploration of the mechanics of one case of early state formation, likely similar to what occurred in north China, see Brian S. Bauer and R. Alan Covey, "Processes of State Formation in the Inca Heartland (Cuzco, Peru)," *American Anthropologist* 104, no. 3 (2002): 846–64.

2. Hung-Hsiang Chou, "Fu-x Ladies of the Shang Dynasty," *Monumenta Serica* 29 (1970–1971): 389.

3. Kate Burridge and Ng Bee-Chin, "Writing the Female Radical: The Encoding of Women in the Writing System," in *Dress, Sex and Text in Chinese Culture*, ed. Antonia Finnane and Anne McLaren (Clayton: Monash Asia Institute, 1999), 123–33; Huang Yanping, "Jiaguwen tixianchu de Shangdai lunli daodeguan," *Xinyu Gaozhuan xuebao* 15, no. 6 (2010): 61–63.

4. Ikeda Suetoshi, *Chūgoku kodai shū kyōshi kenkyū: Seido to shisō* (Tokyo: Tōkai Daigaku shuppankai, 1981), 89–107.

5. K.C. Chang, *Early Chinese Civilization: Anthropological Perspectives* (Cambridge, MA: Harvard University Press, 1976), 157; Riccardo Fracasso, "Holy Mothers of Ancient China: A New Approach to the Hsi-wang-mu Problem," *T'oung Pao* 74 (1988): 19–24; Chang Yuzhi, *Shangdai zongjiao jisi* (Beijing: Zhongguo shehui kexue chubanshe, 2010), 128–32.

6. Chang Yaohua, "Yinxu buci zhong de 'Dongmu' 'Ximu' yu 'Dongwanggong' 'Xiwangmu' shenhua chuanshuo zhi yanjiu," *Zhongguo Guojia Bowuguan guankan* 9 (2013): 47–53.

7. Some scholars have posited that during the *yu* 禦 ceremony a woman had sex with a deity as a form of worship. However, most reject this interpretation. Huang Fengchun, "Guanyu Hanyang Shamaoshan Shangdai zunming de shidu wenti," *Jianghan kaogu* 4 (2012): 61–62.

8. Wang Yuxin, Zhang Yongshan, and Yang Shengnan, "Shilun Yinxu wuhao mu de Fu Hao," *Kaogu xuebao* 2 (1977): 7–10; Jia Shiheng, "Yin Zhou funü shenghuo de jige mian," *Dalu zazhi* 60, no. 5 (1980): 10–13; Zhao Cheng, *Jiaguwen yu Shangdai wenhua* (Shenyang: Liaoning renmin chubanshe, 2000), 144–45; Xu Yihua, "Shangdai zhufu de zongjiao diwei," in *Jinian Yinxu jiaguwen faxian yibai zhounian guoji yantaohui lunwenji*, ed. Wang Yuxin and Song Zhenhao (Beijing: Shehui kexue wenxian chubanshe, 2003), 453–55; Yang Mei, "Qianyi jiaguwen suo fanying de Shangdai funü diwei," *Xuexingtang yuyan wenzi luncong* 1 (2011): 371–73.

9. Chen Mengjia, "Shangdai de shenhua yu wushu," *Yanjing xuebao* 20 (1936): 486–576; Michael J. Puett, *To Become a God: Cosmology, Sacrifice, and Self-Divination in Early China* (Cambridge, MA: Harvard University Press, 2002), 33–40.

10. There is little concrete evidence regarding female shamanism in the Shang. However, grave M2 at the Yanshi site, an early Shang capital, seems suggestive. This grave contains the remains of a middle-aged woman who was interred without the usual grave goods, but in a prestigious location. Some have speculated that she may have been a shaman, which would explain why she was treated with great respect after death despite lacking high family background. Zhongguo Shehui Kexue Xueyuan Kaogu Yanjiusuo, "Henan Yanshi Shengcheng Shangdai zaoqi wangshi jisi yizhi," *Kaogu* 7 (2002): 6–8. Also Edward H. Schafer, "Ritual Exposure in Ancient China," *Harvard Journal of Asiatic Studies* 14, nos. 1/2 (1951): 132; Ngo Van Xuyet, *Divination Magie et Politique dans la Chine Ancienne* (Paris: Presses Universitaires de France, 1976), 197–99; Gilles Boileau, "Wu and Shaman," *Bulletin of the School of Oriental and African Studies* 65, no. 2 (2002): 350–78; Zhao Rongjun, *Yin Shang jiagu buci suo jian zhi wushu* (revised edition) (Beijing: Zhonghua, 2011), 176.

11. Susan Kellogg, "The Woman's Room: Some Aspects of Gender Relations in Tenochtitlan in the Late Pre-Hispanic Period," *Ethnohistory* 42, no. 4 (1995): 563, emphasizes the importance of social class in shaping each woman's experiences.

12. Hu Houxuan, "Zhongguo nuli shehui de renxun he renji (xia)," *Wenwu* 8 (1974): 59; Zhang Yongshan, "Shixi 'xi duo nü zhi bei peng,'" *Gu wenzi yanjiu* 16 (Beijing: Zhonghua shuju, 1989), 31.

13. Yang Shengnan, "Jiaguwen zhong suojian Shangdai de gongna zhidu," *Yindu xuekan* 2 (1999): 28–29. These slave women were called by various names: *nü* 女, *duo nü* 多女, *qie* 妾, and *nüzi* 女子.

14. Zhang, "Shixi 'xi duo nü zhi bei peng,'" 29.

15. Yinxu Xiaomintun Kaogudui, "Henan Anyang shi Xiaomintun Shangdai fangzhi 2003-2004 nian fajue jianbao," *Kaogu* 1 (2007): 3–13.

16. Katheryn M. Linduff, "Women's Lives Memorialized in Burial in Ancient China at Anyang," in *In Pursuit of Gender: Worldwide Archaeological Approaches*, ed. Sarah Milledge Nelson and Myriam Rosen-Ayalon (Walnut Creek, CA: AltaMira Press, 2002), 270.

17. Keightley, "At the Beginning," 7.

18. Ying Wang. "Rank and Power among Court Ladies at Anyang," in *Gender and Chinese Archaeology*, ed. Katheryn M. Linduff and Yan Sun (Walnut Creek, CA: Altamira Press, 2004), 111–12; Hao Xiangping, "Yinxu Xiaotun M5 zai tantao," *Zhongguo Guojia Bowuguan guankan* 12 (2011): 20–26. Li Ya, *Zhongguo lidai zhuangshi* (Beijing: Zhongguo fangzhi chubanshe, 2004), 21–37, discusses the clothing and hairstyles of Shang and Zhou women. Pierre Bourdieu, *Outline of a Theory of Practice*, trans. Richard Nice (Cambridge: Cambridge University Press, 1977), 195, emphasizes the importance of "body habitus"—the ways in which the body is manipulated to reveal a person's social class. People of high status use their bodies to materialize their elite identity.

19. Song Zhenhao, "Xia Shang renkou chutan," *Lishi yanjiu* 4 (1991): 105–06; Luo, "Shilun Shangdai Yindu renkou de ziran goucheng," 350–53.

20. Robert L. Thorp, *China in the Early Bronze Age: Shang Civilization* (Philadelphia: University of Pennsylvania Press, 2006), 102.

21. Yang Baocheng and Yang Xizhang, "Cong Yinxu xiaoxing muzang kan Yindai shehui de pingmin," *Zhongyuan wenwu* 1 (1983): 30, 32.

22. T.F. Mumford, "Death Do Us Unite: Xunzang and Joint Burial in Ancient China," *Papers on Far Eastern History* 27 (2008): 10.

23. Tang Jinqiong, "Yinxu Huayuanzhuang dongdi M60 de sangsu ji qi tezhi," *Kaogu* 3 (2010): 81.

24. Linduff, "Women's Lives Memorialized in Burial in Ancient China at Anyang," 263.

25. For example tomb M5, dating to Anyang phase III. Anyang Wenwu Gongzuodui, "Anyang shi Yindai muzang fajue jianbao," *Huaxia kaogu* 1 (1995): 12.

26. Tomb M207. Yinxu Xiaomintun Kaogudui, "Henan Anyang shi Xiaomintun Shangdai muzang 2003-2004 nian fajue jianbao," *Kaogu* 1 (2007): 34–35.

27. Tomb AXTM18. Linduff, "Women's Lives Memorialized in Burial in Ancient China at Anyang," 269–70.

28. Wang Yonghong, "Ganshou Shangdai Jiangnan - Jiangxi Xingan Dayangzhou Shangdai damu chutu wenwu jingpinzhan," *Shoucangjia* 2 (2006): 7–12.

Some researchers find it hard to believe that a woman received such a lavish burial and argue that she was a religious sacrifice.

29. Hu Binghua, "Tengzhou Qianzhang da Shangdai muzang dimian jianzhu jianxi," *Kaogu* 2 (1994): 146–51.

30. The Shang occasionally buried one woman and one man together, but these tombs are anomalous. For an example see Zhongguo Shehui Kexueyuan Kaogu Yanjiusuo Anyang Gongzuodui, "Henan Anyang Yinxu Huayuanzhuang dongdi 60 hao mu," *Kaogu* 1 (2006): 7–18.

31. Song Zhenhao, *Xia Shang shehui shenghuo shi* (Beijing: Zhongguo shehui kexue chubanshe, 1994), 142–43; Anyang Wenwu Gongzuodui, "Anyang shi Yindai muzang fajue jianbao," 13; Zhongguo Shehui Kexueyuan Kaogu Yanjiusuo Anyang Gongzuodui, "Yinxu Dasikong M303 fajue baogao," *Kaogu xuebao* 3 (2008): 388; Qiao Xin, "Lun Yinxu 'yi xue he zang' mu de tezhi," *Wenxuejie* 4 (2011): 149–50; Geng Chao, "Yinxuzu mudi zhong de 'fufu hezang mu' ji xiangguan wenti," *Shoudu Shifan Daxue xuebao* 2 (2013): 35–9.

32. During the Warring States era, burial positions reversed. Men were placed on the right side of the grave and women on the left side. Cui Ruonan, "Shenti yu xiangzheng: Zhoudai yiqian Zhongguo de 'zuo' 'you' zunbeiguan," *Wenhua yichan* 1 (2015): 95–96.

33. Keightley, "At the Beginning," 29.

34. Mumford, "Death Do Us Unite," 3; Zhu Fenghan, *Shang Zhou jiazu xingtai yanjiu (zengding ban)* (Tianjin: Tianjin guji, 2004), 133–36. Ma Jifan, "Shangai zhongqi de renji zhidu yanjiu - yi Zhengzhou Xiaoshuangqiao Shangdai yizhi de renji yicun wei li," *Zhongyuan wenwu* 3 (2004): 37–44, describes in detail how the Shang carried out human sacrifices.

35. Tang Jigen, "The Burial Ritual of the Shang Dynasty: A Reconstruction," in *Exploring China's Past: New Discoveries and Studies in Archaeology and Art*, trans. and ed. Roderick Whitfield and Wang Tao (London: Saffron, 1999), 176.

36. Hu, "Zhongguo nuli shehui de renxun he renji (xia)," 58–59.

37. Pei Mingxiang, "Lun Zhengzhou shi Xiaoshuangqiao Shangdai qianqi jisi yizhi," *Zhongyuan wenwu* 2 (1996): 6.

38. Zhongguo Shehui Kexueyuan Kaogu Yanjiusuo Anyang Gongzuodui, "Henan Anyang Shi Yinxu Liujiazhuang beidi 2008 nian fajue jianbao," *Kaogu* 7 (2009): 25.

39. Cao Zhaolan, *Jinwen yu Yin Zhou nüxing wenhua* (Beijing: Beijing Daxue, 2004), 52–57.

40. Tomb Houjiazhuang HPKM 1001. Beijing Daxue Lishixi Gujiao Yanshi Shang Zhou zubian ed., *Shang Zhou kaogu* (Beijing: Wenwu chubanshe, 1979), 107.

41. Keightley, "At the Beginning," 28; Tang, "The Burial Ritual of the Shang Dynasty," 179–80; Linduff, "Women's Lives Memorialized in Burial in Ancient China at Anyang," 272; Mumford, "Death Do Us Unite," 4.

42. Wu Cunhao, "Shangdai muzang xingzhi he xiguan yanjiu," *Minsu yanjiu* 4 (1994): 45.

43. Luo, "Shilun Shangdai Yindu renkou de ziran goucheng - jian tan ruhe liyong kaogu ziliao yanjiu lishi," 348.

44. For example, Cao, *Jinwen yu Yin Zhou nüxing wenhua*, 36.

45. Cao, *Jinwen yu Yin Zhou nüxing wenhua*, 39–40. Also Chen Jie, *Shang Zhou xingshi zhidu yanjiu* (Beijing: Shangwu yinshuguan, 2007), 79–89.

46. Zhao Yanxia, *Zhongguo zaoqi xingshi zhidu yanjiu* (Tianjin: Tianjin guji chubanshe, 1996), 126–27.

47. Zheng Huisheng *Shanggu Huaxia funü yu hunyin* (Henan: Henan Renmin, 1988), 118.

48. Cao, *Jinwen yu Yin Zhou nüxing wenhua*, 40–41.

49. Zheng, *Shanggu Huaxia funü yu hunyin*, 129–30; Cao, *Jinwen yu Yin Zhou nüxing wenhua*, 35.

50. Cao, *Jinwen yu Yin Zhou nüxing wenhua*, 36.

51. Li Xusheng, *Shuowen xinzheng* (Fuzhou: Haixia and Fujian renmin, 2010), 884.

52. Cao, *Jinwen yu Yin Zhou nüxing wenhua*, 34–37.

53. *Nüzi* 女子 may have referred to a married woman, in which case this term would have been equivalent to *mu* 母 or *fu* 婦. Alternatively, it might have been a kind of noble title. A third interpretation reads *nü* 女 as *ru* 汝, in which case it would mean "you who are called *zi* 子." Of these possibilities, the first seems most likely. Chen Yingjie, "Shangdai jinwen zhong zhi 'nüzi' mingci shuolue," *Kaogu yu wenwu* 4 (2010): 107.

54. Keightley, "At the Beginning," 3–5; Gu Lijuan, "Jiaguwen nübuzi yu nüxing juese bianqian tanxi," *Yulin Xueyuan xuebao* 22, no. 1 (2012): 74–78.

55. Cao, *Jinwen yu Yin Zhou nüxing wenhua*, 32–33.

56. Cao, *Jinwen yu Yin Zhou nüxing wenhua*, 33.

57. Li, *Shuowen xinzheng*, 887.

58. Wang, "Rank and Power among Court Ladies at Anyang," 103. Wang Guowei, "Nü zi shuo," in *Guantang jilin* (Taipei: Heluo tushu chubanshe, 1975), 163–66, suggests that the formula x-*mu* might have conveyed a woman's style name (*zi* 字).

59. Cheng Chen-hsiang, "A Study of the Bronzes with the 'Ssu T'u Mu' Inscriptions Excavated from the Fu Hao Tomb," in *Studies of Shang Archaeology: Selected Papers from the International Conference on Shang Civilization*, ed. K.C. Chang (New Haven: Yale University Press, 1986), 99. In Shang script, both *mu* and *nü* depict a kneeling woman. However, the orthography of *mu* often emphasizes the breasts. Xu, *Wenzi xiaojiang*, 96–103. Axel Schuessler, *ABC Etymological Dictionary of Old Chinese* (Honolulu: University of Hawaii Press, 2007), 392, notes that the Old Chinese *mu* might be a cognate of the Proto Tibeto-Burman word **mow* which means woman or bride.

60. Chen, "Shangdai jinwen zhong zhi 'nüzi' mingci shuolue," 105.

61. Chen, "Shangdai jinwen zhong zhi 'nüzi' mingci shuolue," 105–06.

62. Cheng, "A Study of the Bronzes with the 'Ssu T'u Mu' Inscriptions Excavated from the Fu Hao Tomb," 82–83; Chen Mengjia, *Yinxu buci zongshu* (Beijing: Zhonghua shuju, 1988), 447.

63. Cheng, "A Study of the Bronzes with the 'Ssu T'u Mu' Inscriptions Excavated from the Fu Hao Tomb," 83, 96–97; Song, *Xia Shang shehui shenghuo shi*, 153–54. Previously this character was often read as *si* 司, but now it is usually considered to be *hou* 后. Cao, *Jinwen yu Yin Zhou nüxing wenhua*, 19. Schuessler,

ABC Etymological Dictionary of Old Chinese, 477, defines *si* as meaning to be in charge, to manage, regulation, and supervisor. Given the limited administrative roles of queens under the Shang and Western Zhou system, *hou* (referring more generally to high social status) seems a much more likely reading of this character than *si*. Yin Shengping, "'Di si' yu 'si mu' kao," *Gu wenzi yanjiu* 13 (Beijing: Zhonghua shuju, 1986), 433, 436, argues that *hou* was the initial orthography for a more complicated later character, pronounced the same way, which meant inheritance or heir. Another possible reading adds a female radical, making it *gou* 姤. Yin, "'Di si' yu 'si mu' kao," 431. This roundabout interpretation seems unlikely.

64. Schuessler, *ABC Etymological Dictionary of Old Chinese*, 279–80, defines *hou* as originally referring to a "'head' in society," with the more specific definitions of sovereign and queen derived from this early meaning.

65. Song, *Xia Shang shehui shenghuo shi*, 148–52; Hu Houxuan, *Jiaguxue Shangshi luncong* (Beijing: Beijing Tushuguan, 2000), vol. 1, 93–97; Chen, *Shang Zhou xingshi zhidu yanjiu*, 59, 112–14, give representative oracle inscriptions regarding *fu* ladies. For detailed discussions of the orthography and history of this character, see Shima Kunio, *Inkyo bokuji kenkyū* (Hirosaki: Chūkokugaku Kenkyūkai, 1958), 94; Cao Zhaolan, "Jinwen 'nü,' 'mu' de xingyi shixi," *Xueshu yanjiu* 7 (2002): 128–31; Qi Wenxin, "'Fu' zi benyi shitan," in *Jinian Yinxu jiaguwen faxian yibai zhounian guoji yantaohui lunwenji*, ed. Wang Yuxin and Song Zhenhao (Beijing: Shehui kexue wenxian chubanshe, 2003), 149–54; Chen, *Shang Zhou xingshi zhidu yanjiu*, 50–54; Wang Taiquan, *Wu diguo: cang zai jiaguwenli* (Taipei: Xiangshi wenhua chubanshe, 2014), 144–46; Li, *Shuowen xinzheng*, 643–44.

66. Zhao Cheng, "Zhufu tansuo," in *Gu wenzi yanjiu* 12 (Beijing: Zhonghua shuju, 1985), 100–01; Chang Cheng-lang, "A Brief Discussion of Fu Tzu," in *Studies of Shang Archaeology: Selected Papers from the International Conference on Shang Civilization*, ed. K.C. Chang (New Haven: Yale University Press, 1986), 109.

67. Zhao, "Zhufu tansuo," 101–02.

68. Cao, *Jinwen yu Yin Zhou nüxing wenhua*, 26–27. Early researchers of oracle inscriptions assumed that all *fu* were married to King Wu Ding. Subsequent research confirmed that these women lived in different periods and were married to different kings. Chou, "Fu-x Ladies of the Shang Dynasty," 347.

69. Keightley, "At the Beginning," 31–33.

70. Chou, "Fu-x Ladies of the Shang Dynasty," 348–51, 355–56.

71. Zhao, "Zhufu tansuo," 102–03.

72. Léon Vandermeersch, *Wangdao ou la Voie Royale: Recherches sur l'Esprit des Institutions de la Chine Archaique* (Paris: Ecole Française d'Extrême-Orient, 1977), vol. 1, 275–76.

73. Chou, "Fu-x Ladies of the Shang Dynasty," 356–60; Zhang Zhenglang, "Fu Hao lueshuo," in *Jiagu jinwen yu Shang Zhou shi yanjiu* (Beijing: Zhonghua shuju, 2012), 194.

74. Cao, *Jinwen yu Yin Zhou nüxing wenhua*, 26–27.

75. Cao, *Jinwen yu Yin Zhou nüxing wenhua*, 30.

76. Shima, *Yinxu buci yanjiu*, 455, holds that in this era the character *fu* 帚 was related to *fu* 服 and *mu* 牧, terms for official positions during the Shang, in which case *fu* 帚 would have been a kind of official. This highly creative interpretation has been received with skepticism.

77. Chang, "A Brief Discussion of Fu Tzu," 109–10, 113, suggests that the "many *fu*" were women sent to the Shang court by conquered peoples and vassals as a hereditary obligation. Chang speculates that these *fu* and *chen* had a status somewhere between slaves and officials. They waited on the king and also performed administrative activities. Also see Zhao, "Zhufu tansuo," 105.

78. Cao, *Jinwen yu Yin Zhou nüxing wenhua*, 24.

79. Cao, *Jinwen yu Yin Zhou nüxing wenhua*, 22.

80. Chang, "A Brief Discussion of Fu Tzu," 104; Schuessler, *ABC Etymological Dictionary of Old Chinese*, 273, 633. Alternatively, *hao* may have been had feminine connotations during the Shang. The original orthography of *hao* depicts a woman holding a child, so it originally probably connoted fertility or motherhood. Xu, *Wenzi xiaojiang*, 137–39.

81. Cao, *Jinwen yu Yin Zhou nüxing wenhua*, 22–23; Cao Dingyun, "'Fuhao' nai 'Zifang' zhi nü," in *Qingzhu Su Bingqi kaogu wushiwu nian lunwenji*, ed. Qingzhu Su Bingqi kaogu wushiwu nian lunwenji bianjizu (Beijing: Wenwu, 1989), 383, believes that the x character in the formula *fu*-x identified a woman's natal state.

82. Song, *Xia Shang shehui shenghuo shi*, 156.

83. Cao, *Jinwen yu Yin Zhou nüxing wenhua*, 34.

84. Huang Mingchong, "Yin Zhou jinwen zhong de qinshu chengwei 'gu' ji qi xiangguan wenti," *Zhongyang yanjiuyuan lishi yuyan yanjiusuo jikan* 75, vol. 1 (2004): 1–98, discusses the evolution of the term *gu* 姑 at great length. In Shang bronze inscriptions *gu* refers to the husband's mother, but in Western Zhou inscriptions it can refer to either a husband's mother or father's sister. The Zhou considered the husband's mother and father's sister analogous kinship roles.

85. Shima, *Inkyo bokuji kenkyū*, 93; Zhao, *Jiaguwen yu Shangdai wenhua*, 125–29; Li, *Shuowen xinzheng*, 166, 885–87. The character *shuang* was written many different ways in Shang script. It originated as a depiction of a person dancing while holding two unidentified objects. Perhaps it represented a shaman performing a ritualistic dance. Xu, *Wenzi xiaojiang*, 183–86. Schuessler, *ABC Etymological Dictionary of Old Chinese*, 355, notes that *shuang* is related to *liang* 俍, which later meant skillful. Similarly, *shuang* eventually meant active or clever. For the orthography of *qi* and *mu*, see Wang, *Wu diguo: cang zai jiaguwenli*, 141–42; Li, *Shuowen xinzheng*, 262–23; Ken-ichi Takashima, *A Little Primer of Chinese Oracle-Bone Inscriptions with Some Exercises* (Wiesbaden: Harrossowitz Verlag, 2015), 125. Xu, *Wenzi xiaojiang*, 403–04, notes that *qi* seems to depict a woman adjusting her hair. Married women may have arranged their hair in a characteristic hairstyle to publicly mark their marital status. In later times, *qie* referred to household women of a debased status. Schuessler, *ABC Etymological Dictionary of Old Chinese*, 311, defines *qie* as referring variously to a slave woman, servant girl, secondary wife, and war captive. The meaning of the term at this early date remains unclear.

86. Song, *Xia Shang shehui shenghuo shi*, 164–71, contends that Shang weddings resembled the marriage rituals described much later in *Liji* and elsewhere. This assertion is highly conjectural. The Shang orthography of the character *gui* 歸 shows a person holding an object, apparently a broom. Xu, *Wenzi xiaojiang*, 423–25, believes that a woman might have brought a broom with her as part of the wedding ceremony.

87. Wang, "Rank and Power among Court Ladies at Anyang," 97, 110. For the *locus classicus* of the custom that a woman's rank derives from that of her son, see Gongyang Gao, *Chongkan Songben Gongyang zhushu fujiao kanji*, annotated He Xiu et al. (Nanchang: 1815; reprinted Taipei: Yiwen yinshuguan, 1965), 1:11b (Yin 1), 3:35a (Yin 5).

88. Zheng, *Shanggu Huaxia funü yu hunyin*, 128.

89. Chang, *Early Chinese Civilization: Anthropological Perspectives*, 84. This was not a unique Shang custom. In other cultures, a mother's background also influenced male identity. For example, see A.G. Miller, *Maya Rulers of Time: A Study of Architectural Sculpture at Tikal, Guatemala* (Philadelphia: University Museum, 1986), 41.

90. Wang, "Rank and Power among Court Ladies at Anyang," 110.

91. Zheng, *Shanggu Huaxia funü yu hunyin*, 117.

92. Hu, *Jiaguxue Shangshi luncong*, vol. 1, 82–85, argued that the Shang were strictly monogamous. In light of subsequent evidence, this assertion now seems dubious. When getting married, a man (either alive or dead) would *qu* 取 (literally "take" or "choose") a wife. Chang, "A Brief Discussion of Fu Tzu," 114–15, 118.

93. Zheng, *Shanggu Huaxia funü yu hunyin*, 117. Li Yanong, "Yindai shehui shenghuo," in *Li Yanong shi lunji* (Shanghai: Shanghai renmin chubanshe, 1962), 419; Ge Yinghui, "Zhouji buci zhong de zhixi xianbi ji xiangguan wenti," *Beijing Daxue xuebao* 1 (1990): 121–28; Keightley, "At the Beginning," 29–31; Cao, *Jinwen yu Yin Zhou nüxing wenhua*, 31, all theorize that the Shang elite went through a series of monogamous and polygynous phases. Alternatively, it is possible that kings with multiple consorts may have had several wives in succession rather than simultaneously. Li, "Yindai shehui shenghuo," 422–23.

94. Li Fang (ed.), *Taiping yulan* (Taipei: Taiwan shangwu yinshuguan, n.d.), 83:11a. Song, *Xia Shang shehui shenghuo shi*, 146; Gao Bing, *Zhoudai hunyin xingtai yanjiu* (Chengdu: Bashu, 2007), 10. Tomb 2 at the late Shang Jingjie site, Lingshi county, Shanxi, a region that belonged to a foreign people (*fang*) who received considerable cultural influence from Shang, contains the joint burial of a man and two women, each interred on opposite sides of the man in her own coffin. Song, *Xia Shang shehui shenghuo shi*, 145.

95. Keith McMahon, *Women Shall Not Rule: Imperial Wives and Concubines in China from Han to Liao* (Lanham, MD: Rowman & Littlefield, 2013), 11.

96. Vandermeersch, *Wangdao ou la Voie Royale*, 280–81; Zheng, *Shanggu Huaxia funü yu hunyin*, 138, 143; Zhao, *Jiaguwen yu Shangdai wenhua*, 128–29.

97. Zheng, *Shanggu Huaxia funü yu hunyin*, 138–39.

98. Wang, "Rank and Power among Court Ladies at Anyang," 97, 100–01, 107–10.

99. Keightley, "At the Beginning," 46–53; Pulleyblank, "Ji and Jiang," 12. Members of a *xing* believed that they had a common remote ancestor. A *shi* was a branch of a *xing*, whose members shared a more recent ancestor. Many imperial scholars mistakenly believed that surnames dated back to high antiquity. Allen J. Chun, "Conceptions of Kinship and Kingship in Classical Chou China," *T'oung P'ao* 76 (1990): 26.

100. Zhao Dongyu, "Shangdai neihun shuo boyi," *Liaoning Shifan Daxue xuebao* 34, no. 5 (2011): 132–34.

101. Zheng, *Shanggu Huaxia funü yu hunyin*, 118; Lu Hong, *Zhoudai Yin Shang liyue jieshou yanjiu* (Beijing: Zhongguo shehui kexue chubanshe, 2013), 119–20.

102. Yang Hsi-chang, "The Shang Dynasty Cemetery System," in *Studies of Shang Archaeology: Selected Papers from the International Conference on Shang Civilization*, ed. K.C. Chang (New Haven: Yale University Press, 1986), 57; Fan Zhoucheng, "Cong Wang Hai 'bin yu you yi' kan Shangdai hunzhi," *Fuling Shifan Xueyuan xuebao* 21, no. 4 (2005): 70–72.

103. Cui Mingde, *Xian Qin zhengzhi hunyin shi* (Jinan: Shandong Daxue, 2004), 37–49. In small-scale societies, intermarriage is a form of reciprocal exchange between kinship groups that serves a political function—creating peaceful and stable bonds with people outside the circle of agnatic kin. Elman R. Service, *Origins of the State and Civilization: The Process of Cultural Evolution* (New York: W.W. Norton & Company, 1975), 60–62.

104. Vandermeersch, *Wangdao ou la Voie Royale*, 297.

105. Song, *Xia Shang shehui shenghuo shi*, 160; Cui, *Xian Qin zhengzhi hunyin shi*, 49–55.

106. Arthur Waley, *The Book of Songs*, ed. Joseph R. Allen (New York: Grove Press, 1996), 229 (Mao 236); Bernhard Karlgren, *The Book of Odes* (Stockholm: Museum of Far Eastern Antiquities, 1950), 187–88; Edward L. Shaughnessy, "Marriage, Divorce, and Revolution: Reading Between the Lines of the *Book of Changes*," *Journal of Asian Studies* 51, no. 3 (1992): 587–99.

107. Paul Wheatley, *The Pivot of the Four Quarters: A Preliminary Enquiry into the Origins and Character of the Ancient Chinese City* (Edinburgh: Edinburgh University Press, 1971), 56, 60; Richard von Glahn, *The Economic History of China: From Antiquity to the Nineteenth Century* (Cambridge: Cambridge University Press, 2016), 12–13.

108. Throughout Chinese history, women often managed to gain important roles within patrilineal Chinese kinship groups. James L. Watson, "Anthropological Overview: The Development of Chinese Descent Groups," in *Kinship Organization in Late Imperial China, 1000–1940*, ed. Patricia Buckey Ebrey and James L. Watson (Berkeley: University of California Press, 1986), 283.

109. This patriarchal system of ranks was not unique to China, and can be found in other early kingdoms as well. For example, Egyptian hieroglypic texts lack a word for "queen." Instead they would use circumlocutions such as "king's wife" and "god's wife." Flannery and Marcus, *The Creation of Inequality*, 417.

110. Tomb M5. Yang, "The Shang Dynasty Cemetery System," 55.

111. Tomb M18. Yang, "The Shang Dynasty Cemetery System," 55. Katheryn M. Linduff, "Many Wives, One Queen in Shang China," in *Ancient Queens: Archaeological Explorations*, ed. Sarah Milledge Nelson (Walnut Creek, CA: AltaMira Press, 2003), 66–71, summarizes information about the tombs of Shang royal spouses.

112. Reconstructions according to Kwang-chih Chang, *Shang Civilization* (New Haven: Yale University Press, 1980), 167–68, and Jia, "Yin Zhou funü shenghuo de jige mian," 8. For less complete versions, see Shima, *Inkyo bokuji kenkyū*, 96–98; Li, "Yindai shehui shenghuo," 418–19; Chen, *Yinxu buci zongshu*, 383–84, 386–88; Song, *Xia Shang shehui shenghuo shi*, 147.

113. Li, "Yindai shehui shenghuo," 419.

114. Zheng, *Shanggu Huaxia funü yu hunyin*, 136. During the Eastern Zhou era it was conventional to compare officials with palace women, as they were similarly dependent on the sovereign. Perhaps this idea had already emerged during the Shang. Lisa Raphals, *Sharing the Light: Representations of Women and Virtue in Early China* (Albany: State University of New York Press, 1998), 12; Paul Rakita Goldin, *The Culture of Sex in Ancient China* (Honolulu: University of Hawaii Press, 2002), 34–35, 40–42; Xiaorong Li, *Women's Poetry of Late Imperial China* (Seattle: University of Washington Press, 2012), 48.

115. Cao, *Jinwen yu Yin Zhou nüxing wenhua*, 73.

116. Cao Zhaolan, "Baojiao de xianqu - Xi Zhou jinwen zhong de nü 'bao,'" *Jiaoyu lilun yu shijian* 25, no. 3 (2005): 63–64.

117. Li Feng, *Bureaucracy and the State in Early China: Governing the Western Zhou* (Cambridge: Cambridge University Press, 2008), 59.

118. Chou, "Fu-x Ladies of the Shang Dynasty," 365, 371–74; Zhao, *Jiaguwen yu Shangdai wenhua*, 142–43; Cao, *Jinwen yu Yin Zhou nüxing wenhua*, 27–28.

119. Zhao, "Zhufu tansuo," 104–05.

120. Cao, *Jinwen yu Yin Zhou nüxing wenhua*, 19, discusses her various names.

121. Linduff, "Women's Lives Memorialized in Burial in Ancient China at Anyang," 263–65.

122. A pair of beautifully crafted bronze cauldrons from the same period have been unearthed. These are believed to have been cast to posthumously honor two of the three known consorts of King Wu Ding. One of these women was called Houmu Wu (or Simu Wu), which was probably a posthumous name of Fu Jing. The other was made for Bi Xin. Cao, *Jinwen yu Yin Zhou nüxing wenhua*, 15.

123. Cao, *Jinwen yu Yin Zhou nüxing wenhua*, 16–20.

124. For a biography of Fu Hao reconstructed mostly from inscriptional records see Yan Yiping, "Fu Hao liezhuan," *Zhongguo wenzi* 3 (1981): 1–104.

125. Cheng, "A Study of the Bronzes with the 'Ssu T'u Mu' Inscriptions Excavated from the Fu Hao Tomb," 81; Cao, *Jinwen yu Yin Zhou nüxing wenhua*, 6; Song Hua, "Fu Hao 'kuilongwen' bianzu fangding yanjiu," *Wenwu jianding yu jianshang* 9 (2013): 50–52; Zhang, "Fu Hao lueshuo," 186.

126. Wang, "Rank and Power among Court Ladies at Anyang," 101–02; Cao, *Jinwen yu Yin Zhou nüxing wenhua*, 11. Li Fan, "Yinxu Fu Hao mu xieshi dongwuxing yuqi chutan," *Jingji yu shehui fazhan* 10, no. 2 (2012): 120–21, describes and classifies the 216 animal-shaped jades from the tomb. Zhang Huian, "Xin'gan Dayangzhou Shangdai muzang yuqi de gongyi ji wenhua yiyun yanjiu," *Jinggangshan Daxue xuebao* 32, no. 6 (2011): 124–30, contends that the symbolism of various jade articles excavated from Shang tombs is related to fertility, goddesses, and other female matters, but offers no evidence for this contention. For a general description of Fu Hao's tomb, see Chang, *Shang Civilization*, 87–90. For a reconstruction of the funerary rituals likely used to inter Fu Hao, see Tang, "The Burial Ritual of the Shang Dynasty," 173–81.

127. Tang, "The Burial Ritual of the Shang Dynasty," 173.

128. Cao, *Jinwen yu Yin Zhou nüxing wenhua*, 11, 13.

129. Thorp, *China in the Early Bronze Age*, 186–87. The posthumous sacrifices that King Wu Ding conducted to Fu Hao included *binji* 賓祭, *jiuji* 酒祭, *kuji* 哭祭, *liaoji* 燎祭, *youji* 侑祭. Cao, *Jinwen yu Yin Zhou nüxing wenhua*, 13.

130. Linduff, "Women's Lives Memorialized in Burial in Ancient China at Anyang," 263.

131. Xu Guangde and He Minling, "Xin shiji Yinxu kaogu de zhongda faxian - ji Anyang Yinxu huayuan dong 54 hao mu de fajue," *Xungen* 4 (2001): 70.

132. Chang, "A Brief Discussion of Fu Tzu," 103, 113; Zhang, "Fu Hao lue-shuo," 186–89.

133. Chang, "A Brief Discussion of Fu Tzu," 104. Cao, *Jinwen yu Yin Zhou nüxing wenhua*, 6–7, discusses the orthography of the characters *fu* and *hao*.

134. Cao, "'Fuhao' nai 'Zifang' zhi nü," 381; Cao Dingyun, *Yinxu Fu Hao mu mingwen yanjiu* (Taipei: Wenjin chubanshe, 1993), 77–84; Li Xueshan and Guo Shengqiang, "Yin Shang wenhua de fanrong yu Zhongguo wenming de jincheng - cong Anyang Yinxu 5 hao mu, 54 hao mu he Xinganshang mu qingtongqi duibi tanqi," *Zhongyuan wenhua yanjiu* 3 (2013): 57; Li, *Shuowen xinzheng*, 1010–11.

135. Cao, *Jinwen yu Yin Zhou nüxing wenhua*, 13–14.

136. Cheng, "A Study of the Bronzes with the 'Ssu T'u Mu' Inscriptions Excavated from the Fu Hao Tomb," 82–83.

137. Cheng, "A Study of the Bronzes with the 'Ssu T'u Mu' Inscriptions Excavated from the Fu Hao Tomb," 83, 96–97. This name has also been read Si Tu Mu. To compare the similar orthographies of *si* 司 and *hou* 后 see Li, *Shuowen xinzheng*, 734–35.

138. Rao Zongyi, "Fu Hao mu tongqi, yuqi suojian shixing fangguo kao," in *Gu wenzi yanjiu* 12 (Beijing: Zhonghua shuju, 1985), 299.

139. Li Xueqin, "Lun 'Fu Hao' mu de niandai ji youguan wenti," *Wenwu* 11 (1977): 33–35, discusses bronzes in her tomb inscribed with other people's names.

140. Lu, "Shangdai nüjie Fu Hao yu nüxing duikang yishi," 94–96.

141. Wang, Zhang, and Yang, "Shilun Yinxu wuhao mu de Fu Hao," 5–7; Yang, "Jiaguwen zhong suojian Shangdai de gongna zhidu," 31.

142. Zheng, *Shanggu Huaxia funü yu hunyin*, 130–31; Wang, "Cong 'pinji zhi chen' xianxiang kan Shangdai funü de shehui diwei," 23.

143. Qi Hangfu, "Cong Yinxu jiaguwen kan Shangdai funü shehui diwei," *Zhongzhou xuekan* 12 (2014): 130.

144. Mary Douglas and Baron Isherwood, *The World of Goods: Towards an Anthropology of Consumption* (New York: W.W. Norton, 1979). For a parallel case, see Elizabeth M. Brumfiel, "Consumption and Politics at Aztec Huexotla," *American Anthropologist* 89, no. 3 (1987): 676.

145. Zheng, *Shanggu Huaxia funü yu hunyin*, 135–36; Zhao, *Jiaguwen yu Shangdai wenhua*, 141; Cao, *Jinwen yu Yin Zhou nüxing wenhua*, 5–6; Xu, "Shangdai zhufu de zongjiao diwei," 450. This preparatory process was called *shi* 示.

146. Yang, "Jiaguwen zhong suojian Shangdai de gongna zhidu," 31; Cao, *Jinwen yu Yin Zhou nüxing wenhua*, 10, 17, 29.

147. Wang, Zhang, and Yang, "Shilun Yinxu wuhao mu de Fu Hao," 7–10; Cao, *Jinwen yu Yin Zhou nüxing wenhua*, 5–6.

148. Zheng, *Shanggu Huaxia funü yu hunyin*, 136.

149. Zheng, *Shanggu Huaxia funü yu hunyin*, 365–68; Zhao, *Jiaguwen yu Shangdai wenhua*, 144–45; Cao, *Jinwen yu Yin Zhou nüxing wenhua*, 5–6.

150. Chou, "Fu-x Ladies of the Shang Dynasty," 365; Zheng, *Shanggu Huaxia funü yu hunyin*, 135; Xu, "Shangdai zhufu de zongjiao diwei," 456–57; Cao, *Jin-*

wen yu Yin Zhou nüxing wenhua, 12. The *yu* 御 ceremony that Fu Hao conducted for King Fu Yi was intended to prevent ancestors from harming the living. Xu, "Shangdai zhufu de zongjiao diwei," 456–57.

151. Chou, "Fu-x Ladies of the Shang Dynasty," 362, 365; Qi, "Cong Yinxu ji-aguwen kan Shangdai funü shehui diwei," 129. Fu Jing was one of the *fu* who sent in tribute to the king. Cao, *Jinwen yu Yin Zhou nüxing wenhua*, 17.

152. Chou, "Fu-x Ladies of the Shang Dynasty," 361.

153. Yang, "Jiaguwen zhong suojian Shangdai de gongna zhidu," 28–30; Wang, "Rank and Power among Court Ladies at Anyang," 104.

154. Li, "Lun 'Fu Hao' mu de niandai ji youguan wenti," 33–35; Cao, *Jinwen yu Yin Zhou nüxing wenhua*, 13–14.

155. Eric C. Mullis, "Toward a Confucian Ethic of the Gift," *Dao* 7, no. 2 (2008): 178–81. For a general anthropological overview of the importance of the exchange of valuables to upholding the social order of prehistoric and Bronze Age societies, see Earle, *Bronze Age Economics*, 19–42.

156. Shirakawa Shizuka, *Kōkotsubun no sekai* (Tokyo: Heibonsha, 1972), 154.

157. Wang, Zhang and Yang, "Shilun Yinxu wuhao mu de Fu Hao," 2–5; Chang Ping-ch'üan, "A Brief Description of the Fu Hao Oracle Bone Inscriptions," in *Studies of Shang Archaeology: Selected Papers from the International Conference on Shang Civilization*, ed. K.C. Chang (New Haven: Yale University Press, 1986), 136; Zheng, *Shanggu Huaxia funü yu hunyin*, 133–34; Keightley, "At the Beginning," 32; Zhao, *Jiaguwen yu Shangdai wenhua*, 139; Cao, *Jinwen yu Yin Zhou nüxing wenhua*, 7–9. Wang, *Wu diguo: cang zai jiaguwenli*, 291–95, discusses Fu Hao's campaigns in detail.

158. Cao, *Jinwen yu Yin Zhou nüxing wenhua*, 8.

159. Cao, *Jinwen yu Yin Zhou nüxing wenhua*, 9; Wang, "Rank and Power among Court Ladies at Anyang," 103.

160. Chou, "Fu-x Ladies of the Shang Dynasty," 368–71; Zhao, *Jiaguwen yu Shangdai wenhua*, 140; Wang, "Cong 'pinji zhi chen' xianxiang kan Shangdai funü de shehui diwei," 22–23; Cao, *Jinwen yu Yin Zhou nüxing wenhua*, 28; Yang, "Qianyi jiaguwen suo fanying de Shangdai funü diwei," 373–74; Qi, "Cong Yinxu jiagu-wen kan Shangdai funü shehui diwei," 129–30. Ironically, a Han dynasty picto-rial stone depicts the Guifang, enemies of Shang, as having female soldiers, even though there is no evidence that Guifang women participated in war. The Han artist uses the presence of women on the battlefield to symbolize the barbarism of the Guifang. Yet it was Shang, not their enemies, who had female soldiers. A. Soper, "King Wu Ting's Victory of the 'Realm of Demons,'" *Artibus Asiae* 17, no. 1 (1954): 55–60.

161. Zhao, *Jiaguwen yu Shangdai wenhua*, 140; Cao, *Jinwen yu Yin Zhou nüxing wenhua*, 16.

162. Wang, "Rank and Power among Court Ladies at Anyang," 102.

163. Zheng, *Shanggu Huaxia funü yu hunyin*, 134. The early Zhou people even engaged in ritualized hunting to symbolize military victory. Yang, *Xi Zhou shi*, 661–70.

164. For an exception see Shanxi sheng Linfen Xingshu Wenhuaju, "Shanxi Lin-fen Xiajin cun Taosi wenhua mudi fajue baogao," 484. Tomb M32 at the Xiajin site

of the Taosi culture belonged to a mature woman. Although the tomb was looted, robbers left behind a stone arrowhead.

165. Thorp, *China in the Early Bronze Age*, 104.

166. Keightley, "At the Beginning," 28.

167. Wang, Zhang, and Yang, "Shilun Yinxu wuhao mu de Fu Hao," 14–16; Cao, *Jinwen yu Yin Zhou nüxing wenhua*, 11; Qi, "Cong Yinxu jiaguwen kan Shangdai funü shehui diwei," 128–29.

168. Victor Turner, *The Forest of Symbols: Aspects of Ndembu Ritual* (Ithaca: Cornell University Press, 1967), 9.

169. Vandermeersch, *Wangdao ou la Voie Royale*, 264–70; Wang, Zhang and Yang, "Shilun Yinxu wuhao mu de Fu Hao," 10–14; Zheng, *Shanggu Huaxia funü yu hunyin*, 129; Keightley, "At the Beginning," 33–34; Hu, *Jiaguxue Shangshi luncong*, vol. 1, 114–24; Cao, *Jinwen yu Yin Zhou nüxing wenhua*, 12; Qi, "Cong Yinxu jiaguwen kan Shangdai funü shehui diwei," 128–32. Wu Qi, "Cong jiagu buci kan Shangdai zhi meieguan," *Mianyang Shifan Xueyuan xuebao* 33, no. 7 (2014): 73–76, asserts that the Shang considered pregnant women particularly beautiful, an interpretation that reads quite a bit into this terse material.

170. Song, *Xia Shang shehui shenghuo shi*, 171–77. The original form of the character *yun* 孕, which denotes pregnancy, depicts a fetus inside the womb. Xu, *Wenzi xiaojiang*, 447–48. Although the Shang valued fertility, on pp. 283–85 Xu contends that the original orthography of the character *qi* 棄 might perhaps depict the abandonment of a newborn baby, who has been placed on a winnowing basket.

171. Not only did the Shang consider the birth of a son auspicious (*jia* 嘉), but oracle bones also use a special character with positive connotations (*yu* 余) to describe this happy event. This terminology reflects the importance that Shang royalty accorded the birth of sons. Hu Xinsheng, "Shangdai 'yuzi' lei buci suo fanying de yuanshi hunyin," *Shandong Daxue xuebao* 1 (1997): 46. The Shang orthography of the character *jia* depicts a kneeling woman beside a digging stick, a phallic symbol representing a son. Thus the term for "auspicious" originally referred to the birth of a son. Xu, *Wenzi xiaojiang*, 134–36. A preference for sons seems to have continued through the ancient era. Han Fei asserted that parents congratulated each other upon the birth of a son but would kill a daughter. Han Fei, *Han Fei zi* (Shanghai: Shangwu yinshuguan, 1930) (*Sibu beiyao* ed.), 18:1b. During the Zhou, the low value of betrothal gifts meant that a family gained little financially when marrying off a daughter, depressing the economic value of women and perhaps leading families to consider daughters of little value.

172. Keightley, "At the Beginning," 43.

173. Keightley, "At the Beginning," 41; Cao, *Jinwen yu Yin Zhou nüxing wenhua*, 13.

174. For the basic procedures regarding sacrifices to female ancestors see Liu Yuan, *Zhou Shang jizu li yanjiu* (Beijing: Shangwu yinshuguan, 2004), 168–72.

175. For an extremely detailed discussion of the character *bi* 妣, see Guo Moruo, "Shi zu bi," *Jiaguwenzi yanjiu* (Hong Kong: Zhonghua shuju, 1976), 1–60. Also Keightley, "At the Beginning," 29–31; Deng Tongxiang, "Shangdai Wu Ding shi guizu 'zi' de yisi liyi kaocha," *Yindu xuekan* 4 (2014): 3.

176. Chang, *Early Chinese Civilization*, 81, 83.

177. Chang, *Shang Civilization*, 171; Chang Yuzhi, *Shangdai zhouji zhidu* (Beijing: Xinhua shudian, 1987), 108–09; Keightley, "At the Beginning," 35–36, 39–40, 43.

178. Chang, *Early Chinese Civilization*, 83.

179. Keightley, "At the Beginning," 36–38.

180. Chang, *Shangdai zhouji zhidu*; Takashima, *A Little Primer of Chinese Oracle-Bone Inscriptions*, 73.

181. Wang, "Rank and Power among Court Ladies at Anyang," 109–10. If two brothers served as king, only the spouse of one of these kings would appear in the official the genealogy for that generation. Chang, *Early Chinese Civilization*, 82–83.

182. Keightley, "At the Beginning," 38.

183. Ren Wei, "Cong kaogu faxian kan Xi Zhou Yan guo Yin yimin zhi shehui zhuangkuang," *Zhongyuan wenwu* 2 (2001): 57.

184. Chang, "A Brief Description of the Fu Hao Oracle Bone Inscriptions," 123.

185. David N. Keightley, "The Religious Commitment: Shang Theology and the Genesis of Chinese Political Culture," *History of Religions* 17, nos. 3-4 (1978): 213.

186. Deng, "Shangdai Wu Ding shi guizu 'zi' de yisi liyi kaocha," 5. For discussions of the mechanics of Shang sacrifices, see Liu, "Ancestor Worship," 123; Liu Yuan, "Shangdai houqi jizu yishi leixing," *Lishi yanjiu* 6 (2002): 80–94; Xu Yuanzhe, "Shangdai jisi de yongsheng fangfa," *Xinxiang Xueyuan xuebao* 23, no. 3 (2009): 72–74; Lian Shaoming, "Shangdai de baiji yu yuji," *Kaogu xuebao* 1 (2011): 23–56.

187. Keightley, "At the Beginning," 41, 43.

188. Chen Zhiyong, "Shixi Shangdai de zongmiao zhidu jiqi zhengzhi gongyong," *Yindu xuekan* 1 (1999): 24.

189. Keightley, "At the Beginning," 42–43.

190. Cao, *Jinwen yu Yin Zhou nüxing wenhua*, 45.

191. Cao, *Jinwen yu Yin Zhou nüxing wenhua*, 46–49.

192. Keightley, "At the Beginning," 42.

193. Keightley, "The Religious Commitment," 217.

194. This ritual was called *bin* 賓. Xu, "Shangdai zhufu de zongjiao diwei," 456–57.

195. In getting married, a man (either alive or dead) would *qu* 取 (literally "take" or "choose") a wife. Chang, "A Brief Discussion of Fu Tzu," 114–15, 118.

CHAPTER 4

1. Du Fangqin, "Shang Zhou xingbie zhidu yu guizu funü diwei zhi bijiao," in *Zhongguo shehui xingbie de lishi wenhua xunzong*, ed. Du Fangqin (Tianjin: Tianjin shehui kexue, 1998), 67–94, compares the conditions faced by Shang and Zhou women.

2. Waley, *The Book of Songs*, 161–63; Karlgren, *The Book of Odes*, 129–31 (Mao 189).

3. Zheng, *Shanggu Huaxia funü yu hunyin*, 186. Zheng speculates that this exemption was intended to preserve a woman's appearance so that men could still use her sexually.

4. Li, *Bureaucracy and the State in Early China*, 11–20, explains why Zhou nobles wrote these texts and how historians should interpret them.

5. Chen Zhaorong, "Xingbie, shenfen yu caifu – cong Shang Zhou qingtongqi yu muzang yiwu suozuo de kaocha," in *Zhongguo shi xinlun – xingbie shi fence*, ed. Li Zhende (Taipei: Zhongyang yanjiu yuan, 2009), 76, notes that of 5,315 bronze items (including weapons) in one catalogue that date to the Western Zhou and Chunqiu eras, 3,276 were commissioned by men and 216 by women. Pairs of men and women together commissioned twenty-three items. So among this sample, men commissioned fifteen times more bronze items than women.

6. Edward L. Shaughnessy, "From Liturgy to Literature: The Ritual Contexts of the Earliest Poems in the Book of Poetry," *Hanxue yanjiu* 13, no. 1 (1995): 133–64; Martin Kern, "Shi Jing Songs as Performance Texts: A Case Study of 'Chu Ci' (Thorny Caltrop)," *Early China* 25 (2000): 49–112.

7. Marcel Granet, *Festivals and Songs of Ancient China*, trans. E.D. Edwards (New York: E.P. Dutton & Co., 1932), 84–86.

8. Anne Behnke Kinney, "The Mao Commentary to the Book of Odes as a Source for Women's History," in *Overt and Covert Treasures: Essays on the Sources for Chinese Women's History*, ed. Clara Wing-Chung Ho (Hong Kong: The City University Press, 2012), 61–111. Yiqun Zhou, *Festivals, Feasts, and Gender Relations in Ancient China and Greece* (Cambridge: Cambridge University Press, 2010), 289–92, 304–11, notes that some of these poems may have been written by men from a female point of view, a common convention in later eras. Fang Zhengyi, "Luelun *Shijing* zhong de nüshiren qun," *Guilin Shi Jiaoyu Xueyuan xuebao* 2 (1997): 43–46, provides a table listing poems traditionally believed to have been composed by women, and those that deal with women's matters.

9. Martin Kern, "Excavated Manuscripts and Their Socratic Pleasures: Newly Discovered Challenges in Reading the 'Airs of the States,'" *Asiatische Studien* 61, no. 3 (2007): 776, 792.

10. Kinney, "The Mao Commentary to the Book of Odes as a Source for Women's History," 65; Katō Minoru, "Lun Liu Xiang guanyu 'Youli' shidai de shijingxue," *Jilin Shifan Xueyuan xuebao* 19, no. 4 (1998): 25–29.

11. Goldin, *The Culture of Sex in Ancient China*, 9–10; Kern, "Excavated Manuscripts and their Socratic Pleasures," 781–82, 787.

12. Jing Jing, "*Shijing* zhong meiren guannian dui Zhongguo shinühua de yingxiang," *Yishu baijia* 7 (2011): 223–25.

13. Rosemary A. Joyce, "Archaeology of the Body," *Annual Review of Anthropology* 34 (2005): 140, 142.

14. Eva Kit Wah Man, "Discourses on Female Bodily Aesthetics and Its Early Revelations in *The Book of Songs*," in *Overt and Covert Treasures: Essays on the Sources for Chinese Women's History*, ed. Clara Wing-Chung Ho (Hong Kong: The City University Press, 2012), 116–19. For example, Waley, *The Book of Songs*, 48–49; Karlgren, *The Book of Odes*, 38 (Mao 57). This technique of naming describing something by enumerating its components, known to literary critics as "the blazon," had a major influence on later portrayals of women in Chinese poetry. Robert Joe Cutter, "To Make Her Mine: Women and the Rhetoric of Property in Early and Early Medieval Fu," *Early Medieval China* 19 (2013): 47–53.

15. Jiang Yuqiu, "Fengya shidai de nüfu zhi mei - cong *Shijing* kan Zhoudai nüzi fushi," *Yishu sheji yanjiu* 3 (2014): 37–42. Wang Fang, "Dong Zhou nüxing faxing fashi chulun," *Kaogu yu wenwu* 3 (2011): 46–57, discusses Zhou hairstyles and hair ornaments.

16. For two examples, see Waley, *The Book of Songs*, 75, 214–15; Karlgren, *The Book of Odes*, 61 (Mao 93), 179 (Mao 225). Li Peng, "Lun *Shijing* nüxing miaoxie de shixing zhihui - yi yu wenhua wei li," *Xianyang Shifan Xueyuan xuebao* 26, no. 5 (2011): 104–07, notes that the sound of tinkling jade ornaments, worn by the nobility, was also considered an important aspect of a woman's beauty. Wu Aiqin, "Shuo ji," *Shixue yuekan* 1 (2007): 134–36, discusses the ritual significance of Zhou hairpins and their use to symbolize social status. Gao Meijin, "Qianxi Chunqiu Zhanguo shiqi de funü zhuangrong," *Guanzi xuekan* 2 (2011): 107–09, describes ancient cosmetics and their application.

17. Joyce, "Archaeology of the Body," 146.

18. Wang Zirong, "*Shijing Guofeng* nüxing xingxiang mianmianguan," *Chuandong xuekan*, vol. 5, no. 3 (1995): 111.

19. Zhang Jing, "Cong 'Mang' deng jishou minge kan Zhongguo gudai funü de xingge guangcai," *Xinzhou Shifa Xueyuan xuebao* 16, no. 4 (2000): 47–51. Chen Ke, "*Shijing* yu *Chuci* zhong nüxing xingxiang zhi bijiao," *Chifeng Xueyuan xuebao*, vol. 33, no. 1 (2012): 138–39, notes how *Shijing* and *Chuci* portray the ideal woman's personality very differently.

20. Cao, *Jinwen yu Yin Zhou nüxing wenhua*, 78.

21. Chen, *Shang Zhou xingshi zhidu yanjiu*, 297–330.

22. Cao, *Jinwen yu Yin Zhou nüxing wenhua*, 113–17; Xie, *Zhoudai jiating xingtai*, 85–100.

23. Li Zhongcao, "Liang Zhou jinwen zhong de funü chengwei," *Gu wenzi yanjiu* 18 (1992): 398–403; Cao Dingyun, "Zhoudai jinwen zhong nüzi chengwei leixing yanjiu," *Kaogu* 6 (1999): 79.

24. Mu Haiting, "Zhoudai jinwen zhong de fuming," *Wenbo* 5 (2007): 54.

25. Li, "Liang Zhou jinwen zhong de funü chengwei," 402–03.

26. Mu, "Zhoudai jinwen zhong de fuming," 15.

27. Zhang Shuyi, "Zhoudai nüzi de xingshi zhidu," *Shixue jikan* 2 (1999): 68; Cao, *Jinwen yu Yin Zhou nüxing wenhua*, 106. Chen, *Shang Zhou xingshi zhidu yanjiu*, 297–330, lists nine formulas used to construct a woman's posthumous name. Other types of names were used as well.

28. Yang, "Jiaguwen zhong suojian Shangdai de gongna zhidu," 28–29.

29. Cao, *Jinwen yu Yin Zhou nüxing wenhua*, 101–04. In the Western Zhou "male and female bondservants" (*chenqie* 臣妾) were attached to the palace, ancestral temple, and aristocratic households. Their status remains a subject of debate. After Shang Yang's reforms in the Eastern Zhou, war captives and convicts were called *li chenqie* 隸臣妾 (bondservants). Thereafter, most "bondservants" were attached to the state. Von Glahn, *The Economic History of China*, 25–26, 34–35, 59.

30. Zhongguo Kexueyuan Kaogusuo, et al., "Beijing fujin faxian de Xi Zhou nuli xunzang mu," *Kaogu* 5 (1974): 310–12; Beijing Daxue Lishixi Gujiao Yanshi Shang Zhou zubian, *Shang Zhou kaogu*, 216; Yu Jiang, "Ritual Practice, Status, and Gender Identity: Western Zhou Tombs at Baoji," in *Gender and Chinese Archaeology,*

ed. Katheryn M. Linduff and Yan Sun (Walnut Creek, CA: Altamira Press, 2004), 124.

31. Cao, *Jinwen yu Yin Zhou nüxing wenhua*, 105; Mumford, "Death Do Us Unite," 4.

32. Cao Jiandun, "Zhoudai jisi yongsheng lizhi kaolue," *Wenbo* 3 (2008): 21.

33. Wang, "*Shijing Guofeng* nüxing xingxiang mianmianguan," 111; Xu Zhuoyun, "Cong *Zhouli* zhong tuice yuangu de funü gongzuo," *Dalu zazhi* 7 (1954): 202–05.

34. Waley, *The Book of Songs*, 108, 120–22; Karlgren, *The Book of Odes*, 87–88, 97–99 (Mao 137, 154); Liu Dehan, *Dong Zhou funü shenghuo* (Taipei: Xuesheng shuju, 1976), 76–80; Yu Tingting, "Dong Zhou shiqi de cansang shengchan quyu tanxi," *Sichou* 1 (2013): 63–66.

35. *Yinsi* 淫祀. Constance A. Cook, *Death in Ancient China: The Tale of One Man's Journey* (Leiden: E.J. Brill, 2006), 4. Imperial authorities wrote about early Zhou shamanistic practices long after the fact, so their descriptions were not necessarily correct.

36. Schafer, "Ritual Exposure in Ancient China," 132–33.

37. Liu Guiying, "Xi Zhou yu Xiwangmu jianjiaokao," *Hebei Daxue xuebao* 33, no. 1 (2008): 89–92.

38. Liu Qiyi, "Xi Zhou jinwen zhong suojian de Zhou wang houfei," *Kaogu yu wenwu* 4 (1980): 85–90; Cao, *Jinwen yu Yin Zhou nüxing wenhua*, 64, 78; Chen Zhaorong, "Cong qingtongqi mingwen kan liang Zhou shi hunyin guanxi," in *Guwenzi yu gudaishi*, ed. Chen Zhaorong (Taipei: Zhongyang yanjiu yuan, Lishi yuyan yanjiusuo, 2007), vol. 1, 256, 259–64.

39. Chen, "Cong qingtongqi mingwen kan liang Zhou shi hunyin guanxi," vol. 1, 256–59. For the orthography of *hou* 后, and its inverted twin *si* 司, see Li, *Shuowen xinzheng*, 734–35.

40. Li Hengmei, *Zhaomu zhidu yanjiu* (Jinan: Qilu shushe, 1996), 11; Chen, "Cong qingtongqi mingwen kan liang Zhou shi hunyin guanxi," 253–92; Xie Naihe, "Jinwen zhong suojian Xi Zhou wanghou shiji kao," *Huaxia kaogu* 4 (2008): 142–52.

41. Although the Chronology Project's dates are often used as general guidelines, many details remain controversial. See Edward L. Shaughnessy, "Chronologies of Ancient China, A Critique of the Xia-Shang-Zhou Chronology Project," in *Windows on the Chinese World: Reflections by Five Historians*, ed. Clara Wing-Chung Ho (Lanham, MD: Lexington Books, 2008), 15–28.

42. Li, *Bureaucracy and the State in Early China*, 69.

43. Zhou, *Festivals, Feasts, and Gender Relations in Ancient China and Greece*, 205–07.

44. Xie, "Jinwen zhong suojian Xi Zhou wanghou shiji kao," 145. For a discussion of the ritual see Yang, *Xi Zhou shi*, 709–35.

45. Cao, *Jinwen yu Yin Zhou nüxing wenhua*, 64–67; Xie, "Jinwen zhong suojian Xi Zhou wanghou shiji kao," 144. Vandermeersh, *Wangdao ou la Voie Royale*, 304–06, describes how Western Zhou queens presided over matters at court in their husbands' absence.

46. Xie, "Jinwen zhong suojian Xi Zhou wanghou shiji kao," 146.

47. Herrlee G. Creel, *The Origins of Statecraft in China, Volume One, The Western Zhou Empire* (Chicago: University of Chicago Press, 1970), 395; Cao, *Jinwen yu Yin*

Zhou nüxing wenhua, 83; Xie, "Jinwen zhong suojian Xi Zhou wanghou shiji kao," 146.

48. Wang Qimin, "Zhoudai zongmiao lizhi kao," *Tangshan Shifan Xueyuan xuebao* 37, no. 1 (2015): 51–52.

49. Earle, *Bronze Age Economics*, 58–59, 82–83, 81–96. The redistributive paradigm continues to undergo critique and refinement. Dimitri Nakassis, William A. Parkinson, and Michael L. Galaty, "Redistribution in Aegean Palatial Societies: Redistributive Economies from a Theoretical and Cross-Cultural Perspective," *American Journal of Archaeology* 115, no. 2 (2011): 177–84.

50. Xie, "Jinwen zhong suojian Xi Zhou wanghou shiji kao," 144, 148–49.

51. Cao, *Jinwen yu Yin Zhou nüxing wenhua*, 70; Xie, "Jinwen zhong suojian Xi Zhou wanghou shiji kao," 145.

52. Xie, "Jinwen zhong suojian Xi Zhou wanghou shiji kao," 144.

53. Sunjoo Pang, "The Consorts of King Wu and King Wen in the Bronze Inscriptions of Early China," *Momumenta Serica* 33 (1977–1978): 129–30; Cao, *Jinwen yu Yin Zhou nüxing wenhua*, 64–69; Xie, "Jinwen zhong suojian Xi Zhou wanghou shiji kao," 143–44, 147–49.

54. Creel, *The Origins of Statecraft in China*, 395; Cao, *Jinwen yu Yin Zhou nüxing wenhua*, 83–84.

55. Xie, "Jinwen zhong suojian Xi Zhou wanghou shiji kao," 146, 148–49. One inscription shows a queen in charge of a group of people called *Jiangshi ren* 姜氏人, perhaps her natal relatives.

56. Takigawa Kamitaro, *Shiki kaichū kōshō* (Tokyo: 1934; reprinted Taipei: Zhonghua shuju, 1977), 35:2.

57. Creel, *The Origins of Statecraft in China*, 394–95; Xie, "Jinwen zhong suojian Xi Zhou wanghou shiji kao," 144, 146–47.

58. Tsui-mei Huang, "Gender Differentiation in Jin State Jade Regulations," in *Gender and Chinese Archaeology*, ed. Katheryn M. Linduff and Yan Sun (Walnut Creek, CA: Altamira Press, 2004), 146.

59. Yu, "Ritual Practice, Status, and Gender Identity," 133.

60. T'ang Chün-I, "The T'ien Ming [Heavenly Ordinance] in Pre-Ch'in China," *Philosophy East and West* 11, no. 4 (1962): 195–218.

61. Goldin, *The Culture of Sex in Ancient China*, 53–54; Yang Yun, "Zhoudai shengmu songge tanxi," *Shehui kexue zhanxian* 1 (2009): 277–78.

62. Cook, *Death in Ancient China*, 74.

63. Ying Yong, "Gender, Status, Ritual Regulations, and Mortuary Practice in the State of Jin," in *Gender and Chinese Archaeology*, ed. Katheryn M. Linduff and Yan Sun (Walnut Creek, CA: Altamira Press, 2004), 161.

64. Yu, "Ritual Practice, Status, and Gender Identity," 119, 123, 127.

65. Yu, "Ritual Practice, Status, and Gender Identity," 129–30.

66. Ying, "Gender, Status, Ritual Regulations, and Mortuary Practice in the State of Jin," 161–62, 174–75, 182, 196–97; Huang, "Gender Differentiation in Jin State Jade Regulations," 142–43.

67. Ying, "Gender, Status, Ritual Regulations, and Mortuary Practice in the State of Jin," 189–90; Alain Thote, "Shang and Zhou Funeral Practices: Interpretation of Material Vestiges," in *Early Chinese Religion: Part One: Shang through Han (1250 BC–220 AD)*, ed. John Lagerwey and Marc Kalinowski (Leiden: E.J. Brill,

2009), 123. Tombs from the state of Guo exemplify the use of jade in Western Zhou burials. See Jiang Tao, Wang Longzheng, and Qiao Bin, *Sanmenxia Guo guo nüguizu mu chutu yuqi jingsui* (Taipei: Zhongzhi meishu, 2002); Zhang Shuaifeng, "Guo guo guizu de yu xiangshi wenhua," *Zhonghua wenwu huabao* 6 (2012): 115–16.

68. Creel, *The Origins of Statecraft in China*, 394; Cao, *Jinwen yu Yin Zhou nüxing wenhua*, 85.

69. Cao, *Jinwen yu Yin Zhou nüxing wenhua*, 99.

70. Cao, *Jinwen yu Yin Zhou nüxing wenhua*, 82.

71. Cao, *Jinwen yu Yin Zhou nüxing wenhua*, 84.

72. Cao, *Jinwen yu Yin Zhou nüxing wenhua*, 78–81.

73. Cao, *Jinwen yu Yin Zhou nüxing wenhua*, 81.

74. Waley, *The Book of Songs*, 229; Karlgren, *The Book of Odes*, 187–88 (Mao 236), describes a political marriage between Shang and Zhou. Also see Shaughnessy, "Marriage, Divorce, and Revolution," 587–99; Pulleyblank, "Ji and Jiang," 9.

75. Chen, "Cong qingtongqi mingwen kan liang Zhou wangshi hunyin guanxi," 39–45.

76. Cao Zhaolan, "Cong jinwen kan liang Zhou hunyin guanxi," *Wuhan Daxue xuebao* 1 (2004): 108–14, and Cao, *Jinwen yu Yin Zhou nüxing wenhua*, 182–88, discuss bronze inscriptions documenting political marriages among the nobility. For evidence from tomb goods, see Ying, "Gender, Status, Ritual Regulations, and Mortuary Practice in the State of Jin," 195.

77. Ying, "Gender, Status, Ritual Regulations, and Mortuary Practice in the State of Jin," 196–97.

78. Chen Fangmei, "Jin hou mu qingtongqi suojian xingbie yanjiu de xin xiansuo," in *Jin hou mudi chuti qingtongqi guoji xueshu yantaohui wenji*, ed. Shanghai Bowuguan (Shanghai: Shanghai shuhua, 2002), 164–66; Ying, "Gender, Status, Ritual Regulations, and Mortuary Practice in the State of Jin," 194–95.

79. Li, *Bureaucracy and the State in Early China*, 59.

80. Cao, *Jinwen yu Yin Zhou nüxing wenhua*, 74–75; Xie, "Jinwen zhong suojian Xi Zhou wanghou shiji kao," 143.

81. Waley, *The Book of Songs*, 244–47, 313–17; Karlgren, *The Book of Odes*, 199–202, 257–61 (Mao 245, 300). For ceremonies in honor of Jiang Yuan, see Lu, *Zhoudai Yin Shang liyue jieshou yanjiu*, 285–88.

82. Pulleyblank, "Ji and Jiang," 8. Hou Xudong and Howard Goodman, "Rethinking Chinese Kinship in the Han and the Six Dynasties: A Preliminary Observation," *Asia Major* 23, no. 1 (2010): 29–63, emphasize the instability of surnames up until the end of the Northern Dynasties.

83. Tian Fu (Xing Yitian), "Cong *Lienü zhuan* kan Zhongguoshi muai de liulu," in *Zhongguo funüshi lunwenji sanji*, ed. Bao Jialin (Taipei: Sanlian, 1993), 22; Anne Behnke Kinney, "Infant Abandonment in Early China," *Early China* 18 (1993): 129.

84. Liu, *Zhou Shang jizu li yanjiu*, 93.

85. Cao, *Jinwen yu Yin Zhou nüxing wenhua*, 199.

86. Cao Wei, "San Bo Che Fu qi yu Xi Zhou hunyin zhidu," *Wenwu* 3 (2000): 63–65; Cao, *Jinwen yu Yin Zhou nüxing wenhua*, 85, 111–12; Constance A. Cook, "Education and the Way of the Former Kings," in *Writing & Literacy in Early China: Studies from the Columbia Early China Seminar*, ed. Li Feng and David Prager Branner (Seattle: University of Washington Press, 2011), 315. During the Western Zhou,

Shang remnants continued to maintain some of their unique traditional practices regarding ancestral sacrifices to deceased women. Ren, "Cong kaogu faxian kan Xi Zhou Yan guo Yin yimin zhi shehui zhuangkuang," 57.

87. Feng Shi, "Wo fangding mingwen yu Xi Zhou sangdianli," *Kaogu xuebao* 3 (2013): 185–212. Geng Chao, "Zhoudai jiazu jisi yu liangxing guanxi lunlüe," in *Lifa yu xinyang - Zhongguo gudai nüxing yanjiu lunkao*, ed. Pu Muzhou (Hong Kong: Shangwu yinshuguan, 2013), 9–22, describes how the husband took the leading role in conducting family sacrifices, and how his wife assisted him.

88. The *zudian* ceremony consisted of two parts: the summer sacrifice (*yueji* 礿祭, 禴祭) and the thanksgiving sacrifice (*saiji* 奈祭).

89. Cao Dingyun, "Jinwen zhong de nüxing xiangjizhe ji qi shehui diwei," *Shenzhen Daxue xuebao*, vol. 19, no 3 (2002): 80, 84; Ying, "Gender, Status, Ritual Regulations, and Mortuary Practice in the State of Jin," 184; Cao, *Jinwen yu Yin Zhou nüxing wenhua*, 199, 201–02, 203–06.

90. Susan Carol Rogers, "Female Forms of Power and the Myth of Male Dominance: A Model of Female/Male Interaction in Peasant Society," *American Ethnologist* 2, no. 4 (1975): 727–56.

91. Waley, *The Book of Songs*, 14, 194–96; Karlgren, *The Book of Odes*, 8, 161–64 (Mao 13, 209).

92. Zhou, *Festivals, Feasts, and Gender Relations in Ancient China and Greece*, 186–94.

93. Granet, *Festivals and Songs of Ancient China*, 124–25, 129–30; Chen Yongxiang, "Tantan *Shijing* zhong de 'aiqing' shi," *Chuxiong Shizhuan xuebao* 14, no. 4 (1999): 47–48; Deng Qihua, "Qian gu fengliu xun jiuzong - Shijing hunlian shi pingxi zhi er," *Simao Shifan Gaodeng Zhuanke Xuexiao xuebao*, 15, no. 1 (1999): 36–37; Yang Xiaoli, "*Shijing* qifu xingxiang qianxi," *Dali Xueyuan xuebao* 1, no. 1 (2002): 101.

94. Granet, *Festivals and Songs of Ancient China*, 147.

95. Hu, "Shangdai 'yuzi' lei buci suo fanying de yuanshi hunyin," 47–48.

96. Li Tong, "*Shijing* zhong nüxing de duli yishi," *Shandong Guangbo Dianshi Daxue xuebao* 2 (2010): 37–39.

97. Waley, *The Book of Songs*, 47–48; Karlgren, *The Book of Odes*, 37–38 (Mao 56).

98. Waley, *The Book of Songs*, 61–62; Karlgren, *The Book of Odes*, 48–49 (Mao 71).

99. Waley, *The Book of Songs*, 112; Karlgren, *The Book of Odes*, 91–92 (Mao 145).

100. Waley, *The Book of Songs*, 116–17; Karlgren, *The Book of Odes*, 94–95 (Mao 151).

101. Liang Ping, "Cai li jing fan, mei bu sheng shou - *Shijing Guofeng* zhong nüxing xingxiang mei de tanxi," *Xibei Nonglin Keji Daxue xuebao* 4, no. 3 (2004): 125, argues that fertility constitutes an important aspect of female beauty in the *Shijing* poems.

102. Tse-tsung Chow, "The Childbirth Myth and Ancient Chinese Medicine: A Study of Aspects of the *Wu* Tradition," in *Ancient China: Studies in Early Civilization*, ed. David T. Roy and Tsuen-hsuin Tsien (Hong Kong: Chinese University Press, 1978), 49–52; Wen Yiduo, "Shuo yu," in *Wen Yiduo quanji* (Taipei: Liren shuju, 1993), vol. 1, 117–38; Wen Yiduo, "Gao Tang shennü chuanshuo zhi fenxi," in *Wen Yiduo quanji* (Taipei: Liren shuju, 1993), vol. 1, 81–82; Huang Weihua, "'Gu' yu *Shijing* zhong sanshou nüxing beiyuan shi," *Wenshizhe* 1 (1998): 26; Zhang Li-

anju, "*Shijing* zhong de shengzhi chongbai mima dujie," *Beifang luncong* 2 (2001): 92–95; Yang Yi, "*Shijing* zhong 'lian' yu shengzhi chongbai," *Qingnian zuojia* 7 (2010): 5–6; Man, "Discourses on Female Bodily Aesthetics and Its Early Revelations in *The Book of Songs*," 120–21.

103. Yu Liangjie, "Lun sanglin yu Chunqiu shiqi hunyin zhi guanxi," *Jiangsu Ligong Daxue xuebao* 5 (1995): 99–102; Gong Yanbing and Wei Gengyuan, "*Shijing* shu yu muti de chouyang kaocha - sangyuan he nannü mishi," *Shaanxi Shifan Daxue xuebao* 25, no. 2 (1996): 43.

104. Waley, *The Book of Songs*, 18; Karlgren, *The Book of Odes*, 10 (Mao 20).

105. Waley, *The Book of Songs*, 80; Karlgren, *The Book of Odes*, 65–66 (Mao 101) (changing "match-maker" to "matchmaker"). Also Waley, 126; Karlgren, 103 (Mao 158). For a marriage delayed for lack of a matchmaker, see Waley, 49–51; Karlgren, 38–41 (Mao 58). The term *gui* 歸 has two meanings that are almost opposite. It refers to a woman leaving home to get married and also to a married woman returning home to visit her parents. Yang Lianmin and Ma Xiaoxue, "'Guining fumu' yu 'guining' zhidu kaolue," *Liaocheng Daxue xuebao* 6 (2003): 14, 18.

106. Granet, *Festivals and Songs of Ancient China*, 130.

107. Waley, *The Book of Songs*, 54; Karlgren, *The Book of Odes*, 44 (Mao 64).

108. Cao, *Jinwen yu Yin Zhou nüxing wenhua*, 176–81. Waley, *The Book of Songs*, 160–61; Karlgren, *The Book of Odes*, 129 (Mao 188), implies that a man sometimes married a woman for her dowry.

109. Zheng, *Shanggu Huaxia funü yu hunyin*, 197–98.

110. Waley, *The Book of Songs*, 277–79; Karlgren, *The Book of Odes*, 230–32 (Mao 261).

111. Anthropologists describe these sorts of marriages as sororal polygyny or accompanying concubinage. For detailed analyses of *ying* marriage see Marcel Granet, *La polygynie sororale et le sororat dans la Chine féodale* (Paris: Editions Ernest Leroux, 1920); Kurihara Keisuke, *Kodai Chūgoku koninsei no rei rinen to keitai* (Tokyo: Tōhō shoten, 1982), 301–81. Xia Mailing, "Yuan shi fu yu Chunqiu hunzhi," *Zhengzhou Daxue xuebao* 1 (1993): 70–71, discusses in detail three specific cases of *ying* marriage between rulers of the state of Song and groups of related women.

112. Jia, "Yin Zhou funü shenghuo de jige mian," 17–18; Li, "Liang Zhou jinwen zhong de funü chengwei," 401; Cao Zhaolan, "Cong jinwen kan Zhou dai yingqie hunzhi," *Shenzhen Daxue xuebao* 6 (2001): 100–07; Cao, *Jinwen yu Yin Zhou nüxing wenhua*, 232.

113. *Shijing*: Shang Lixin, "*Shijing* yingjia shi yu Zhoudai yinghun wenhua," *Shanghai Shifan Daxue xuebao*, vol. 31, no. 1 (2002): 65–70; Zhou Yanliang, "*Shijing* yinghun shi yu yinghun wenhua," *Wenyi yanjiu* 3 (2002): 63–73; Qin Yangang and Sun Yingwei, "'Zhou Nan Guanju' he Zhoudai guizu de yinghunzhi," *Zhonghua wenhua luntan* 3 (2006): 34–39; Deng Qihua, "Yizhong huangdan de hunzhi - cong shijing kan Xi Zhou Chunqiu zhuhou ying hun," *Puer Xueyuan xuebao* 30, no. 1 (2014): 90–94. *Zuo zhuan*: Cao Xiaowei, "Chunqiu shiqi yinghun yanjiu," *Lilun xuekan* 4 (2014): 105–09.

114. For a discussion of the orthography of this character, which varied considerably in bronze script, see Cao, *Jinwen yu Yin Zhou nüxing wenhua*, 151, 153–56. Schuessler, *ABC Etymological Dictionary of Old Chinese*, 564, 577, links *ying* to the related characters *yi* 詒 and *yi* 貽, meaning to transmit, bequeath, hand down, or

give. Cai Feng, "Chunqiu shiqi guizu shixing yingqie, zhidi hunzhi ma?" *Yunnan Minzu Daxue xuebao* 3 (2014): 112, cautions that scholars have misinterpreted this character when reading some inscriptions, falsely assuming that it refers to sororal polygyny when it sometimes simply means sending a dowry along with a bride.

115. Chen Xiaofang, *Chunqiu hunyin lisu yu shehui lilun* (Chengdu: Bashu shushe, 2000), 23–31.

116. Melvin P. Thatcher, "Marriages of the Ruling Elite in the Spring and Autumn Period," in *Marriage and Inequality in Chinese Society*, ed. Rubie S. Watson and Patricia B. Ebrey (Berkeley: University of California Press, 1991), 31–32.

117. Thatcher, "Marriages of the Ruling Elite in the Spring and Autumn Period," 31–32; Cai, "Chunqiu shiqi guizu shixing yingqie, zhidi hunzhi ma?" 111.

118. Cao, *Jinwen yu Yin Zhou nüxing wenhua*, 233–35. Li Yanong, "Zhouzu de shizu zhidu yu Tuobazu de qianfengjian zhi," in *Li Yanong shi lunji* (Shanghai: Shanghai renmin chubanshe, 1962), 244–46, argues that accompanying women were wives and not concubines.

119. Chen, "Chunqiu hunyin lisu yu shehui lilun," 31–34; Cao, *Jinwen yu Yin Zhou nüxing wenhua*, 151–52, 171–75.

120. Zhang Nan and Li Yaguang, "Lun Zhoudai de ying hun zhidu," *Liaoning Gongcheng Jishu Daxue xuebao* 2 (2008): 170; Cao, "Chunqiu shiqi yinghun yanjiu," 105.

121. Cai, "Chunqiu shiqi guizu shixing yingqie, zhidi hunzhi ma?" 111; Cao, "Chunqiu shiqi yinghun yanjiu," 106.

122. Cai, "Chunqiu shiqi guizu shixing yingqie, zhidi hunzhi ma?" 113–15.

123. Zhu Liuyu, "Cong yingqie zhengbao zhidu kan Zhoudai zhengzhi hunyin," *Tianjin Shida xuebao* 4 (2000): 43; Zhang and Li, "Lun Zhoudai de ying hun zhidu," 172; Cao, "Chunqiu shiqi yinghun yanjiu," 105.

124. Gao, *Zhoudai hunyin xingtai yanjiu*, 200–02. Even so, this custom endured into the Han dynasty. The Tang dynasty commentator Yan Shigu (581–645) notes that during the Han, *ying* referred to a concubine who entered the palace at the same time as the future empress. Ban Gu, *Hanshu*, annotated Yan Shigu (Beijing: Zhonghua, 1962), 12:360, n. 5.

125. Li, "Zhouzu de shizu zhidu yu Tuobazu de qianfengjian zhi," 239.

126. Xie, *Zhoudai jiating xingtai*, 58–63; Kurihara, *Kodai Chūgoku koninsei no rei rinen to keitai*, 383–455; Cao, *Jinwen yu Yin Zhou nüxing wenhua*, 144–49. Sixteen *Shijing* poems mention surname exogamy. See Liu Dongying, "*Shijing* zhong suojian de Zhoudai tongxing bu hun lisu," *Zhida xuebao* 1 (2003): 92–93, 101. Unlike the customs of later eras, under the *zongfa* 宗法 kinship system only the eldest son succeeded to the *xing* 姓. The remaining sons remained members of the *shi* 氏 but not the *xing*. Chun, "Conceptions of Kinship and Kingship in Classical Chou China," 31–33.

127. Cao Zhaolan, "Jinwen nüxing chengwei zhong de guxing," *Kaogu yu wenwu* 2 (2002): 51–60; Cao, *Jinwen yu Yin Zhou nüxing wenhua*, 127–44.

128. Xu Zhongshu, "Zhongguo gudai de fuxi jiating ji qi qinshu chengwei," *Sichuan Daxue xuebao* 1 (1980): 110–12; Cao, "Jinwen nüxing chengwei zhong de guxing," 58.

129. Cao, *Jinwen yu Yin Zhou nüxing wenhua*, 210. When the elite in a stratified society puts a high value on obtaining the best marriage partner, they are more likely to ignore incest taboos. Flannery and Marcus, *The Creation of Inequality*, 313.

130. Xie, *Zhoudai jiating xingtai*, 50–54.

131. Zheng, *Shanggu Huaxia funü yu hunyin*, 166; Wu Yumei, "Cong *Shijing* kan Zhoudairen de hunlian shenghuo," *Liaoning Daxue xuebao* 1 (1996): 91. Jia, "Yin Zhou funü shenghuo de jige mian," points out that in Western Zhou bronze inscriptions, the character *qie* 妾 still meant wife. The Zhou referred to minor wives in other ways, although the terminology of concubinage was still not standard in this era.

132. Zheng, *Shanggu Huaxia funü yu hunyin*, 211–12; Liu Jie, "Zhoudai de fuqi hezangmu," *Qingdao Daxue Shifan Xueyuan xuebao* 2 (2009): 78–83.

133. Mumford, "Death Do Us Unite," 10.

134. Zhou, *Festivals, Feasts, and Gender Relations in Ancient China and Greece*, 207–08. Engesi, "Jiazu, sichan yu guojia de qiyuan," trans. Pan Guangdan, in *Pan Guangdan wenji*, ed. Shen Kunpeng (Beijing: Beijing Daxue chubanshe, 2000), vol. 13, 231–34, fn. 214, discusses the concept of avunculate and the privileges of maternal uncles in historic China.

135. Waley, *The Book of Songs*, 51; Karlgren, *The Book of Odes*, 41 (Mao 59). Zheng Qun, "You 'gui' kan *Shijing* zhong de nüxing zai hunyin zhong de juese," *Simao Shifan Gaodeng Zhuanke Xuexiao xuebao* 20, no. 1 (2004): 42; Zhou, *Festivals, Feasts, and Gender Relations in Ancient China and Greece*, 301–02.

136. Waley, *The Book of Songs*, 61; Karlgren, *The Book of Odes*, 48–49 (Mao 71).

137. Waley, *The Book of Songs*, 49–51; Karlgren, *The Book of Odes*, 38–41 (Mao 58).

138. Waley, *The Book of Songs*, 156; Karlgren, *The Book of Odes*, 125 (Mao 181); Zhou, *Festivals, Feasts, and Gender Relations in Ancient China and Greece*, 292–97.

139. Keith Knapp, "The Ru Reinterpretation of *Xiao*," *Early China* 20 (1995): 200–02; Waley, *The Book of Songs*, 95, 134, 158–59; Karlgren, *The Book of Odes*, 78–79, 105, 127 (Mao 121, 162, 185). Shimomi Takao, *Kō to bosei no mekanizumu - Chūgoku joseishi no shigi* (Tokyo: Kenbun, 1997), explores the impact of filial values on early ideas of motherhood in great detail.

140. Cao, *Jinwen yu Yin Zhou nüxing wenhua*, 110–11.

141. Cao, *Jinwen yu Yin Zhou nüxing wenhua*, 107–09.

142. Waley, *The Book of Songs*, 160–61; Karlgren, *The Book of Odes*, 129 (Mao 188).

143. Yang Guangyu, "Zhenmian rensheng bubei buqu - qianlun 'Mang' zhong de qifu xingxiang," *Hefei Lianhe Daxue xuebao* 9, no. 2 (1999): 26–29; Yang, "*Shijing* qifu xingxiang qianxi," 101, 103.

144. Waley, *The Book of Songs*, 20; Karlgren, *The Book of Odes*, 13 (Mao 23).

145. Alice Schlegel, "Status, Property, and the Value on Virginity," *American Ethnologist* 18, no. 4 (1991): 719–34.

146. Waley, *The Book of Songs*, 65; Karlgren, *The Book of Odes*, 51 (Mao 76).

147. Waley, *The Book of Songs*, 39–40; Karlgren, *The Book of Odes*, 31 (Mao 47). The management of desire became a topic of discussion. Xunzi considered the management of the emotions, and desire in particular, an important goal of cultivation. He believed that if our desires are proper, our behavior will be orderly and harmonious. Zhan Shiyou and Peng Chuanhua, "Cultivation (Jiaohua): The Goal of Xunzi's Ethical Thought," *Frontiers of Philosophy in China*, vol. 2, no. 1 (2007): 35, 42.

148. Waley, *The Book of Songs*, 124–25; Karlgren, *The Book of Odes*, 100–02 (Mao 156).

CHAPTER 5

1. Zheng Xuan, et al. (annotators), *Chongkan Songben Yili zhushu fujiao kanji* (Nanchang: Nanchangfu xuekanben, 1815; reprinted Taipei: Yiwen, 1955, 35:408; Liu Zenggui, "Handai funü de mingzi," *Xin shixue* 7, no. 4 (1996): 35. During this era, *xing* 姓 and *shi* 氏 merged.

2. Pulleyblank, "Ji and Jiang," 5–6; Cao, *Jinwen yu Yin Zhou nüxing wenhua*, 241–46.

3. According to ritual regulations, a girl received the title *mu* 母 when she underwent the pinning ceremony and changed her hairstyle at age fifteen *sui* 歲. Cho-yun Hsu and Katheryn M. Linduff, *Western Chou Civilization* (New Haven: Yale University Press, 1988), 374.

4. Cao, *Jinwen yu Yin Zhou nüxing wenhua*, 247–50, 258–59.

5. Cao, *Jinwen yu Yin Zhou nüxing wenhua*, 252–57; Gao Bing, "Qin guo hunyin zhidu yanjiu," *Xibei Shida xuebao* 3 (2006): 90–95.

6. The wife of a deceased marquis whose son had inherited the marquisate was called *tai furen* 太夫人. Ban, *Hanshu*, 4:122, n. 1.

7. The wives of polygynous rulers were distinguished by rank as *yuanfei* 元妃, *erfei* 二妃, and *xiafei* 下妃. Thatcher, "Marriages of the Ruling Elite in the Spring and Autumn Period," 29. Chu had a different system of titles for harem women. Luo Yunhuan, "Chu guo de taizi zhidu yanjiu," *Jianghan luntan* 7 (2000): 71.

8. Huang Fengchun, "Chu guo sanggui zhidu yanjiu," *Jianghan kaogu* 2 (1999): 58, 64–67. Xu Fu, *Qin huiyao dingbu* (Taipei: Dingwen shuju, 1978), 1:12–15, provides detailed information about female names and titles in Qin.

9. By the Zhanguo era, the nuclear family consisting of an average of five people had become the norm. Qi Fa, "Zhanguo shiqi de jiating jiegou," *Huazhong Keji Daxue xuebao* 2 (2003): 58–61. For a description of the breakdown of clans and the rise of small families, attributed to improvements in agricultural technology, see Nishijima Sadao, "The Economic and Social History of the Former Han," in *The Cambridge History of China, Volume I, The Ch'in and Han Empires, 221 B.C.–A.D. 220*, ed. Denis Twitchett and Michael Loewe (Cambridge: Cambridge University Press, 1986), 546–47. H.J. Habakkuk, "Family Structure and Economic Change in Nineteenth Century Europe," *Journal of Economic History* 15, no. 1 (1955): 1–12, is a classic article that demonstrates the relation between partible inheritance and small family size. For the higher status of wives in smaller families, see Rebecca L. Warner, Gary R. Lee, and Janet Lee, "Social Organization, Spousal Resources, and Marital Power: A Cross-Cultural Study," *Journal of Marriage and Family* 48, no. 1 (1986): 121–28.

10. Archaeological remains attest to intermarriage between Chinese and foreign elites. For example, some unusual bronze vessels in the tombs of Jin noblewomen resemble the pottery of steppe peoples. These women were probably relatives of the rulers of steppe peoples who married Jin nobility. Chen, "Jin hou mu qingtongqi suojian xingbie yanjiu de xin xiansuo," 161–63; Ying, "Gender, Status, Ritual Regulations, and Mortuary Practice in the State of Jin," 194–95. Mencius writes that some people of the time considered marriages between Huaxia and foreigners a disgraceful necessity. Bryan W. Van Norden (trans.), *Mengzi: With*

Selections from Traditional Commentaries (Indianapolis: Hackett Publishing, 2008), 92 (4A:7.2).

11. Jennifer Holmgren, "Imperial Marriage in the Native Chinese and Non-Han State, Han to Ming," in *Marriage and Inequality in Chinese Society*, ed. Rubie S. Watson and Patricia Buckley Ebrey (Berkeley: University of California Press, 1991), 61; Thatcher, "Marriages of the Ruling Elite in the Spring and Autumn Period," 44. Mutual mourning obligations helped bind affines together. Cao, *Jinwen yu Yin Zhou nüxing wenhua*, 229–31. Du Zhengsheng, "Cong wufu lun chuantong de zuqun jiegou ji qi lunli," in *Zhonghua wenhua de guoqu xianzai he weilai* (Beijing: Zhonghua shuju, 1992), 267–72, emphasizes the inequality of mourning regulations regarding women and men. Although mourning rites recognized women as members of the patrilineal family, within the kinship system their status was inferior to men.

12. Wang Xuan, "Shilun *Zuozhuan* zhong de hunyinguan," *Jingji yu shehui fazhan* 1, no. 4 (2003): 116–17. Thatcher, "Marriages of the Ruling Elite in the Spring and Autumn Period," 25–57, lists all marriages from the Chunqiu era that were recorded in transmitted texts. Bai Lu, "Xian Qin nüxing yanjiu - cong shehui xingbie shijiao de kaocha yu fenxi" (PhD dissertation, Nankai University, 2009), 166–83, provides an appendix listing political marriages between Zhou noble families, classified according to state. Cui, *Xian Qin zhengzhi hunyin shi*, 25, 110–48; and Newell Ann Van Auken, "A Formal Analysis of the Chuenchiou (Spring and Autumn Classic)" (part 1) (PhD dissertation, University of Washington, 2006), 110–23, examine in detail the marriages of the ruling house of the state of Lu during the Chunqiu era. For bronze inscriptions recording political marriges see Cao, *Jinwen yu Yin Zhou nüxing wenhua*, 216–25.

13. Chang, *Early Chinese Civilization*, 90. Thatcher, "Marriages of the Ruling Elite in the Spring and Autumn Period," 41, contests Chang's interpretation.

14. Cui, *Xian Qin zhengzhi hunyin shi*, 25, 110–48.

15. Zhang Hongliang, "Dong Zhou Chu guo lianhun kaoshu," *Jianghan kaogu* 2 (2007): 52–57.

16. Egashira Hiroshi, "Kinbun naka no kazoku seido ni kan suru nisan no mondai," *Nihon Chūgoku gakkaihō* 19 (1967): 85–86; Zhang Bangwei, *Hunyin yu shehui (Songdai)* (Chengdu: Sichuan renmin chubanshe, 1989), 46; Chang, *Early Chinese Civilization*, 89; Xie, *Zhoudai jiating xingtai*, 63–71; Zhao Jianli, "Jin guo furen kao," *Nei Menggu Nongye Daxue xuebao* 1 (2012): 314. Some scholars have speculated that the Shang elite practiced cross-cousin marriage. See Vandermeersch, *Wangdao ou la Voie Royale*, 288–92. Marcel Granet, *Danses et Légendes de la Chine Ancienne* (Paris: Librairie Félix Alcan, 1926), 13–14, sees repeated intermarriage between moities as the basis for Zhou society. S. Baştuğ, "Kinship, Marriage and Descent in Early China," *Journal of Asian History* 29, no. 2 (1995): 149–87, argues that the Zhou practiced what anthropologists refer to as Dravidian kinship, centered on cross-cousin marriage. Hugh D.R. Baker, *Chinese Family and Kinship* (New York: Columbia University Press, 1979), 43, suggests that cross-cousin marriage would improve relations between mother-in-law and daughter-in-law, as they were already relatives. Chinese anthropologists call cross-cousin marriage *zhongbiao hun* 中表婚.

17. Cai Feng, "Chunqiu shiqi Song 'nei hunzhi' kaocha," *Hebei Shifan Daxue xuebao* 5 (2004): 117–18.

18. Van Auken, "A Formal Analysis of the *Chuenchiou*," 361–63.

19. Hsu Cho-yun, "Development of State-Society Relationship in Early China," in *La Société Civile Face à l'État Dans la Tradition Chinoise, Japonaise, Coréen et Vietnamienne*, ed. Léon Vandermeersch (Paris: École Française d'Extrême-Orient, 1994), 5.

20. Xie, *Zhoudai jiating xingtai*, 36.

21. Geng Chao, "Dong Zhou zhengzhi waijiao hunzhong de xingbie chayi jiqi yingxiang," *Yunnan shehui kexue* 2 (2009): 134.

22. Thatcher, "Marriages of the Ruling Elite in the Spring and Autumn Period," 44.

23. Thatcher, "Marriages of the Ruling Elite in the Spring and Autumn Period," 44; Geng, "Dong Zhou zhengzhi waijiao hunzhong de xingbie chayi jiqi yingxiang," 135–36; Chen Xiaofang, "Chunqiu shiqi de zhenjieguan," *Xinan Minzu Xueyuan xuebao* 21, no. 1 (2000): 105–09; Wai-yee Li, *The Readability of the Past in Early Chinese Historiography* (Cambridge, MA: Harvard University Asia Center, 2007), 151. The position of some noblewomen at the center of power in a rival state allowed them to serve as spies for their natal state. Wang Zijin and Zhang Jing, *Zhongguo funü tongshi: Xian Qin juan* (Hangzhou: Hangzhou chubanshe, 2010), 122–25.

24. Zuo Qiuming, *Chongkan Songben Zuozhuan zhushu fujiao kanji* (Nanchang: Nanchangfu xuekanben, 1815; reprinted Taipei: Yiwen yinshuguan, 1965), 7: 126b (Huan 15). Thatcher, "Marriages of the Ruling Elite in the Spring and Autumn Period," 45; Li, *The Readability of the Past in Early Chinese Historiography*, 150.

25. Imperial historians recognized the importance of filial piety as a major source of female power under the imperial system. See Wei, *Weishu*, 108C: 2786–87.

26. Olivia Milburn, "Gender, Sexuality and Power in Early China: The Changing Biographies of Lord Ling of Wei and Lady Nanzi," *Nan Nü* 12, no. 1 (2010): 1–29; Goldin, *The Culture of Sex in Ancient China*, 28–29.

27. Goldin, *The Culture of Sex in Ancient China*, 60.

28. Wang Chaochao, "Zhanguo houqi Qin guo waiqi yanjiu," *Bohai Daxue xuebao* 2 (2011): 108, 110–11.

29. Keith McMahon, "Women Rulers in Imperial China," *Nan Nü* 15, no. 2 (2013): 193.

30. For example, the state of Jin had forty rulers. Information about thirty consorts of eleven rulers has survived. Some facts are known from transmitted texts and other from inscriptions. Zhao, "Jin guo furen kao," 313.

31. During times of war, women sometimes played a supporting role, such as building defensive fortifications and mending the clothing of soldiers. Wang Zijin and Sun Zhongjia, "Zhanguo Qin Han shiqi de nüjun," *Shehuixue yanjiu* 6 (1996): 113–18; Wang Zijin, *Zhongguo nüzi congjun shi* (Beijing: Junshi yiwen chubanshe, 1998), 45–53. With rare exceptions, weapons disappeared from female graves, in spite of the intensification of warfare. Jiang Zhanghua, "Zhanguo shiqi gu Shu shehui de bianqian - cong muzang fenxi rushou," *Chengdu kaogu yanjiu* (2009): 341.

32. Hebei Sheng Wenwu Yanjiusuo and Tang Xian Wenwu Baoguansuo, "Tang Xian Shulü Dong Zhou muzang fajue jianbao," *Wenwu chunqiu* 1 (2012): 42; Li Xiating and Li Jiansheng, "Ye tan Changzhi Fenshuiling Dong Zhou mudi," *Zhongguo Guojia Bowuguan guankan* 3 (2012): 17.

33. Chen, "Xingbie, shenfen yu caifu," 25, notes that the items in women's tombs came from increasingly diverse sources. They could include things that she used in life, those given by a husband, ritual paraphanalia, items given to her by her natal family, and dowry goods. Whether a wife was buried before or after her husband could also affect the quantity and contents of her tomb. Chen, 60–63.

34. Huang, "Gender Differentiation in Jin State Jade Regulations," 144–45.

35. The number of burial goods with ritual significance in women's tombs declined over time. Chen, "Xingbie, shenfen yu caifu," 54–55.

36. Cao, *Jinwen yu Yin Zhou nüxing wenhua*, 238–41.

37. Zhou Yiqun, "Virtue and Talent: Women and *Fushi* in Early China," *Nan Nü*, 5, no. 1 (2003): 14–16.

38. Gao Fang, *Zuozhuan nüxing yanjiu* (Harbin: Heilongjiang Daxue chubanshe, 2010), 151; Bai Lu and Du Fangqin, "Zhoudai quangui funü jieru 'gong' 'wai' shiwu de sanzhong leixing - cong shehui xingbie shijiao de guancha yu fenxi," *Shanxi Shida xuebao* 2 (2009): 94–9.

39. For specific examples of women who interfered in dynastic succession, see Wang and Zhang, *Zhongguo funü tongshi*, 190–92.

40. Zhao Dongyu and Lu Cui, "Chunqiu shiqi Qi guo guifu 'luanzheng' tanxi," *Liaoning Shifan Daxue xuebao* 1 (2009): 120–21.

41. Geng Chao and Liu Shan, "Chunqiu shiqi guizu funü de canzheng yu liangxing guanxi," *Guanzi xuekan* 3 (2012): 97–101.

42. "But if you have Xi Shi's lovely face, / The slanderer will get in and supplant you." David Hawkes, *The Songs of the South: An Ancient Chinese Anthology of Poems by Qu Yuan and Other Poets* (Harmondsworth, UK: Penguin Books, 1985), 177; Wang Siyuan, *Chuci jiaoshi* (Beijing: Renmin jiaoyu, 1990), 192 ("Xi wangri").

43. Zhen Hongyong, "Shanggu Jiang shi buzu minsu yicun yu Chunqiu shiqi funü congzheng guanxi shixi," *Qinghai Minzu Daxue xuebao* 7 (2011): 77–80.

44. Zhou, "Virtue and Talent: Women and *Fushi* in Early China," 1–42.

45. Stephen W. Durrant, *The Cloudy Mirror: Tension and Conflict in the Writings of Sima Qian* (Albany: State University of New York Press, 1995), 108; Lisa Raphals, "Arguments by Women in Early Chinese Texts," *Nannü* 3, no. 2 (2001): 157–95.

46. Patricia Ebrey, "Education Through Ritual: Efforts to Formulate Family Rituals During the Sung Period," in *Neo-Confucian Education: The Formative Stage*, ed. William Theodore de Bary and John Chaffee (Berkeley: University of California Press, 1989), 277; Michael David Kaulana Ing, *The Dysfunction of Ritual in Early Confucianism* (Oxford: Oxford University Press, 2012), 57–58.

47. Goldin, *The Culture of Sex in Ancient China*, 58.

48. Liu, *Dong Zhou funü shenghuo*, 31–35; Cook, "Education and the Way of the Former Kings," 321.

49. Constance A. Cook, "Ancestor Worship During the Eastern Zhou," in *Early Chinese Religion: Part One: Shang through Han (1250 BC - 220 AD)*, ed. John Lagerwey and Marc Kalinowski (Leiden: E.J. Brill, 2009), 254, 260–61.

50. Van Norden, *Mengzi*, 114–15 (4B33.1).

51. Even though Confucian thinkers recognized the moral equality of the sexes, they did not believe that men and women should be treated equally. Goldin, *The Culture of Sex in Ancient China*, 69–70. And the capacity to remonstrate did not

imply elevated social status. In Han dynasty narratives, many of the men who remonstrated with nobles had lowly positions, such as servants and fishermen.

52. Goldin, *The Culture of Sex in Ancient China*, 53–54.

53. Cook, "Education and the Way of the Former Kings," 334. During the Western Han, learning shifted away from performance to become primarily textual. See Cook, 307.

54. Raphals, "Arguments by Women in Early Chinese Texts," 157–95; Zhou, "Virtue and Talent," 1–3.

55. Guisso, "Thunder Over the Lake," 56.

56. Roger T. Ames and Henry Rosemont, Jr., *The Analects of Confucius: A Philosophical Translation* (New York: Ballantine, 1998), 211 (17.25). Bruce E. Brooks and A. Taeko Brooks, *The Original Analects: Sayings of Confucius and His Successors* (New York: Columbia University Press, 1998), 240–41 (17.23), suggest that this line might be an interpolation from about two centuries after the death of the sage. But at the very least it reflects a point of view held by some of his followers.

57. Goldin, *The Culture of Sex in Ancient China*, 55–57.

58. Zheng, *Shanggu Huaxia funü yu hunyin*, 232–44.

59. Robin D.S. Yates, "Social Status in the Ch'in: Evidence from the Yün-meng Legal Documents. Part One: Commoners," *Harvard Journal of Asiatic Studies* 47, no. 1 (1987): 221.

60. Mumford, "Death Do Us Unite," 11–12.

61. A man was said to "take" *qu* 娶 a wife. This character derived from the homophonous character *qu* 取 ("to take"). When a woman married she was "familied" (*jia* 嫁), a character taken from the homophonous *jia* 家 (family). Pulleyblank, "Ji and Jiang," 5. He Dan, "Chunqiu shiqi hunyin tedian zhi tanjiu," *Huanan Ligong Daxue xuebao* 2 (2014): 75, attributes the standardization of marriage terminology to ritualization. The character *gui* 歸, which could mean "leave home," was also used to refer to a woman's marriage. Zheng, "You 'gui' kan *Shijing* zhong de nüxing zai hunyin zhong de juese," 41. Arlen Lian, "The 'Shesheng' Adjustments to the Rites in Early China," *Journal of the American Oriental Society* 128, no. 4 (2008): 723–35, contrasts descriptions of ideal weddings in the ritual canon with actual practices.

62. Kurihara, *Kodai Chūgoku koninsei no rei rinen to keitai*, 73–79; Li Jinhe, *Wei Jin Sui Tang hunyin xingtai yanjiu* (Jinan: Qi Lu shushe, 2005), 20. According to ritualists, even the music chosen for performance at weddings should help differentiate the sexes. Joseph S.C. Lam, "The Presence and Absence of Female Musicians and Music in China," in *Women and Confucian Cultures in Premodern China, Korea, and Japan*, ed. Dorothy Ko, JaHyun Kim Haboush, and Joan R. Piggott (Berkeley: University of California Press, 2003), 99.

63. Kong Yingda (annotator), *Liji zhengyi* (Taipei: Zhonghua shuju, *Sibu beiyao* ed., 1980), 61:12a.

64. Granet, *La polygynie sororale et le sororat dans la Chine féodale*, 59–62. For this reason, a noblewoman often entered a marriage dowered with ritual vessels appropriate for use in the ancestral sacrifices. Cao, *Jinwen yu Yin Zhou nüxing wenhua*, 212–14, 216–18. Shiga Shūzō, *Chūgoku kazokuhō no genri* (Tokyo: Sōbunsha, 1967), 459–56, emphasizes the wife's participation in ancestral sacrifices as a key step to becoming a member of her husband's family.

65. Van Norden, *Mengzi*, 118 (5A2.1).

66. Zhou, *Festivals, Feasts, and Gender Relations in Ancient China and Greece*, 247–48.

67. Under the laws of various Zhou dynasty states, male and female convicts suffered different punishments. While male convicts performed various forms of labor, women were often sentenced to pound grain. Ban, *Hanshu*, 23: 1091.

68. Gao Bing, "Cong 'Shuihudi Qin jian' kan Qin guo de hunyin lunli guannian," *Yantai Shifan Xueyuan xuebao* 4 (2005): 36; Gao, "Qin guo hunyin zhidu yanjiu," 94; Zhu Honglin, "Zhanguo shiqi youguan hunyin guanxi falü de yanjiu - zhujian Qin Han lü yu 'Zhouli' bijiao yanjiu (si)," *Jilin Shifan Daxue xuebao* 3 (2011): 47, 49.

69. Zu Jingran, "Cong Shuihudi Qin jian kan Qin guo funü de hunyin zhuangkuang," *Suzhou Keji Xueyuan xuebao* 28, no. 5 (2011): 54–55.

70. For polygyny, see Yang Junru, "Chunqiu shidai zhi nannü fengji," in *Zhongguo funüshi lunwenji* (second edition), ed. Li Youning and Zhang Yufa (Taipei: Taiwan Shangwu, 1988), 24–26; Gao, "Qin guo hunyin zhidu yanjiu," 93; Zu, "Cong Shuihudi Qin jian kan Qin guo funü de hunyin zhuangkuang," 54. For the architecture of polygyny, see Xie, *Zhoudai jiating xingtai*, 278–86.

71. Yang, "Chunqiu shidai zhi nannü fengji," 21–22. There were even occasional instances of incest between close relatives. See Yang, 27–28, and Chen, *Chunqiu hunyin lisu yu shehui lilun*, 64.

72. Xie, *Zhoudai jiating xingtai*, 74–75. For quotations documenting *zheng* and *bao*, see Qian Zongfan, *Zhoudai zongfa zhidu yanjiu* (Guilin: Guangxi Shifan Daxue chubanshe, 1989), 53–60. There were also instances of men marrying their niece. Xie, 75.

73. Xie, *Zhoudai jiating xingtai*, 72–74; Liu Zongtang and Zhang Tai, "Lun Chunqiu shiqi 'zheng' hunzhi de he 'li' xing," *Xueshu luntan* 2 (2006): 169–71; Zhao, "Jin guo furen kao," 314. Sometimes a man would marry the wife of his deceased brother, a practice that anthropologists call junior levirate.

74. Lü Yahu, "Dong Zhou shiqi 'zheng' 'bao' hun xianxiang kaobian," *Renwen zazhi* 6 (2004): 144.

75. Huang Yi, "Gudai Xila yu Zhongguo Zhouchao jichengzhi de bijiao," *Minzushi yanjiu* (2005): 446.

76. Service, *Origins of the State and Civilization*, 63.

77. Sun Hongbin, "*Shijing* zhong de mei yu Zhoudai de benzhe bu jin," *Wenbo* 4 (2002): 24–25.

78. Lü Yahu and Feng Lizhen, "Dong Zhou shiqi nannü shihun nianling wenti kaobian," *Shaanxi Ligong Xueyuan xuebao* 2 (2005): 80–83; Zhao Huili, "*Shijing* zhong Zhoudai hunsu tanwei," *Xueshu jiaoliu* 2 (2014): 155; J. Michael Farmer, "Classical Scholarship in the Shu Region: The Case of Qiao Zhou," in *Early Medieval China: A Sourcebook*, ed. Wendy Swartz, Robert Ford Campany, Yang Lu, and Jessey J.C. Choo (New York: Columbia University Press, 2014), 118.

79. Pinning was called *ji* 筓. Du You, *Tongdian* (Beijing: Zhonghua shuju, 1988), 59: 1674–76, quotes ancient sources that give ideal ages for female pinning, male capping, and marriage. Confucius allegedly said that women should marry at age fifteen.

80. Gao, *Zhoudai hunyin xingtai yanjiu,* 205–08. Du You, *Tongdian,* 59: 1676–79, quotes ancient sources that specify spring as the ideal time of year for weddings.

81. Yang, "Chunqiu shidai zhi nannü fengji," 22–23.

82. Sun Dehua, "Cong *Shijing* de aiqing shi kan Zhoudai de pinhunli ji hunzhi tedian," *Changchun Daxue xuebao* 7 (2007): 58–60.

83. Hsu and Linduff, *Western Chou Civilization,* 374–75; Patricia Buckley Ebrey, "Shifts in Marriage Finance from the Sixth to the Thirteenth Century," in *Marriage and Inequality in Chinese Society,* ed. Rubie S. Watson and Patricia B. Ebrey (Berkeley: University of California Press, 1991), 97.

84. Thatcher, "Marriages of the Ruling Elite in the Spring and Autumn Period," 36–37. For an example of a dowry see Cao, *Jinwen yu Yin Zhou nüxing wenhua,* 216–18.

85. Thatcher, "Marriages of the Ruling Elite in the Spring and Autumn Period," 35–36; Hsu and Linduff, *Western Chou Civilization,* 374–75. Hawkes, *The Songs of the South,* 24 ("Shao's South"), describes the wedding of a granddaughter of King Ping of Zhou, the first Eastern Zhou king.

86. Zu, "Cong Shuihudi Qin jian kan Qin guo funü de hunyin zhuangkuang," 57.

87. Gu Hongli, "Zhoudai chema yu *Shijing* hunjia shi," *Lantai shijie* 341 (2011): 59–60; Xu Mangui, "Fuqi he jin jie liangyuan lian li jiaobei shang yinhuan - gudai hunsu yin jiao bei jiu ji jiubei yuanshi chengxu jianshang," *Dongfang shoucang* 12 (2012): 60–62.

88. Li, *The Readability of the Past in Early Chinese Historiography,* 150.

89. Zhou, *Festivals, Feasts, and Gender Relations in Ancient China and Greece,* 206, 244–45.

90. Zhou, *Festivals, Feasts, and Gender Relations in Ancient China and Greece,* 242.

91. For example, Mencius mourned more lavishly for his mother than his father because his official rank was higher when his mother died than when his father died. In each case he conducted mourning in a manner appropriate to his official rank, so his mother's status rose in tandem with that of her son. Van Norden, *Mengzi,* 31–32 (1B16.1).

92. Zhou, *Festivals, Feasts, and Gender Relations in Ancient China and Greece,* 209–10, 260.

93. For example, in 651 BCE Duke Huan, the most accomplished of the Five Hegemons, assembled the nobility to subscribe to a document that included an injunction against treating a concubine as a wife. Moreover, there does not seem to have been a ritual for promoting a concubine to wifely status. Van Norden, *Mengzi,* 166 (6B7.3); Thatcher, "Marriages of the Ruling Elite in the Spring and Autumn Period," 29–30. For general information on early concubines, see Patricia Ebrey, "Concubines in Sung China," *Journal of Family History* 11, no. 1 (1986): 3.

94. Zheng, *Shanggu Huaxia funü yu hunyin,* 164–65.

95. Thatcher, "Marriages of the Ruling Elite in the Spring and Autumn Period," 32–33.

96. Thatcher, "Marriages of the Ruling Elite in the Spring and Autumn Period," 33.

97. Gao Qingcong, "Zhoudai zongfa zhidu xia de 'mudi,'" *Gudai wenming* 6, no 1 (2012): 41–47.

98. Zheng, *Shanggu Huaxia funü yu hunyin,* 162–64. Chu had different kinship customs. Because Chu lacked the custom of primogeniture of a son of the legitimate wife, younger sons could inherit. Moreover, the people of Chu did not rigorously distinguish wife from concubine. Zheng, 232–36. The son of a concubine was called a *shuzi* 庶子.

99. Yan Ming, *Zhongguo mingji yishu shi* (Taipei: Wenjin, 1992), 13–14; Xiao Guoliang, *Zhongguo changji shi* (Taipei: Wenjin chubanshe, 1996), 13.

100. Cao Yingchun, "'Zhongfu' yu 'qingfu' - xian Qin Zhao guo yu Yan guo fengsu chayi jiedu," *Zhonghua wenhua luntan* 1 (2010): 30–31.

101. Mi Yongying, "Dong Zhou shiqi nüxing yiren shehui diwei guankui - yi youguan Qi guo nüyue de wenxian yu kaogu faxian wei shijiao," *Hubei shehui kexue* 8 (2014): 118–20.

102. Mumford, "Death Do Us Unite," 5.

103. Jin Guiyun, "Dong Zhou Qi guo guizu maizang zhidu yanjiu," *Guanzi xuekan* 3 (1994): 61–62; Yin Qun, "Dong Zhou shiqi Qin Qi xunren mu de bijiao yanjiu," *Dongfang kaogu* 4 (2012): 323.

104. Cook, *Death in Ancient China,* 67; Thote, "Shang and Zhou Funeral Practices," 133, 135.

105. Yin Qun, "Lun Dabaozishan Qin gong lingyuan de renxun - jian tan Ying Qin xianren xiqian zhi diwang," *Fudan xuebao* 6 (2014): 82; Yang Mao, "Churen sheng, renxun shitan," *Xinan Nongye Daxue xuebao* 5 (2009): 95–96. Qin Shihuang reportedly had all of his childless consorts sacrificed and entombed with him, the last major incident of human sacrifice in the Chinese heartland. A small cemetery near Qin Shihuang's tomb contains several human sacrifices, including a woman strangled with a cord. Gan Xiaohua, "Luelun Qin de renxun wenhua," *Xi'an Caijing Xueyuan xuebao* 21, no. 4 (2008): 15. During the Han dynasty, human sacrifice continued for a time in the marginal regions. The deceased king of Nanyue was entombed with female and male sacrificial victims. Guo Junran, "Qin Han shiqi de renxun xianxiang shulun," *Suzhou Jiaoyu Xueyuan xuebao* 16, no. 6 (2013): 34–35.

106. Feng Rujun, "Zhanguo shiqi hunyin guannian qianlun," *Xueshu luntan* 2 (2002): 109–10, discusses the Zhou emphasis on virginity, attributing it to the rise of private property. Also Sun, "*Shijing* zhong de mei yu Zhoudai de benzhe bu jin," 25; Van Norden, *Mengzi,* 79 (3B3.5).

107. Zheng, *Shanggu Huaxia funü yu hunyin,* 213–14, 218–19, gives many examples of noblewomen who remarried. Also Yang, "Chunqiu shidai zhi nannü fengji," 23–24; Chen, "Chunqiu shiqi de zhenjieguan," 105–09.

108. Wang, "Shilun *Zuo zhuan* zhong de hunyinguan," 118; Yang, "Chunqiu shidai zhi nannü fengji," 26. Zhou Haixia, "Chunqiu shiqi de liangxing xisu yu zhenjieguan," *Hanshan Shifan Xueyuan xuebao* 1 (2008): 56, provides a table documenting twenty cases of adultery.

109. Liu Zenggui, *Handai hunyin zhidu* (Taipei: Huashi, 1980), 14.

110. For specific examples of Zhou divorces, see Zheng, *Shanggu Huaxia funü yu hunyin,* 215–16. If a political tie between two noble families was particularly useful, sometimes the husband's family continued to treat a divorced woman as kin for mourning purposes as a way of maintaining the political bond. Thatcher, "Marriages of the Ruling Elite in the Spring and Autumn Period," 45–46. During

the Eastern Zhou, divorce began to be called *lihun* 離婚. Yang Jiping, "Dunhuang chutu de fangqi shu suoyi," *Ximen Daxue xuebao* 4 (1999): 34.

111. Li, "Zhouzu de shizu zhidu yu Tuobazu de qianfengjian zhi," 250; Sun Jie, "Cong *Shijing* kan Zhoudai de chuqizhi," *Anhui wenxue* 5 (2007): 63–64.

112. Zheng, *Shanggu Huaxia funü yu hunyin*, 218.

113. This procedure was called called *xiuqi* 休妻. Zu, "Cong Shuihudi Qin jian kan Qin guo funü de hunyin zhuangkuang," 55–56.

114. The absconding of a wife was termed *taowang* 逃亡.

115. Yuri Pines, *Foundations of Confucian Thought: Intellectual Life in the Chunqiu Period, 722-453 B.C.E.* (Honolulu: University of Hawaii Press, 2002), 149, 152.

116. Goldin, *The Culture of Sex in Ancient China*, 28–29; Li, *The Readability of the Past in Early Chinese Historiography*, 149.

117. Goldin, *The Culture of Sex in Ancient China*, 28–29.

118. Chen, *Chunqiu hunyin lisu yu shehui lunli*, 106–18.

119. Zhou, "Chunqiu shiqi de liangxing xisu yu zhenjieguan," 57–58; Gao, *Zhoudai hunyin xingtai yanjiu*, 78.

120. For example Gongyang, *Chongkan Songben Gongyang zhushu fujiao kanji*, 21:268b (Xiang 30); Zuo, *Chongkan Songben Zuozhuan zhushu fujiao kanji*, 9:156a (Zhuang 14). Also Gao, *Zhoudai hunyin xingtai yanjiu*, 75–76, 172.

121. Zhou, *Festivals, Feasts, and Gender Relations in Ancient China and Greece*, 196–201.

122. Gao, *Zhoudai hunyin xingtai yanjiu*, 73-8, 170–74.

123. Zhou Mi and Huang Yuhong, "Yun Xian Qiaojiayuan mudi Dong Zhou - Xi Han jumin yachi de xingtai guancha yu celiang," *Jiang Han kaogu* 3 (2010): 106–12, analyzes the skeletons of women in an Eastern Zhou cemetery.

124. Li Hengmei and Yu Xia, "Lu guo zhaomu zhidu lice," *Henan Daxue xuebao* 4 (2000): 44; Liu Zheng, *Jinwen miaozhi yanjiu* (Beijing: Zhongguo shehui kexue, 2004), 14–17.

125. Cao, *Jinwen yu Yin Zhou nüxing wenhua*, 260–67; Cook, "Education and the Way of the Former Kings," 329.

126. Katherine K. Young, "Introduction," in *Women in World Religions*, ed. Arvind Sharma (Albany: State University of New York Press, 1987), 31.

127. Hawkes, *The Songs of the South*, 46.

128. Zheng Xuan (annotator), *Chongkan Songben Zhouli zhushu fujiao kanji* (Nanchang: Nanchangfu xuekanben, 1815; reprinted Taipei: Yiwen yinshuguan, 1955), 17:265b; Lin Fushi, *Handai de wuzhe* (Taipei: Daoxiang chubanshe, 1988), 13–20.

129. Jia Dongyue and Zhang Xianhua, "*Zuozhuan* zhong de Qi guo nüxing," *Taishan Xueyuan xuebao* 9 (2006): 51–52; Marc Kalinowski, "Diviners and Astrologers Under the Eastern Zhou: Transmitted Texts and Recent Archaeological Discoveries," in *Early Chinese Religion: Part One: Shang through Han (1250 BC–220 AD)*, ed. John Lagerwey and Marc Kalinowski (Leiden: E.J. Brill, 2009), 351, 359.

130. Cai Feng, "Qi guo 'gu jiemei bujia' yu 'wuer' zhi su bianyi," *Zhonghua nüzi xueyuan xuebao* 2 (1999): 45–49. This unmarried religious specialist was called a *wuer* 巫兒.

131. Wang and Zhang, *Zhongguo funü tongshi*, 45; Wang Zheng, "Gudai wenyan xiaoshuo yu Zhoudai de yuji qiuyu," *Xiaoshuo pinglun* 6 (2012): 52–53.

132. Constance A. Cook, "Moonshine and Millet: Feasting and Purification Rituals in Ancient China," in *Of Tripod and Palate: Food, Politics and Religion in Traditional China*, ed. Roel Sterckx (New York: Palsgrave Macmillan, 2005), 15.

133. Chow, "The Childbirth Myth and Ancient Chinese Medicine," 43–90; Wang and Zhang, *Zhongguo funü tongshi*, 147–51. There were numerous shamanistic methods to induce fertility and additional ways to evoke the birth of a son. Lü Yahu, *Zhanguo Qin Han jianbo wenxian suo jian wushu yanjiu* (Beijing: Kexue, 2010), 65–100.

134. Zhao Fulin, "Kongzi yu Wanqiu - jian lun Zhoudai wuxi diwei de bianhua yu wunü bujia zhi su," *Gansu shehui kexue* 1 (2006): 52–56.

135. Hawkes, *The Songs of the South*, 106, 115.

136. Anne Birrell, *Chinese Mythology: An Introduction* (Baltimore: The Johns Hopkins University Press, 1993), 160; Mark Edward Lewis, "The Mythology of Early China," in *Early Chinese Religion: Part One: Shang through Han (1250 BC–220 AD)*, ed. John Lagerwey and Marc Kalinowski (Leiden: E.J. Brill, 2009), 585.

137. Goldin, *The Culture of Sex in Ancient China*, 17–18.

138. Chang, *Early Chinese Civilization*, 158–59.

139. Birrell, *Chinese Mythology*, 69; Chen Jianxian, *Shenqi yu yingxiong: Zhongguo gudai shenhua de muti* (Beijing: Sanlian shuju, 1994), 47–48; Yang Lihui, *Nü Wa suyuan - Nü Wa xinyang qiyuan di de zai tuice* (Beijing: Beijing Shifan Daxue chubanshe, 1999), 61–69. Chen, 58–59, argues that Nü Wa may have been considered an earth goddess. This interpretation seems far-fetched.

140. Birrell, *Chinese Mythology*, 33–35.

141. Birrell, *Chinese Mythology*, 164.

142. Durrant, *The Cloudy Mirror*, 124.

143. Chen Zhiyong, "Lun Zhoudai de hexie wenhua," *Tangdu xuekan* 5 (2008): 81–85.

144. Chenyang Li, "The Confucian Ideal of Harmony," *Philosophy East and West* 56, no. 4 (2006): 589.

145. Gary G. Hamilton, "Patriarchy, Patrimonialism, and Filial Piety: A Comparison of China and Western Europe," *The British Journal of Sociology* 41, no. 1 (1990): 92.

146. Zhou, *Festivals, Feasts, and Gender Relations in Ancient China and Greece*, 254, 322.

147. Elvin Hatch, "Theories of Social Honor," *American Anthropologist* 91, no. 2 (1989): 346–47. The possibility that women often adhered to a social norm as a strategy to gain status, even when they did not agree with it, can help explain the eventual rise of radical expressions of chastity such as self-mutilation and suicide.

148. Knapp, "The Ru Reinterpretation of *Xiao*," 200–02; Donald Holzman, "The Place of Filial Piety in Ancient China," *Journal of the American Oriental Society* 118, no. 2 (1998): 1–15. Kang Xuewei, *Xian Qin xiaodao yanjiu* (Taipei: Wenjin, 1992), discusses the origins and early development of filial piety in detail.

149. Qingping Liu, "Filiality versus Sociality and Individuality: On Confucianism and Consanguinitism," *Philosophy East and West* 53, no. 2 (2003): 234; Van Norden, *Mencius*, 101 (4A27.1).

150. Jen-der Lee, "Childbirth in Early Imperial China," *Nan Nü* 7, no. 2 (2005): 220.

151. Henry Rosemont, Jr. and Roger T. Ames, *The Chinese Classic of Family Reverence: A Philosophical Translation of the* Xiaojing (Honolulu: University of Hawaii Press, 2009), 107; Jian Zhaoliang, ed. *Xiaojing jizhu shushu – fu dushutang dawen*, annotated by Zhou Chunjian (Shanghai: Huadong Shifan Daxue chubanshe, 2011), 5:37.

152. Rosemont and Ames, *The Chinese Classic of Family Reverence*, 110; Jian *Xiaojing jizhu shushu*, 9:71. Trigger, *Understanding Early Civilizations*, 271, notes that the tendency of ancient societies to model family relations after the state reinforced patriarchy.

153. Miranda Brown, "Sons and Mothers in Warring States and Han China, 453 BCE–220 CE," *Nan Nü* 5, no. 2 (2003): 142–43; Gao, Zuozhuan *nüxing yanjiu*, 41–44.

154. Rosemont and Ames, *The Chinese Classic of Family Reverence*, 71, 114; Jian *Xiaojing jizhu shushu*, 15:100.

155. Trigger, *Understanding Early Civilizations*, 189–90.

156. Bret Hinsch, "The Origins of Separation of the Sexes in China," *Journal of the American Oriental Society* 123, no. 3 (2003): 595–616.

157. A similar association of men with grain production and women with textiles occurred in many early societies. Trigger, *Understanding Early Civilizations*, 360.

158. Tamara T. Chin, *Savage Exchange: Han Imperialism, Chinese Literary Style, and the Economic Imagination* (Cambridge, MA: Harvard University Asia Center, 2014), 57–58.

159. Bret Hinsch, "Textiles and Female Virtue in Early Imperial Chinese Historical Writing," *Nan Nü* 5, no. 2 (2003): 170–202.

160. Raphals, *Sharing the Light*, 195–234.

161. Eric L. Hutton (trans.), *Xunzi: The Complete Text* (Princeton: Princeton University Press, 2014), 179; Xun Kuang, *Xunzi jiaoshi*, annotated by Wang Tianhai (Shanghai: Shanghai guji, 2005), 17: 687.

162. Wu Congxiang, *Handai nüxing lijiao yanjiu* (Jinan: Qilu, 2013), 14–15, 16–17. Granet, *La polygynie sororale et le sororat dans la Chine féodale*, 60, theorizes that separation of the sexes was an outgrowth of exogamy. He argues that because husband and wife represented different kinship groups, people believed that they ought to keep apart.

163. James Legge and Robin R. Wang, "The Record of Rites (*Liji*)," in *Images of Women in Chinese Thought and Culture: Writings from the Pre-Qin Period through the Song Dynasty*, ed. Robin R. Wang (Indianapolis: Hackett Publishing, 2003), 56.

164. Goldin, *The Culture of Sex in Ancient China*, 66.

165. Zhou, "Virtue and Talent," 13; Zhou, *Festivals, Feasts, and Gender Relations in Ancient China and Greece*, 260–62.

166. Yang, "Chunqiu shidai zhi nannü fengji," 36.

167. Van Norden, *Mengzi*, 97 (4A17.1).

168. Van Norden, *Mengzi*, 78 (3B2.2); Hutton, *Xunzi*, 120; Xun, *Xunzi jiaoshi*, 12:532.

169. Liu, *Handai hunyin zhidu*, 21.

170. Edward L. Shaughnessy, "The Composition of the 'Qian' and 'Kun' Hexagrams of the *Zhouyi*," in *Before Confucius: Studies in the Creation of the Chinese Classics* (Albany: State University of New York Press, 1997), 197–219; Raphals, *Sharing the Light*, 144–50; Bret Hinsch, *Women in Early Imperial China* (Lanham, Maryland: Rowman & Littlefield, 2002), 143–57; Li, *The Readability of the Past in Early Chinese Historiography*, 147.

171. Goldin, *The Culture of Sex in Ancient China*, 69–70.

EPILOGUE

1. Zheng, *Shanggu Huaxia funü yu hunyin*, 170–71; Goldin, *The Culture of Sex in Ancient China*, 57. Yi Jiang was probably her name while she was alive, and Wen Mu her posthumous appellation. Many posthumous names included the character *wen* 文. The orthography of *wen* (depicting a person with a design on the chest) seems to recall an extremely ancient Shang ritual in which mourners would tattoo their chests. Xu, *Wenzi xiaojiang*, 4–6. Similar customs were practiced in other regions of the world. For example, some African cultures also practice tattooing as a mourning ritual. Betty Schneider, "Body Decoration in Mozambique," *African Arts* 6, no. 2 (1973): 26–31.

2. Ames and Rosemont, *The Analects of Confucius*, 124–25 (8.20).

3. For example Wei, *Weishu*, 108C:2786–87. She eventually became a symbol of general female virtue. Liu Xu, et al., *Jiu Tangshu*, annotated by Liu Jie and Chen Naiqian (Beijing: Zhonghua, 1975), 62:2390.

4. Goldin, *The Culture of Sex in Ancient China*, 58.

5. Tamara Chin, "Orienting Mimesis: Marriage and the Book of Songs," *Representations* 94, no. 1 (2006): 60.

6. Cook, "Ancestor Worship During the Eastern Zhou," 260–61.

7. Cao, *Jinwen yu Yin Zhou nüxing wenhua*, 238–41.

8. Gao, *Zuozhuan nüxing yanjiu*, 141–45.

9. Li, *The Readability of the Past in Early Chinese Historiography*, 143, 145–49; Wang Xiuchen, *Sanli yongshi kaolun* (Beijing: Zhongguo shehui kexue chubanshe, 2007), 316–19.

10. Bai and Du, "Zhoudai quangui funü jieru 'gong' 'wai' shiwu de sanzhong leixing," 98–99; Zheng, *Shanggu Huaxia funü yu hunyin*, 173; Wu, *Handai nüxing lijiao yanjiu*, 33–38.

11. Goldin, *The Culture of Sex in Ancient China*, 37; Li, *The Readability of the Past in Early Chinese Historiography*, 154–57, 159–60. For an extremely detailed discussion of the concept of licentiousness (*yin* 淫) and its various manifestations see Kurihara, *Kodai Chūgoku koninsei no rei rinen to keitai*, 538–624.

12. Vandermeersch, *Wangdao ou la Voie Royale*, 306.

13. Li, *The Readability of the Past in Early Chinese Historiography*, 151–52.

14. Tong Zhe (ed.), *Han Fei zi jijie* (Beijing: Zhonghua, 1998), 745 (*wai chu shui*).

15. Raphals, *Sharing the Light*, 12; Goldin, *The Culture of Sex in Ancient China*, 24, 34–35, 40–42. This idea grew out of the belief that the state and the family are

analogous institutions. Chang Jincang, *Zhoudai lisu yanjiu* (Harbin: Heilongjiang renmin chubanshe, 2004), 17–22. This became a standard idea repeated by writers in later eras. Jowen R. Tung, *Fables for the Patriarchs: Gender Politics in Tang Discourse* (Lanham, MD: Rowman & Littlefield, 2000), 33–40. This metaphorical comparison of state and family led people to compare the relationship between ruler and subject with that of father and son. Isamu Ogata, *Chūgoku kodai no ie to kokka - kōtei shipaika no chitsujo kekkō* (Tokyo: Iwanami shoten, 1975), 187–97.

16. Waley, *The Book of Songs*, 169, 283–85; Kalgren, *The Book of Odes*, 136 (Mao 192), 236–28 (Mao 264), expresses similar sentiments without naming Bao Si.

17. Li Feng, *Landscape and Power in Early China: The Crisis and Fall of the Western Zhou 1045–771 BC* (Cambridge: Cambridge University Press, 2006), 199. For a cogent retelling and detailed discussion of the Bao Si narrative, see pp. 195, 200, 214.

18. Li, *Landscape and Power in Early China*, 201, translates these later versions. Ban, *Hanshu*, 27D:1465 used concepts from Han dynasty portent studies to interpret the Bao Si story.

19. Here I use the term myth as analogous with ideology. Halpern, "'Myth' and 'Ideology' in Modern Usage," 129–49.

20. Li, *Landscape and Power in Early China*, 199, 202–3.

21. Li, *Landscape and Power in Early China*, 196–98, 232.

22. Raphals, *Sharing the Light*, 63; Bret Hinsch, "Evil Women and Dynastic Collapse: Tracing the Development of an Ideological Archetype," *Quarterly Journal of Chinese Studies* 1, no. 2 (2012): 62–81.

23. Kong Anguo, *Shangshu*, annotated Kong Yingda, et al., collated Ruan Yuan (N.p. Ruan Yuan edition, 1815; reprinted Taipei: Yiwen, 1955), 11: 158.

24. Mo Di, *Mozi*, annotated Sun Yirang (Taipei: Huazheng, 1987), 19: 139; Ian Johnson, *The Mozi: A Complete Translation* (New York: Columbia University Press, 2010), 191.

25. A few other cryptic references prior to Xunzi also hint at an evil female presence at the end of the Shang. Hinsch, "Evil Women and Dynastic Collapse," 67–68.

26. Hutton, *Xunzi*, 225; Xun, *Xunzi jiaoshi*, 21: 832.

27. Raphals, *Sharing the Light*, 15–20, 61–70; Hinsch, "Evil Women and Dynastic Collapse," 71–79.

28. For example, Cao Pi (Emperor Wen of Wei) (187–226 CE) issued an edict prohibiting women from interfering in politics. He justified this prohibition by declaring women's interference in politics to be the root of chaos. Chen Shou, *Sanguozhi* (Beijing; Zhonghua shuju, 1959), 2: 80. For this reason, Cao Cao and his successors deliberately chose empresses from minor families who would be less likely to interfere with government. Robert Joe Cutter, "To the Manner Born? Nature and Nurture in Early Medieval Chinese Literary Thought," in *Culture and Power in the Reconstitution of the Chinese Realm, 200–600*, ed. Scott Pearce, Audrey Spiro, and Patricia Ebrey (Cambridge, MA: Harvard University Asia Center, 2001), 70. Similar prohibitions were repeated for the remainder of imperial history.

29. Goldin, *The Culture of Sex in Ancient China*, 51, 53, 65.

30. Goldin, *The Culture of Sex in Ancient China*, 61–62. For example, the Qing dynasty historian Zhao Yi emphasized the sexual dimension of female-induced chaos in the Tang dynasty. Zhao Yi, *Nianer shi zhaji* (Taipei: Shijie shuju, 1974), 19:256. Ancient records claimed that in remote antiquity, a naked woman was

sometimes exposed in shamanistic rituals to ward off evil, as her body was believed to emit a kind of potent force. Hu Xinsheng, *Zhongguo gudai wushu* (Beijing: Renmin, 2010), 197.

31. Lam, "The Presence and Absence of Female Musicians and Music in China," 99–100, 104.

32. Trigger, *Understanding Early Civilizations*, 188.

Bibliography

Ai Guangkuo 袁廣闊. "Henan Erlitou wenhua muzang de jige wenti" 河南二里頭文化墓葬的幾個問題. *Kaogu* 考古 12 (1996): 62–69.

Allen, Ann Taylor. "Feminism, Social Science, and the Meanings of Modernity: The Debate on the Origin of the Family in Europe and the United States, 1860–1914." *The American Historical Review* 104, no. 4 (1999): 1085–13.

Allen, W.L., and J.B. Richardson. "The Reconstruction of Kinship from Archaeological Data: The Concepts, the Methods, and the Feasibility." *American Antiquity* 36, no. 1 (1971): 41–53.

Ames, Roger T., and Henry Rosemont, Jr. *The Analects of Confucius: A Philosophical Translation.* New York: Ballantine, 1998.

Anyang Wenwu Gongzuodui 安陽文物工作隊. "Anyang shi Yindai muzang fajue jianbao" 安陽市殷代墓葬發掘簡報. *Huaxia kaogu* 華夏考古 1 (1995): 1–13.

Bachofen, Johann Jacob. *An English Translation of Bachofen's Mutterrecht (Mother Right) (1861): A Study of the Religious and Juridical Aspects of Gynecocracy in the Ancient World,* translated by David Partenheimer. Lewistown, NY: Edwin Mellen Press, 2003.

Bacus, Elisabeth A. "Gender in East and Southeast Asian Archaeology." In *Worlds of Gender: The Archaeology of Women's Lives Around the Globe,* edited by Sarah Milledge Nelson, 39–72. Lanham, MD: AltaMira Press, 2007.

Bai Lu 白路. "Xian Qin nüxing yanjiu - cong shehui xingbie shijiao de kaocha yu fenxi" 先秦女性研究 – 從社會性別視角的考察與分析. PhD dissertation, Nankai University, 2009.

Bai Lu 白路 and Du Fangqin 杜芳琴. "Zhoudai quangui funü jieru 'gong' 'wai' shiwu de sanzhong leixing - cong shehui xingbie shijiao de guancha yu fenxi" 周代權貴婦女介入公外事務的三種類型 – 從社會性別視角的觀察與分析. *Shanxi Shida xuebao* 山西師大學報 2 (2009): 94–99.

Baker, Hugh D.R. *Chinese Family and Kinship*. New York: Columbia University Press, 1979.

Bamberger, Joan. "The Myth of Matriarchy: Why Men Rule in Primitive Society." In *Woman, Culture, and Society*, edited by Michelle Zimbalist Rosaldo and Louise Lamphere, 263–80. Stanford: Stanford University Press, 1974.

Ban Gu 班固. *Hanshu* 漢書, annotated by Yan Shigu 顏師古. Beijing: Zhonghua, 1962.

Bao Ximing 暴希明. "Cong jiaguwen, jinwen 'xing' de yigou kan gudai hunyin xingtai de yanjin" 從甲骨文金文姓的異構看古代婚姻型態的演進. *Anyang Shifan Xueyuan xuebao* 安陽師範學院學報 4 (2012): 89–91.

Barnes, R.H., and Ruth Barnes, trans. *Joseph Kohler, On the Prehistory of Marriage: Totemism, Group Marriage, Mother Right*. Chicago: University of Chicago Press, 1975.

Baştuğ, S. "Kinship, Marriage and Descent in Early China." *Journal of Asian History* 29, no. 2 (1995): 149–87.

Bauer, Brian S., and R. Alan Covey. "Processes of State Formation in the Inca Heartland (Cuzco, Peru)." *American Anthropologist* 104, no. 3 (2002): 846–64.

Beijing Daxue Lishixi Gujiao Yanshi Shang Zhou zubian 北京大學歷史系古教研室商周組編 ed. *Shang Zhou kaogu* 商周考古. Beijing: Wenwu chubanshe, 1979.

Birrell, Anne. *Chinese Mythology: An Introduction*. Baltimore: The Johns Hopkins University Press, 1993.

Boileau, Gilles. "Wu and Shaman," *Bulletin of the School of Oriental and African Studies* 65, no. 2 (2002): 350–78.

Bolger, Diane. "Figurines, Fertility, and the Emergence of Complex Society in Prehistoric Cyprus." *Current Anthropology* 37, no. 2 (1996): 365–73.

Booth, Alison. "The Mother of All Cultures: Camille Paglia and Feminist Mythologies." *The Kenyon Review* 21, no. 1 (1999): 27–45.

Bourdieu, Pierre. *Outline of a Theory of Practice*, translated by Richard Nice. Cambridge: Cambridge University Press, 1977.

Brooks, Bruce E., and A. Taeko Brooks. *The Original Analects: Sayings of Confucius and His Successors*. New York: Columbia University Press, 1998.

Brown, Judith. "Note on the Division of Labor by Sex." *American Anthropologist* 72 (1970): 1075–76.

Brown, Miranda. "Sons and Mothers in Warring States and Han China, 453 BCE–220 CE." *Nan Nü* 5, no. 2 (2003): 137–69.

Brumfiel, Elizabeth M. "Cloth, Gender, Continuity, and Change: Fabricating Unity in Anthropology." *American Anthropologist* 108, no. 4 (2006), 862–77.

———. "Consumption and Politics at Aztec Huexotla." *American Anthropologist* 89, no. 3 (1987): 676–86.

Burridge, Kate, and Ng Bee-Chin. "Writing the Female Radical: The Encoding of Women in the Writing System." In *Dress, Sex and Text in Chinese Culture*, edited by Antonia Finnane and Anne McLaren, 123–33. Clayton: Monash Asia Institute, 1999.

Cai Feng 蔡鋒. "Chunqiu shiqi guizu shixing yingqie, zhidi hunzhi ma?" 春秋時期貴族實行媵妾, 侄娣婚制嗎? *Yunnan Minzu Daxue xuebao* 雲南民族大學學報 3 (2014): 111–17.

———. "Chunqiu shiqi Song 'nei hunzhi' kaocha" 春秋時期宋内婚制考察. *Hebei Shifan Daxue xuebao* 河北師範大學學報 5 (2004): 117–20.

———. "Qi guo 'gu jiemei bujia' yu 'wuer' zhi su bianyi" 齊國姑姐妹不嫁與巫兒之俗辨疑. *Zhonghua nüzi xueyuan xuebao* 中華女子學院學報 2 (1999): 45–49.

Cao Dingyun 曹定雲. "'Fuhao' nai 'Zifang' zhi nü" 婦好乃子方之女. In *Qingzhu Su Bingqi kaogu wushiwu nian lunwenji* 慶祝蘇秉崎考古五十五年論文集, edited by Qingzhu Su Bingqi kaogu wushiwu nian lunwenji bianjizu 慶祝蘇秉崎考古五十五年論文集編輯組, 381–85. Beijing: Wenwu, 1989.

———. "Jinwen zhong de nüxing xiangjizhe ji qi shehui diwei" 金文中的女性享祭者及其社會地位. *Shenzhen Daxue xuebao* 深圳大學學報 19, no.2 (2002): 78–87.

———. *Yinxu Fu Hao mu mingwen yanjiu* 殷墟婦好墓銘文研究. Taipei: Wenjin chubanshe, 1993.

———. "Zhoudai jinwen zhong nüzi chengwei leixing yanjiu" 周代金文中女子稱謂類型研究. *Kaogu* 考古 6 (1999): 78–87.

Cao Jiandun 曹建敦. "Zhoudai jisi yongsheng lizhi kaolue" 周代祭祀用牲禮制考略. *Wenbo* 文博 3 (2008): 18–21.

Cao Wei 曹瑋. "San Bo Che Fu qi yu Xi Zhou hunyin zhidu" 散伯車父器與西周婚姻制度. *Wenwu* 文物 3 (2000): 63–65.

Cao Xiaowei 曹曉偉. "Chunqiu shiqi yinghun yanjiu" 春秋時期媵婚研究. *Lilun xuekan* 理論學刊 4 (2014): 105–09.

Cao Yingchun 曹迎春. "'Zhongfu' yu 'qingfu' - xian Qin Zhao guo yu Yan guo fengsu chayi jiedu" 重婦與輕婦 - 先秦趙國與燕國風俗差異解讀. *Zhonghua wenhua luntan* 中華文化論壇 1 (2010): 29–33.

Cao Zhaolan 曹兆蘭. "Baojiao de xianqu - Xi Zhou jinwen zhong de nü 'bao'" 保教的先驅 - 西周金文中的女保. *Jiaoyu lilun yu shijian* 教育理論與實踐 25, no. 3 (2005): 63–64.

———. "Cong jinwen kan liang Zhou hunyin guanxi" 從金文看兩周婚姻關係. *Wuhan Daxue xuebao* 武漢大學學報 1 (2004): 108–14.

———. "Cong jinwen kan Zhou dai yingqie hunzhi" 從金文看周代媵妾婚制. *Shenzhen Daxue xuebao* 深圳大學學報 6 (2001): 100–7.

———. "Jinwen 'nü,' 'mu' de xingyi shixi" 金文女母的形義試試析. *Xueshu yanjiu* 學術研究 7 (2002): 128–31.

———. "Jinwen nüxing chengwei zhong de guxing" 金文女性稱謂中的古姓. *Kaogu yu wenwu* 考古與文物 2 (2002): 51–60.

———. *Jinwen yu Yin Zhou nüxing wenhua* 金文與殷周女性文化. Beijing: Beijing Daxue, 2004.

Chang Bin 常彬. "Cong Shijing kan shanggu xianmin de shengzhi chongbai" 從詩經看上古先民的生殖崇拜. *Guizhou minzu xueyuan xuebao* 貴州民族學院學報 2 (2000): 19–20.

Chang Cheng-lang. "A Brief Discussion of Fu Tzu." In *Studies of Shang Archaeology: Selected Papers from the International Conference on Shang Civilization*, edited by K.C. Chang, 103–19. New Haven: Yale University Press, 1986.

Chang Jincang 常金倉. *Zhoudai lisu yanjiu* 周代禮俗研究. Harbin: Heilongjiang renmin chubanshe, 2004.

Chang, K.C. (Kwang-chih). *Early Chinese Civilization: Anthropological Perspectives*. Cambridge, MA: Harvard University Press, 1976.

———. *Shang Civilization*. New Haven: Yale University Press, 1980.

Chang Ping-ch'üan. "A Brief Description of the Fu Hao Oracle Bone Inscriptions." In *Studies of Shang Archaeology: Selected Papers from the International Conference on Shang Civilization*, edited by K.C. Chang, 121–40. New Haven: Yale University Press, 1986.

Chang Yaohua 常耀華. "Yinxu buci zhong de 'Dongmu' 'Ximu' yu 'Dongwanggong' 'Xiwangmu' shenhua chuanshuo zhi yanjiu" 殷墟卜辭中的東母西母與東王公西王母神話傳說之研究. *Zhongguo Guojia Bowuguan guankan* 中國國家博物館館刊 9 (2013): 47–53.

Chang Yuzhi 常玉芝. *Shangdai zhouji zhidu* 商代周祭制度. Beijing: Xinhua shudian, 1987.

———. *Shangdai zongjiao jisi* 商代宗教祭祀. Beijing: Zhongguo shehui kexue chubanshe, 2010.

Changzhou Shi Bowuguan 常州市博物館. "Changzhou Weidun xinshiqi shidai yizhi disanci fajue jianbao" 常州圩墩新石器時代遺址第三次發掘簡報. *Shiqian yanjiu* 史前研究 2 (1984): 68–69.

Chen Dongyuan 陳東原. *Zhongguo funü shenghuo shi* 中國婦女生活史. Shanghai: Shangwu yinshuguan, 1937.

Chen Fangmei 陳芳妹. "Jin hou mu qingtongqi suojian xingbie yanjiu de xin xiansuo" 晉侯墓青銅器所見性別研究的新線索. In *Jin hou mudi chuti qingtongqi guoji xueshu yantaohui wenji* 晉侯墓地出土青銅器國際學術研討會論文集, edited by Shanghai Bowuguan 上海博物館, 157–96. Shanghai: Shanghai shuhua, 2002.

Chen Guoqiang 陳國強. "Luelun Dawenkou muzang de shehui xingzhi – yu Tang Lan tongzhi shangque" 略論大汶口墓葬的社會性質 - 與唐蘭先生商榷. In *Dawenkou wenhua taolun wenji* 大汶口文化討論文集, edited by Shandong Daxue Lishixi Kaogu Jiaoyanshi 山東大學歷史系考古教研室, 96–109. Ji'nan: Jilu Sushe, 1979.

Chen Jianxian 陳建憲. *Shenqi yu yingxiong: Zhongguo gudai shenhua de muti* 神祇與英雄: 中國古代神話的母體. Beijing: Sanlian shuju, 1994.

Chen Jie 陳絜. *Shang Zhou xingshi zhidu yanjiu* 商周姓氏制度研究. Beijing: Shangwu yinshuguan, 2007.

Chen Ke 陳珂. "*Shijing* yu *Chuci* zhong nüxing xingxiang zhi bijiao" 詩經與楚辭中女性形象之比較. *Chifeng Xueyuan xuebao* 赤峰學院學報 33, no. 1 (2012): 138–39.

Chen Mengjia 陳夢家. "Shangdai de shenhua yu wushu" 商代的神話與巫術. *Yanjing xuebao* 燕京學報 20 (1936): 486–576.

———. *Yinxu buci zongshu* 殷墟卜辭綜述. Beijing: Zhonghua shuju, 1988.

Chen Shou 陳壽. *Sanguozhi* 三國志. Beijing; Zhonghua shuju, 1959.

Chen Tiemei 陳鐵梅. "Zhongguo xin shiqi muzang chengnianren gu xing bi yichang de wenti" 中國新石器墓葬成年人骨性比異常的問題. *Kaogu xuebao* 考古學報 4 (1990): 511–22.

Chen Xiaofang 陳筱芳. *Chunqiu hunyin lisu yu shehui lilun* 春秋婚姻禮俗與社會倫理. Chengdu: Bashu shushe, 2000.

———. "Chunqiu shiqi de zhenjieguan" 春秋時期的貞節觀. *Xinan Minzu Xueyuan xuebao* 西南民族學院學報 21, no. 1 (2000): 105–09.

Chen Yingjie 陳英杰. "Shangdai jinwen zhong zhi 'nüzi' mingci shuolue" 商代金文中之女子銘辭說略. *Kaogu yu wenwu* 考古與文物 4 (2010): 105–09.

Chen Yongxiang 陳永香. "Tantan *Shijing* zhong de 'aiqing' shi" 談談詩經中的愛情詩. *Chuxiong Shizhuan xuebao* 楚雄師專學報 14, no. 4 (1999): 46–51.

Chen Zhaorong 陳昭容. "Cong qingtongqi mingwen kan liang Zhou shi hunyin guanxi" 從青銅器銘文看兩周室婚姻關係. In *Guwenzi yu gudaishi* 古文字與古代史, edited by Chen Zhaorong, vol. 1, 253–92. Taipei: Zhongyang yanjiu yuan, Lishi yuyan yanjiusuo, 2007.

———. "Xingbie, shenfen yu caifu – cong Shang Zhou qingtongqi yu muzang yiwu suozuo de kaocha" 性別身分與財富從商周青銅器與墓葬遺物所作的考察. In *Zhongguo shi xinlun – xingbie shi fence* 中國史新論性別史分冊, edited by Li Zhende 李貞德, 19–86. Taipei: Zhongyang yanjiu yuan, 2009.

Chen Zhiyong 陳智勇. "Lun Zhoudai de hexie wenhua" 論周代的和諧文化. *Tangdu xuekan* 唐都學刊 5 (2008): 81–85.

———. "Shixi Shangdai de zongmiao zhidu jiqi zhengzhi gongyong" 試析商代的宗廟制度及其政治功用. *Yindu xuekan* 殷都學刊 1 (1999): 22–26, 53.

Cheng Chen-hsiang. "A Study of the Bronzes with the 'Ssu T'u Mu' Inscriptions Excavated from the Fu Hao Tomb." In *Studies of Shang Archaeology: Selected Papers from the International Conference on Shang Civilization*, edited by K.C. Chang, 81–119. New Haven: Yale University Press, 1986.

Chin, Tamara. "Orienting Mimesis: Marriage and the Book of Songs." *Representations* 94, no. 1 (2006): 53–79.

———. *Savage Exchange: Han Imperialism, Chinese Literary Style, and the Economic Imagination*. Cambridge, MA: Harvard University Asia Center, 2014.

Chou, Hung-Hsiang. "Fu-x Ladies of the Shang Dynasty." *Monumenta Serica* 29 (1970–1971): 346–90.

Chow, Tse-tsung. "The Childbirth Myth and Ancient Chinese Medicine: A Study of Aspects of the *Wu* Tradition." In *Ancient China: Studies in Early Civilization*, edited by David T. Roy and Tsuen-hsuin Tsien, 43–90. Hong Kong: Chinese University Press, 1978.

Chun, Allen J. "Conceptions of Kinship and Kingship in Classical Chou China." *Toung P'ao* 76 (1990): 16–48.

Conkey, Margaret W., and Joan M. Gero. "Gender and Feminism in Archaeology." *Annual Review of Anthropology* 26 (1997): 411–37.

Conkey, Margaret W., and Janet D. Spector. "Archaeology and the Study of Gender." In *Advances in Archaeological Method and Theory, Volume 7*, edited by Michael B. Schiffer, 1–38. Orlando: Academic Press, 1984.

Cook, Constance A. "Ancestor Worship During the Eastern Zhou." In *Early Chinese Religion: Part One: Shang through Han (1250 BC–220 AD)*, edited by John Lagerwey and Marc Kalinowski, 237–79. Leiden: E.J. Brill, 2009.

———. A. *Death in Ancient China: The Tale of One Man's Journey*. Leiden: E.J. Brill, 2006.

———. "Education and the Way of the Former Kings." In *Writing & Literacy in Early China: Studies from the Columbia Early China Seminar*, edited by Li Feng and David Prager Branner, 302–36. Seattle: University of Washington Press, 2011.

———. "Moonshine and Millet: Feasting and Purification Rituals in Ancient China." In *Of Tripod and Palate: Food, Politics and Religion in Traditional China*, edited by Roel Sterckx, 9–23. New York: Palsgrave Macmillan, 2005.

Creel, Herrlee G. *The Origins of Statecraft in China, Volume One, The Western Zhou Empire.* Chicago: University of Chicago Press, 1970.

Crown, Patricia L., and Suzanne K. Fish. "Gender and Status in the Hohokam Pre-Classic to Classic Transition." *American Anthropologist* 98, no. 4 (1996): 803–17.

Cui Mingde 崔明德. *Xian Qin zhengzhi hunyin shi* 先秦政治婚姻史. Ji'nan: Shandong Daxue, 2004.

Cui Ruonan 崔若男. "Shenti yu xiangzheng: Zhoudai yiqian Zhongguo de 'zuo' 'you' zunbeiguan" 身體與象徵: 周代以前中國的左右尊卑觀. *Wenhua yichan* 文化遺產 1 (2015): 89–97.

Cutter, Robert Joe. "To Make Her Mine: Women and the Rhetoric of Property in Early and Early Medieval Fu." *Early Medieval China* 19 (2013): 39–57.

———. "To the Manner Born? Nature and Nurture in Early Medieval Chinese Literary Thought." In *Culture and Power in the Reconstitution of the Chinese Realm, 200-600*, edited by Scott Pearce, Audrey Spiro, and Patricia Ebrey, 53–71. Cambridge, MA: Harvard University Asia Center, 2001.

Danforth, Marie Elaine. "Nutrition and Politics in Prehistory." *Annual Review of Anthropology* 28 (1999): 1–25.

Debaine-Francfort, Corinne. *Du Néolithique à l'âge du bronze en Chine du nord-ouest: La Culture de Qijia et ses Connexions.* Paris: Éditions Recherche sur les Civilisations, 1995.

Deng Qihua 鄧啓華. "Qian gu fengliu xun jiuzong - Shijing hunlian shi pingxi zhi er" 千古風流尋舊蹤 – 詩經婚戀詩評析之二. *Simao Shifan Gaodeng Zhuanke Xuexiao xuebao* 思茅師範高等專科學校學報 15, no. 1 (1999): 36–48.

———. "Yizhong huangdan de hunzhi - cong shijing kan Xi Zhou Chunqiu zhuhou ying hun" 一種荒誕的婚制 - 從詩經看西周春秋諸侯媵婚. *Puer Xueyuan xuebao* 普洱學院學報 30, no. 1 (2014): 90–94.

Deng Tongxiang 鄧統湘. "Shangdai Wu Ding shi guizu 'zi' de yisi liyi kaocha" 商代武丁時貴族子的祭祀禮儀考察. *Yindu xuekan* 殷都學刊 4 (2014): 3–8.

Ding Huiyu 丁滙宇. "Luelun Daxi wenhua muzang fanying de shehui xingtai" 略論大溪文化墓葬反映的社會型態. *Sanxia luntan* 三峽論壇 1 (2014): 19–23.

Douglas, Mary, and Baron Isherwood. *The World of Goods: Towards an Anthropology of Consumption.* New York: W.W. Norton, 1979.

Du Fangqin 杜芳琴. "Shang Zhou xingbie zhidu yu guizu funü diwei zhi bijiao" 商周性別制度與貴族婦女地位之比較. In *Zhongguo shehui xingbie de lishi wenhua xunzong* 中國社會性別的歷史文化尋蹤, edited by Du Fangqin, 67–94. Tianjin: Tianjin shehui kexue, 1998.

Du You 杜佑. *Tongdian* 通典. Beijing: Zhonghua shuju, 1988.

Du Zhengsheng 杜正勝. "Cong wufu lun chuantong de zuqun jiegou ji qi lunli" 從五服論傳統的族群結構及其倫理. In *Zhonghua wenhua de guoqu xianzai he weilai* 中華文化的過去現在和未來, 256–75. Beijing: Zhonghua shuju, 1992.

Durrant, Stephen W. *The Cloudy Mirror: Tension and Conflict in the Writings of Sima Qian.* Albany: State University of New York Press, 1995.

Earle, Timothy. *Bronze Age Economics: The Beginnings of Political Economies.* Boulder, CO: Westview Press, 2002.

———. "Specialization and the Production of Wealth: Hawaiian Chiefdoms and the Inka Empire." In *Specialization, Exchange, and Complex Societies*, edited by

Elizabeth M. Brumfiel and Timothy K. Earle, 64–75. Cambridge: Cambridge University Press, 1987.

Ebrey, Patricia. "Concubines in Sung China." *Journal of Family History* 11, no. 1 (1986): 1–24.

———. "Education Through Ritual: Efforts to Formulate Family Rituals During the Sung Period." In *Neo-Confucian Education: The Formative Stage*, edited by William Theodore de Bary and John Chaffee, 277–306. Berkeley: University of California Press, 1989.

———. "Shifts in Marriage Finance from the Sixth to the Thirteenth Century." In *Marriage and Inequality in Chinese Society*, edited by Rubie S. Watson and Patricia B. Ebrey, 97–132. Berkeley: University of California Press, 1991.

Egashira Hiroshi 江頭廣. "Kinbun naka no kazoku seido ni kan suru nisan no mondai" 金文中の家族制度に關する二三の問題. *Nihon Chūgoku gakkaihō* 日本中國學會報 19 (1967): 77–92.

Eller, Cynthia. *Gentlemen and Amazons: The Myth of Matriarchal Prehistory*. Berkeley: University of California Press, 2011.

———. "Matriarchy and the Volk." *Journal of the American Academy of Religion* 81, no. 1 (2013): 188–221.

———. *The Myth of Matriarchal Prehistory: Why an Invented Past Won't Give Women a Future*. Boston: Beacon Press, 2000.

Engels, Frederick. *The Origin of the Family, Private Property, and the State*. New York: Pathfinder, 1972.

Engesi 恩格斯. "Jiazu, sichan yu guojia de qiyuan" 家族私產與國家的起源, translated by Pan Guangdan 潘光旦. In *Pan Guangdan wenji* 潘光旦文集, edited by Shen Kunpeng 沈昆朋, vol. 13, 83–470. Beijing: Beijing Daxue chubanshe, 2000.

Fan Zhoucheng 范州成. "Cong Wang Hai 'bin yu you yi' kan Shangdai hunzhi" 從王亥濱于有易看商代婚制. *Fuling Shifan Xueyuan xuebao* 涪陵師範學院學報 21, no. 4 (2005): 70–72.

Fang Zhengyi 方正已. "Luelun *Shijing* zhong de nüshiren qun" 略論詩經中的女詩人群. *Guilin Shi Jiaoyu Xueyuan xuebao* 桂林市教育學院學報 2 (1997): 38–47.

Farmer, J. Michael. "Classical Scholarship in the Shu Region: The Case of Qiao Zhou." In *Early Medieval China: A Sourcebook*, edited by Wendy Swartz, Robert Ford Campany, Yang Lu, and Jessey J.C. Choo, 108–24. New York: Columbia University Press, 2014.

Feng Rujun 馬汝軍. "Zhanguo shiqi hunyin guannian qianlun" 戰國時期婚姻觀念淺論. *Xueshu luntan* 學術論壇 2 (2002): 107–10.

Feng Shi 馮時. "Wo fangding mingwen yu Xi Zhou sangdianli" 我方鼎銘文與西周喪奠禮. *Kaogu xuebao* 考古學報 3 (2013): 185–212.

Flanagan, James G. "Hierarchy in Simple 'Egalitarian' Societies." *Annual Review of Anthropology* 18 (1989): 245–66.

Flannery, Kent, and Joyce Marcus. *The Creation of Inequality: How Our Prehistoric Ancestors Set the Stage for Monarchy, Slavery, and Empire*. Cambridge, MA: Harvard University Press, 2012.

Fluehr-Lobban, Carolyn. "A Marxist Reappraisal of the Matriarchate." *Current Anthropology* 20, no. 2 (1979): 341–59.

Fox, Robin. *Kinship and Marriage: An Anthropological Perspective*. Cambridge: Cambridge University Press, 1967.

Fracasso, Riccardo. "Holy Mothers of Ancient China: A New Approach to the Hsi-wang-mu 西王母 Problem. *T'oung Pao* 74 (1988): 1–46.

Fu Shaonan 付曉男. "Cong *Shuowen jiezi* nüzi bu tanxi Zhongguo gudai funü wenhua" 從 說文解字女子部探析中國古代婦女文化. *Yuyan jianshe* 語言建設 9 (2014): 73–74.

Gan Xiaohua 甘小華. "Luelun Qin de renxun wenhua" 略論秦的人殉文化. *Xi'an Caijing Xueyuan xuebao* 西安財經學院學報 21, no. 4 (2008): 14–17.

Gansu Sheng Wenwu Kaogu Yanjiusuo 甘肅省文物考古研究所 and Xibei Daxue Sichou zhi Lu Wenhua Yichan Baohu yu Kaogu Yanjiu Zhongxin 西北大學絲綢之路文化遺產保護與考古研究中心. "Gansu Lintan Mogou mudi Qijia wenhua muzang 2009 nian fajue jianbao" 甘肅臨潭磨溝墓地齊家文化墓葬 2009 年發掘簡報. *Wenwu* 文物 6 (2014): 4–23.

Gao Bing 高兵. "Cong 'Shuihudi Qin jian' kan Qin guo de hunyin lunli guannian" 睡虎地秦簡看秦國的婚姻倫理觀念. *Yantai Shifan Xueyuan xuebao* 煙台師範學院學報 4 (2005): 36–9.

———. "Qin guo hunyin zhidu yanjiu" 秦國婚姻制度研究. *Xibei Shida xuebao* 西北師大學報 3 (2006): 90–95.

———. *Zhoudai hunyin xingtai yanjiu* 周代婚姻形態研究. Chengdu: Bashu, 2007.

Gao Fang 高方. Zuozhuan *nüxing yanjiu* 左傳女性研究. Harbin: Heilongjiang Daxue chubanshe, 2010.

Gao Guangren 高廣仁. "Shandong diqu shiqian wenhua gailun" 山東地區史前文化概論. In *Shandong shiqian wenhua lunwenji* 山東史前文化論文集, edited by Shandong sheng jilu kaogu congkan bianjibu 山東省紀錄考古叢刊編輯部, 40–55. Ji'nan: Shandong renmin, 1986.

Gao Meijin 高梅進. "Qianxi Chunqiu Zhanguo shiqi de funü zhuangrong" 淺析春秋戰國時期的婦女妝容. *Guanzi xuekan* 管子學刊 2 (2011): 107–09.

Gao, Qiang, and Yun Kuen Lee. "A Biological Perspective on Yangshao Kinship." *Journal of Anthropological Archaeology* 12, no. 3 (1993): 266–98.

Gao Qingcong 高婧聰. "Zhoudai zongfa zhidu xia de 'mudi'" 周代宗法制度下的母弟. *Gudai wenming* 古代文明 6, no 1 (2012): 41–7.

Gao Wei 高煒, Gao Tianlin 高天麟, and Zhang Daihai 張岱海. "Guanyu Taosi mudi de jige wenti" 關於陶寺墓地的幾個問題. *Kaogu* 考古 6 (1983): 231–36.

Ge Yinghui 葛英會. "Zhouji buci zhong de zhixi xianbi ji xiangguan wenti" 周祭卜辭中的直系先妣及相關問題. *Beijing Daxue xuebao* 北京大學學報 1 (1990): 121–28.

Geng Chao 耿超. "Dong Zhou zhengzhi waijiao hunzhong de xingbie chayi jiqi yingxiang" 東周政治外交婚中的性別差異及其影響. *Yunnan shehui kexue* 雲南社會科學 2 (2009): 132–36.

———. "Yinxuzu mudi zhong de 'fufu hezang mu' ji xiangguan wenti" 殷墟族墓地中的夫婦合葬墓及相關問題. *Shoudu Shifan Daxue xuebao* 首都師範大學學報 2 (2013): 35–9.

———. "Zhoudai jiazu jisi yu liangxing guanxi lunlüe" 周代家族祭祀與兩性關係論略. In *Lifa yu xinyang - Zhongguo gudai nüxing yanjiu lunkao* 禮法與信仰 - 中國古代女性研究論考, edited by Pu Muzhou 蒲慕州, 9–22. Hong Kong: Shangwu yinshuguan, 2013.

Geng Chao 耿超 and Liu Shan 劉姍. "Chunqiu shiqi guizu funü de canzheng yu liangxing guanxi" 春秋時期貴族婦女的參政與兩性關係. *Guanzi xuekan* 管子學刊 3 (2012): 97–101.

Gero, Joan M. "Genderlithics: Women's Roles in Stone Tool Production." In *Engendering Archaeology: Women and Prehistory*, edited by Joan M. Gero and Margaret W. Conkey, 163–93. Oxford: Basil Blackwell, 1991.

Goldberg, Steven. *The Inevitability of Patriarchy*. New York: William Morrow, 1973.

Goldin, Paul Rakita. *The Culture of Sex in Ancient China*. Honolulu: University of Hawaii Press, 2002.

Gong Qiming 鞏啓明. "Cong kaogu ziliao kan Yangshao wenhua de shehui zuzhi he shehui fazhan jieduan" 從考古資料看仰韶文化的社會組織和社會發展階段. *Zhongyuan wenwu* 中原文物 5 (2001): 29–37.

Gong Wen 鞏文. "Yangshao wenhua zhuishi shulun" 仰韶文化墜飾述論. *Zhongyuan wenwu* 中原文物 5 (2014): 24–32.

Gong Yanbing 公炎冰 and Wei Gengyuan 魏耕原. "*Shijing* shu yu muti de chouyang kaocha - sangyuan he nannü mishi" 詩經樹與母體的抽樣考察 - 桑園和男女秘事. *Shaanxi Shifan Daxue xuebao* 陝西師範大學學報 25, no. 2 (1996): 42–47.

Gongyang Gao 公羊高. *Chongkan Songben Gongyang zhushu fujiao kanji* 重栞宋本公羊注疏附校堪記, annotated by He Xiu 何休 et al. Nanchang: Nanchangfu xuekanben, 1815; reprinted Taipei: Yiwen yinshuguan, 1965.

Good, Irene. "Archaeological Textiles: A Review of Current Research." *Annual Review of Anthropology* 30 (2001): 209–26.

Gough, Kathleen. "An Anthropologist Looks at Engels." In *Woman in a Man-Made World*, edited by Nona Glazer-Malbin and Helen Youngelson Waehrer, 156–68. Chicago: Rand McNally, 1972.

Graburn, Nelson. "On Marxism and the Matriarchate." *Current Anthropology* 20, no. 3 (1979): 608–09.

Granet, Marcel. *Danses et Légendes de la Chine Ancienne*. Paris: Librairie Félix Alcan, 1926.

———. *Festivals and Songs of Ancient China*, translated by E.D. Edwards. New York: E.P. Dutton & Co., 1932.

———. *La polygynie sororale et le sororat dans la Chine féodale*. Paris: Editions Ernest Leroux, 1920.

Gu Hongli 谷紅麗. "Zhoudai chema yu *Shijing* hunjia shi" 周代車馬與詩經婚嫁詩. *Lantai shijie* 蘭台世界 341 (2011): 59–60.

Gu Lijuan 谷麗娟. "Jiaguwen nübuzi yu nüxing juese bianqian tanxi" 甲骨文女部字與女性角色變遷探析. *Yulin Xueyuan xuebao* 榆林學院學報 22, no. 1 (2012): 74–78.

Gu Yan. "Chiang Ch'ing's Wolfish Ambition in Publicizing 'Matriarchal Society.'" *Chinese Studies in History* 12, no. 3 (1979): 75–79.

Guisso, Richard W. "Thunder Over the Lake: The Five Classics and Perceptions of Woman in Early China." In *Women in China: Current Directions in Historical Scholarship*, edited by Richard Guisso, 47–61. Youngstown, NY: Philo Press, 1981.

Guo Junran 郭俊然. "Qin Han shiqi de renxun xianxiang shulun" 秦漢時期的人殉現象述. *Suzhou Jiaoyu Xueyuan xuebao* 宿州教育學院學報 16, no. 6 (2013): 34–35.

Guo Min 郭敏. "Shiqian xianmin de toushi xisu" 史前先民的頭飾習俗. *Zhongyuan wenwu* 中原文物 2 (2007): 25–31.

Guo Moruo 郭沫若. "Shangceng jianzhu de shehui zuzhi" 上層建築的社會組織. In *Guo Moruo quanji: lishi bian* 郭沫若全集, 歷史編, vol. 1, 217–50. Beijing: Renmin wenxue, 1982.

———. "Shi zu bi" 釋祖妣, in *Jiaguwenzi yanjiu* 甲骨文字研究, 1.1a–23b. Hong Kong: Zhonghua shuju, 1976.

Guo Ting 郭婷. "*Shuowen jiezi*, nübu hanzi, yu shanggu hunyu wenhua" 說文解字女部漢字與上古婚育文化. *Mingzuo xinshang* 名作欣賞 9 (2015): 150–51.

Habakkuk, H.J. "Family Structure and Economic Change in Nineteenth Century Europe." *Journal of Economic History* 15, no. 1 (1955): 1–12.

Halpern, Ben. "'Myth' and 'Ideology' in Modern Usage." *History and Theory* 1, no. 2 (1961): 129–49.

Hamilton, Gary G. "Patriarchy, Patrimonialism, and Filial Piety: A Comparison of China and Western Europe." *The British Journal of Sociology* 41, no. 1 (1990): 77–104.

Han Dao 韓疇. "Cong Taosi yizhi kan Zhongguo Longshan shidai wangquan de xingcheng" 從陶寺遺址看中國龍山時代王權的形成. *Lishi gouchen* 歷史鈎沈 3 (2014): 177–78.

Han Fei 韓非. *Han Fei zi* 韓非子. Shanghai: Shangwu yinshuguan (*Sibu beiyao* edition), 1930.

Han Jianye 韓建業. "Dawenkou mudi fenxi" 大汶口墓地分析. *Zhongyuan wenwu* 中原文物 2 (1994): 48–61.

Han Longfu 韓隆福 and Qiu Zhiyong 邱智勇. "Lun muquan shehui de xingcheng he yiyi" 論母權社會的形成和意義. *Wuling xuekan* 武陵學刊 5 (1995): 55–59.

Hao Xiangping 郝向平. "Yinxu Xiaotun M5 zai tantao" 殷墟小屯 M5 再探討. *Zhongguo Guojia Bowuguan guankan* 中國國家博物館館刊 12 (2011): 20–26.

Hatch, Elvin. "Theories of Social Honor." *American Anthropologist* 91, no. 2 (1989): 341–53.

Hawkes, David. *The Songs of the South: An Ancient Chinese Anthology of Poems by Qu Yuan and Other Poets.* Harmondsworth, UK: Penguin Books, 1985.

He Dan 何丹. "Chunqiu shiqi hunyin tedian zhi tanjiu" 春秋時期婚姻特點之探究. *Huanan Ligong Daxue xuebao* 華南理工大學學報 2 (2014): 75–81.

He Deliang 何德亮. "Lun Zaozhuang Jianxin Dawenkou wenhua yicun" 論棗庄建新大汶口文化遺存. *Huaxia kaogu* 華夏考古 4 (1998): 47–56.

He Deliang 何德亮 and Niu Ruihong 牛瑞紅. "Dawenkou Yilongshan wenhua quzhi zangsu tanxi" 大汶口一龍山文化屈肢葬俗探析. *Liaohai wenwu xuekan* 遼海文物學刊 1 (1996): 79–84, 33.

———. "Zaozhuang Jianxin Dawenkou wenhua muzang fenxi" 棗庄建新大汶口文化墓葬分析. *Zhongyuan wenwu* 中原文物 4 (1996): 23–34.

He Deliang 何德亮 and Sun Po 孫波. "Shilun Lunan Subei diqu de Dawenkou wenhua" 試論魯南蘇北地區的大汶口文化. *Dongnan wenwu* 東南文化 3 (1997): 23–31.

He Xingliang 何星亮. "Banpo yuwen shi tuteng biaozhi haishi nüyin xiangzheng" 半坡魚紋是圖騰標誌還是女陰象徵. *Zhongyuan wenwu* 中原文物 3 (1996): 63–69, 118.

He Zhoude 何周德. "Hulu xingqiwu yu shengyu chongbai" 葫蘆形器物與生育崇拜. *Kaogu yu wenwu* 考古與文物 3 (1996): 47–52.

Hebei Sheng Wenwu Yanjiusuo 河北省文物研究所 and Tang Xian Wenwu Baoguansuo 唐縣文物保管所. "Tang Xian Shulü Dong Zhou muzang fajue jianbao" 唐縣淑闊東周墓葬發掘簡報. *Wenwu chunqiu* 文物春秋 1 (2012): 41–45.

Hendon, Julia A. "Archaeological Approaches to the Organization of Domestic Labor: Household Practice and Domestic Relations." *Annual Review of Anthropology* 25 (1996): 45–61.

Hinsch, Bret. "Evil Women and Dynastic Collapse: Tracing the Development of an Ideological Archetype." *Quarterly Journal of Chinese Studies* 1, no. 2 (2012): 62–81.

———. "The Origins of Separation of the Sexes in China." *Journal of the American Oriental Society* 123, no. 3 (2003): 595–616.

———. "Prehistoric Images of Women from the North China Region: The Origins of Chinese Goddess Worship?" *Journal of Chinese Religions* 32 (2004): 47–82.

———. "Textiles and Female Virtue in Early Imperial Chinese Historical Writing." *Nan Nü* 5, no. 2 (2003): 170–202.

———. *Women in Early Imperial China.* Lanham, Maryland: Rowman & Littlefield, 2002.

Holmgren, Jennifer. "Imperial Marriage in the Native Chinese and Non-Han State, Han to Ming." In *Marriage and Inequality in Chinese Society*, edited by Rubie S. Watson and Patricia Buckley Ebrey, 58–96. Berkeley: University of California Press, 1991.

Holzman, Donald. "The Place of Filial Piety in Ancient China." *Journal of the American Oriental Society* 118, no. 2 (1998): 1–15.

Hou Xudong and Howard Goodman. "Rethinking Chinese Kinship in the Han and the Six Dynasties: A Preliminary Observation." *Asia Major* 23, no. 1 (2010): 29–63.

Hsu Cho-yun. "Development of State-Society Relationship in Early China." In *La Société Civile Face à l'État Dans la Tradition Chinoise, Japonaise, Coréen et Vietnamienne*, edited by Léon Vandermeersch, 1–16. Paris: École Française d'Extrême-Orient, 1994.

Hsu, Cho-yun, and Katheryn M. Linduff. *Western Chou Civilization.* New Haven: Yale University Press, 1988.

Hu Binghua 胡秉華. "Tengzhou Qianzhang da Shangdai muzang dimian jianzhu jianxi" 滕州前掌大商代墓葬地面建築簡析. *Kaogu* 考古 2 (1994): 146–51.

Hu Houxuan 胡厚宣. *Jiaguxue Shangshi luncong* 甲骨學商史論叢. Beijing: Beijing Tushuguan, 2000.

———. "Zhongguo nuli shehui de renxun he renji (xia)" 中國奴隸社會的人殉和人祭 (下). *Wenwu* 文物 8 (1974): 56–67, 72.

Hu Xinsheng 胡新生. "Shangdai 'yuzi' lei buci suo fanying de yuanshi hunyin" 商代余子類卜辭所反映的原始婚姻. *Shandong Daxue xuebao* 山東大學學報 1 (1997): 46–49.

———. *Zhongguo gudai wushu* 中國古代巫術. Beijing: Renmin, 2010.

Huang Fengchun 黃鳳春. "Chu guo sanggui zhidu yanjiu" 楚國喪歸制度研究. *Jianghan kaogu* 江漢考古 2 (1999): 64–67, 58.

———. "Guanyu Hanyang Shamaoshan Shangdai zunming de shidu wenti" 關於漢陽紗帽山商代尊銘的釋讀問題. *Jianghan kaogu* 江漢考古 4 (2012): 61–62.

Huang Mingchong 黃銘崇. "Yin Zhou jinwen zhong de qinshu chengwei 'gu' ji qi xiangguan wenti" 殷周金文中的親屬稱謂姑及其相關問題. *Zhongyang yanjiuyuan lishi yuyan yanjiusuo jikan* 中央研究院歷史語言研究所集刊 75, vol. 1 (2004): 1–98.

Huang, Tsui-mei. "Gender Differentiation in Jin State Jade Regulations." In *Gender and Chinese Archaeology*, edited by Katheryn M. Linduff and Yan Sun, 137–60. Walnut Creek, CA: Altamira Press, 2004.

Huang Weihua 黃維華. "'Gu' yu *Shijing* zhong sanshou nüxing beiyuan shi" 谷與詩經中三首女性悲怨詩. *Wenshizhe* 文史哲 1 (1998): 26–31.

Huang Yanping 黃艷萍. "Jiaguwen tixianchu de Shangdai lunli daodeguan" 甲骨文體現出的商代倫理道德觀. *Xinyu Gaozhuan xuebao* 新余高專學報 15, no. 6 (2010): 61–63.

Huang Yi 黃誼. "Gudai Xila yu Zhongguo Zhouchao jichengzhi de bijiao" 古代希臘與中國周朝繼承制的比較. *Minzushi yanjiu* 民族史研究 (2005): 438–47.

Hutton, Eric L., trans. *Xunzi: The Complete Text*. Princeton: Princeton University Press, 2014.

Ikeda Suetoshi 池田末利. *Chūgoku kodai shū kyōshi kenkyū: Seido to shisō* 中國古代宗教史研究: 制度と思想. Tokyo: Tōkai Daigaku Shuppankai, 1981.

Ing, Michael David Kaulana. *The Dysfunction of Ritual in Early Confucianism*. Oxford: Oxford University Press, 2012.

Ingham, John M. "Human Sacrifice at Tenochtitlan." *Comparative Studies in Society and History* 26, no. 3 (1984): 379–400.

Isaac, Glynn. "The Food-Sharing Behavior of Protohuman Hominids." *Scientific American* 238 (1978): 90–108.

Isamu Ogata 尾形勇. *Chūgoku kodai no ie to kokka - kōtei shipaika no chitsujo kekkō* 中國古代の家と國家 – 皇帝支配下の秩序結構. Tokyo: Iwanami shoten, 1975.

Jay, Jennifer W. "Imagining Matriarchy: 'Kingdoms of Women' in Tang China." *Journal of the American Oriental Society* 116, no. 2 (1996): 220–29.

Jia Dongyue 賈冬月 and Zhang Xianhua 張憲華. "*Zuozhuan* zhong de Qi guo nüxing" 左傳中的齊國女性. *Taishan Xueyuan xuebao* 泰山學院學報 9 (2006): 51–54.

Jia Guiyun 靳桂雲. "Longshan shiqi de gucheng yu muzang" 龍山時期的古城與墓葬. *Huaxia kaogu* 華夏考古 1 (1998): 38–45, 5.

Jia Shiheng 賈士蘅. "Yin Zhou funü shenghuo de jige mian" 殷周婦女生活德幾個. *Dalu zazhi* 大陸雜誌 60, no. 5 (1980): 10–13.

Jia Zhiqiang 賈志强 and Mu Wenjun 穆文軍. "Taosi leixing shehui xingzhi de kaoguxue fenxi" 陶寺類型社會性質的考古學分析. *Xinzhou Shifan Xueyuan xuebao* 忻州師範學院學報 27, no. 3 (2011): 127–31.

Jian Bozan翦伯贊. *Xian Qin shi* 先秦史. Beijing: Daxue, 1990.

Jian Zhaoliang 簡朝亮, ed. *Xiaojing jizhu shushu – fu dushutang dawen* 孝經集注述疏 - 附讀書堂答問, annotated by Zhou Chunjian 周春健. Shanghai: Huadong Shifan Daxue chubanshe, 2011.

Jiang Huapeng 江華鵬. "Zhong Ri nüxing xingshi zhidu bijiao yanjiu" 中日女性姓氏制度比較研究. *Haixia kexue* 海峽科學 9 (2014): 77–79.

Jiang Tao 姜濤, Wang Longzheng 王龍正, and Qiao Bin 喬斌. *Sanmenxia Guo guo nüguizu mu chutu yuqi jingsui* 三門峽虢國女貴族墓出土玉器精髓. Taipei: Zhongzhi meishu, 2002.

Jiang Yuqiu 蔣玉秋. "Fengya shidai de nüfu zhi mei - cong *Shijing* kan Zhoudai nüzi fushi" 風雅時代的女服之美 - 從詩經看周代女子服飾.*Yishu sheji yanjiu* 藝術設計研究 3 (2014): 37–42.

Jiang Zhanghua 江章華. "Zhanguo shiqi gu Shu shehui de bianqian - cong muzang fenxi rushou" 戰國時期古蜀社會的變遷 - 從墓葬分析入手. *Chengdu kaogu yanjiu* 成都考古研究 (2009): 335–46.

Jiao, Tianlong. "Gender Studies in Chinese Neolithic Archaeology." In *Gender and the Archaeology of Death*, edited by Bettina Arnold and Nancy L. Wicker, 51–62. Walnut Creek: Rowman & Littlefield, 2001.

Jin Guiyun 靳桂雲. "Dong Zhou Qi guo guizu maizang zhidu yanjiu" 東周齊國貴族埋葬制度研究. *Guanzi xuekan* 管子學刊 3 (1994): 59–63.

———. "Longshan wenhua jumin shiwu jiegou yanjiu" 龍山文化居民食物結構研究. *Wenshizhe* 文史哲 2 (2013): 99–111.

Jing Jing 井精. "*Shijing* zhong meiren guannian dui Zhongguo shinühua de yingxiang" 詩經中美人觀念對中國仕女畫的影響. *Yishu baijia* 藝術百家 7 (2011): 223–25.

Johnson, Ian. *The Mozi: A Complete Translation*. New York: Columbia University Press, 2010.

Joyce, Rosemary A. "Archaeology of the Body." *Annual Review of Anthropology* 34 (2005): 139–58.

Kalinowski, Marc. "Diviners and Astrologers Under the Eastern Zhou: Transmitted Texts and Recent Archaeological Discoveries." In *Early Chinese Religion: Part One: Shang through Han (1250 BC–220 AD)*, edited by John Lagerwey and Marc Kalinowski, 341–96. Leiden: E.J. Brill, 2009.

Kandiyoti, Deniz. "Bargaining with Patriarchy." *Gender and Society* 2, no. 3 (1988): 274–90.

Kang Xuewei 康學偉. *Xian Qin xiaodao yanjiu* 先秦孝道研究. Taipei: Wenjin, 1992.

Kaplan, Hillard, Kim Hill, A. Magdalena Hurtado, and Jane Lancaster. "The Embodied Capital Theory of Human Evolution." In *Reproductive Ecology and Human Evolution*, edited by Peter T. Ellison, 293–317. Hawthorne, NY: Aldine de Gruyter, 2001.

Kaplan, Hillard S., Paul L. Hooper, and Michael Gurven. "The Evolutionary and Ecological Roots of Human Social Organization." *Philosophical Transactions of the Royal Society: Biological Sciences* 364, no. 1533 (2009): 3289–99.

Karlgren, Bernhard. *The Book of Odes*. Stockholm: Museum of Far Eastern Antiquities, 1950.

Katō Minoru 加藤實. "Lun Liu Xiang guanyu 'Youli' shidai de shijingxue" 論劉向關於幽厲時代的詩經學. *Jilin Shifan Xueyuan xuebao* 吉林師範學院學報 19, no. 4 (1998): 25–29.

Keightley, David N. "At the Beginning: The Status of Women in Neolithic and Shang China." *Nan Nü* 1, no. 1 (1999): 1–63.

———. "The Religious Commitment: Shang Theology and the Genesis of Chinese Political Culture." *History of Religions* 17, nos. 3–4 (1978): 211–25.

Kellogg, Susan. "The Woman's Room: Some Aspects of Gender Relations in Tenochtitlan in the Late Pre-Hispanic Period." *Ethnohistory* 42, no. 4 (1995): 563–76.

Kern, Martin. "Excavated Manuscripts and their Socratic Pleasures: Newly Discovered Challenges in Reading the 'Airs of the States.'" *Asiatische Studien* 61, no. 3 (2007): 775–93.

———. "Shi Jing Songs as Performance Texts: A Case Study of 'Chu Ci' (Thorny Caltrop)." *Early China* 25 (2000): 49–112.

Kinney, Anne Behnke. "Infant Abandonment in Early China." *Early China* 18 (1993): 107–38.

————. "The Mao Commentary to the Book of Odes as a Source for Women's History." In *Overt and Covert Treasures: Essays on the Sources for Chinese Women's History*, edited by Clara Wing-Chung Ho, 61–111. Hong Kong: The City University Press, 2012.

Knapp, Keith. "The Ru Reinterpretation of *Xiao*." *Early China* 20 (1995): 195–222.

Kong Anguo 孔安國. *Shangshu* 尚書, annotated by Kong Yingda 孔穎達 et al., collated by Ruan Yuan 阮元, n.p. Ruan Yuan edition, 1815; reprinted Taipei: Yiwen, 1955.

Kong Yingda 孔穎達, annotator. *Liji zhengyi* 禮記正義. Taipei: Zhonghua shuju (*Sibu beiyao* ed.), 1980.

Kurihara Keisuke 栗原圭介. *Kodai Chūgoku koninsei no rei rinen to keitai* 古代中國婚姻制の禮理念と形態. Tokyo: Tōhō shoten, 1982.

Lam, Joseph S.C. "The Presence and Absence of Female Musicians and Music in China." In *Women and Confucian Cultures in Premodern China, Korea, and Japan*, edited by Dorothy Ko, JaHyun Kim Haboush, and Joan R. Piggott, 97–122. Berkeley: University of California Press, 2003.

LeCount, Lisa J. "Like Water for Chocolate: Feasting and Political Ritual Among the Late Classic Maya at Xunantunich, Belize." *American Anthropologist* 103, no. 4 (2001): 935–53.

Lee, Jen-der. "Childbirth in Early Imperial China." *Nan Nü* 7, no. 2 (2005): 216–86.

Legge, James, and Robin R. Wang. "The Record of Rites (*Liji*)." In *Images of Women in Chinese Thought and Culture: Writings from the Pre-Qin Period through the Song Dynasty*, edited by Robin R. Wang, 48–60. Indianapolis: Hackett Publishing, 2003.

Leick, Gwendolyn. *Mesopotamia: The Invention of the City*. London: Penguin Books, 2001.

Lewis, Mark Edward. "The Mythology of Early China." In *Early Chinese Religion: Part One: Shang through Han (1250 BC–220 AD)*, edited by John Lagerwey and Marc Kalinowski, 543–94. Leiden: E.J. Brill, 2009.

Li, Chenyang. "The Confucian Ideal of Harmony." *Philosophy East and West* 56, no. 4 (2006): 583–603.

Li Fan 李凡. "Yinxu Fu Hao mu xieshi dongwuxing yuqi chutan" 殷墟婦好墓寫實動物形玉器初探. *Jingji yu shehui fazhan* 經濟與社會發展 10, no. 2 (2012): 120–21.

Li Fang 李昉, ed. *Taiping yulan* 太平預覽. Taipei: Taiwan shangwu yinshuguan, n.d.

Li Feng. *Bureaucracy and the State in Early China: Governing the Western Zhou*. Cambridge: Cambridge University Press, 2008.

————. *Landscape and Power in Early China: The Crisis and Fall of the Western Zhou 1045–771 BC*. Cambridge: Cambridge University Press, 2006.

Li Genpan 李根蟠, Huang Chongyue 黃崇岳, and Lu Xun 盧勳. *Zhongguo yuanshi shehui jingji yanjiu* 中國原始社會經濟研究. Beijing: Zhongguo shehui kexue, 1987.

Li Hengmei 李衡眉. *Zhaomu zhidu yanjiu* 昭穆制度研究. Jinan: Qilu shushe, 1996.

Li Hengmei 李衡眉 and Yu Xia 于霞. "Lu guo zhaomu zhidu lice" 魯國昭穆制度蠡測. *Henan Daxue xuebao* 河南大學學報 4 (2000): 42–46.

Li Jinhe 李金河. *Wei Jin Sui Tang hunyin xingtai yanjiu* 魏晉隋唐婚姻形態研究. Jinan: Qi Lu shushe, 2005.

Li Longhai 李龍海. "Cong Shangzu de hunyin yange ji shenghuo fangshi kan Shangdai de jicheng zhidu" 從商族的婚姻沿革及生活方式看商代的繼承制度. *Yindu xuekan* 殷都學刊 3 (2001): 14–20.

Li Peng 李鵬. "Lun *Shijing* nüxing miaoxie de shixing zhihui - yi yu wenhua wei li" 論詩經女性描寫的詩性智慧 - 以玉文化為例. *Xianyang Shifan Xueyuan xuebao* 咸陽師範學院學報 26, no. 5 (2011): 104–07.

Li Tong 李瞳. "*Shijing* zhong nüxing de duli yishi" 詩經中女性的獨立意識. *Shandong Guangbo Dianshi Daxue xuebao* 山東廣播電視大學學報 2 (2010): 37–39.

Li, Wai-yee. *The Readability of the Past in Early Chinese Historiography*. Cambridge, MA: Harvard University Asia Center, 2007.

Li, Xiaorong. *Women's Poetry of Late Imperial China*. Seattle: University of Washington Press, 2012.

Li Xiating 李夏廷 and Li Jiansheng 李建生. "Ye tan Changzhi Fenshuiling Dong Zhou mudi" 也談長治分水嶺東周墓地. *Zhongguo Guojia Bowuguan guankan* 中國國家博物館館刊 3 (2012): 15–31.

Li Xueqin 李學勤. "Lun 'Fu Hao' mu de niandai ji youguan wenti" 論婦好墓的年代及有關問題. *Wenwu* 文物 11 (1977): 33–35.

Li Xueshan 李雪山 and Guo Shengqiang 郭勝强. "Yin Shang wenhua de fanrong yu Zhongguo wenming de jincheng - cong Anyang Yinxu 5 hao mu, 54 hao mu he Xinganshang mu qingtongqi duibi tanqi" 殷商文化的繁榮與中國文明的進程 - 從安陽殷墟 5 號墓, 54 號墓和新干商墓青銅器對比談起. *Zhongyuan wenhua yanjiu* 中原文化研究 3 (2013): 53–58.

Li Xusheng 李旭昇. *Shuowen xinzheng* 說文新證. Fuzhou: Haixia and Fujian renmin, 2010.

Li Ya 李芽. *Zhongguo lidai zhuangshi* 中國歷代妝飾. Beijing: Zhongguo fangzhi chubanshe, 2004.

Li Yanong 李亞農. "Yindai shehui shenghuo" 殷代社會生活. In *Li Yanong shi lunji* 李亞農史論集, 399–602. Shanghai: Shanghai renmin chubanshe, 1962.

———. "Zhouzu de shizu zhidu yu Tuobazu de qianfengjian zhi" 周族的氏族制度與拓拔族的前封建制. In *Li Yanong shi lunji* 李亞農史論集, 323–96. Shanghai: Shanghai renmin chubanshe, 1962.

Li Yongkui 李永魁, Zhang Xiaopo 張曉波, and Zhang Xian 張弦. "Linxia shi faxian Machang leixing renxiang caotao" 臨夏市發現馬廠類型人像彩陶. *Kaogu yu wenwu* 考古與文物 3 (2003): 96.

Li Zhongcao 李仲操. "Liang Zhou jinwen zhong de funü chengwei" 兩周金文中的婦女稱謂. *Gu wenzi yanjiu* 古文字研究 18 (1992): 398–405.

Lian, Arlen. "The 'Shesheng' Adjustments to the Rites in Early China." *Journal of the American Oriental Society* 128, no. 4 (2008): 723–35.

Lian Shaoming 連劭名. "Shangdai de baiji yu yuji" 商代的拜祭與御祭. *Kaogu xuebao* 考古學報 1 (2011): 23–56.

Liang Anhe 梁安和. "Xian Qin shiqi de zhongnong sixiang ji qi cuoshi" 先秦時期的重農思想及其措施. *Gujin nongye* 古今農業 3 (1998): 31–36.

Liang Lei 梁蕾. "Lun Nü Wa yu Xiwangmu xingxiang ji yanbian" 論女媧與希望母形象及演變. *Shaanxi Qingnian Qiye Xueyuan xuebao* 陝西青年企業學院學報 1 (2014): 70–74.

Liang Ping 梁平. "Cai li jing fan, mei bu sheng shou - *Shijing Guofeng* zhong nüxing xingxiang mei de tanxi" 彩麗競繁美不勝收 - 詩經國風中女性形象美的探析. *Xibei Nonglin Keji Daxue xuebao* 西北農林科技大學學報 4, no. 3 (2004): 124–27.

Liang Xingpeng 梁星彭. "Shilun Keshengzhuang erqi wenhua" 試論客省莊二期文化. *Kaogu xuebao* 考古學報 4 (1994): 397–423.

Liaoning Sheng Wenwu Kaogu Yanjiusuo 遼寧省文物考古研究所. "Liaoning Niuheliang Hongshan wenwu 'nüshen miao' yu jishi zhongqun fajue jianbao" 遼寧牛河梁紅山文化女神廟與積石冢群發掘簡報. *Wenwu* 文物 8 (1986): 1–17.

Lin Fushi 林富士. *Handai de wuzhe* 漢代的巫者. Taipei: Daoxiang chubanshe, 1988.

Linduff, Katheryn M. "Many Wives, One Queen in Shang China." In *Ancient Queens: Archaeological Explorations,* edited by Sarah Milledge Nelson, 59–75. Walnut Creek, CA: AltaMira Press, 2003.

———. "Women's Lives Memorialized in Burial in Ancient China at Anyang." In *In Pursuit of Gender: Worldwide Archaeological Approaches,* edited by Sarah Milledge Nelson and Myriam Rosen-Ayalon, 257–87. Walnut Creek, CA: AltaMira Press, 2002.

Linduff, Katheryn M., Robert D. Drennan, and Gideon Shelach. "Early Complex Societies in NE China: The Chifeng International Collaborative Archaeological Research Project." *Journal of Field Archaeology* 29, nos. 1/2 (2002–2004): 45–73.

Liu Dehan 劉德漢. *Dong Zhou funü shenghuo* 東周婦女生活. Taipei: Xuesheng shuju, 1976.

Liu Dongying 劉冬穎. "'Shijing' zhong suojian de Zhoudai tongxing bu hun lisu" 詩經中所見的周代同姓不婚禮俗. *Zhida xuebao* 職大學報 1 (2003): 92–93, 101.

Liu Guiying 劉桂英. "Xi Zhou yu Xiwangmu jianjiaokao" 西周與西王母建交考. *Hebei Daxue xuebao* 河北大學學報 33, no. 1 (2008): 89–92.

Liu Houqin 劉厚琴. "Handai muxi yishi yanjiu" 漢代母系意識研究. *Xianyang Shifan Xueyuan xuebao* 咸陽師範學院學報 29, no. 3 (2014): 27–31.

Liu Hui 劉慧. "Ye shuo Dawenkou wenhua baya xiguan de yuanyin" 也說大汶口文化拔牙習慣的因由. *Minsu yanjiu* 民俗研究 4 (1996): 26–29.

Liu Jie 劉潔. "Zhoudai de fuqi hezangmu" 周代的夫妻合葬墓. *Qingdao Daxue Shifan Xueyuan xuebao* 青島大學師範學院學報 2 (2009): 78–83.

Liu Li. "Ancestor Worship: An Archaeological Investigation of Ritual Activities in Neolithic North China." *Journal of East Asian Archaeology* 2, nos. 1–2 (2000): 129–64.

Liu Li 劉莉. "Shandong Longshan wenhua muzang xingtai yanjiu: Longshan shiqi shehui fenhua, yili huodong, ji jiaohuan guanxi de kaoguxue fenxi" 山東龍山文化墓葬形態研究: 龍山時期社會分化, 禮儀活動, 及交換關係的考古學分析. *Wenwu jikan* 文物季刊 2 (1999): 32–49.

Liu Pu 劉溥. *Qinghai caitao wenshi* 青海彩陶紋飾. Xining: Qinghai Renmin, 1989.

Liu, Qingping. "Filiality versus Sociality and Individuality: On Confucianism and Consanguinitism." *Philosophy East and West* 53, no. 2 (2003): 234–50.

Liu Qiyi 劉啓益. "Xi Zhou jinwen zhong suojian de Zhou wang houfei" 西周金文中所見的周王后妃. *Kaogu yu wenwu* 考古與文物 4 (1980): 85–90.

Liu Weiwei 劉瑋瑋. "Daoxue zunchong nüxing yuanyuan tanxi" 道學尊崇女性淵源探析. *Qinghai shehui kexue* 青海社會科學 5 (2012): 13–17.

Liu Xianzhang 劉憲章. "Dawenkou zangsu de zongjiao neihan" 大汶口葬俗的宗教內涵. *Taishan Xiangzhen Qiye Zhigong Daxue xuebao* 泰山鄉鎮企業職工大學學報 3 (2001): 12–15.

Liu Xu 劉昫 et al. *Jiu Tangshu* 舊唐書, annotated by Liu Jie 劉節 and Chen Naiqian 陳乃乾. Beijing: Zhonghua, 1975.

Liu Yi 劉毅, Zhou Wenjie 周文杰, and Cao Jingzhuang 曹敬庄. "Yandi Yandi ling shiji zhi yanjiu" 炎帝炎帝陵史籍之研究. *Hunan shehui kexue* 湖南社會科學 2 (2014): 250–55.

Liu Yuan 劉源. *Zhou Shang jizu li yanjiu* 周商祭祖禮研究. Beijing: Shangwu yinshuguan, 2004.

———. "Shangdai houqi jizu yishi leixing" 商代後期祭祖儀式類型. *Lishi yanjiu* 歷史研究 6 (2002): 80–94.

Liu Zenggui 劉增貴. "Handai funü de mingzi" 漢代婦女的名字. *Xin shixue* 新史學 7, no. 4 (1996): 33–94.

———. *Handai hunyin zhidu* 漢代婚姻制度. Taipei: Huashi, 1980.

Liu Zheng 劉正. *Jinwen miaozhi yanjiu* 金文廟制研究. Beijing: Zhongguo shehui kexue, 2004.

Liu Zongtang 劉宗棠 and Zhang Tai 張泰. "Lun Chunqiu shiqi 'zheng' hunzhi de he 'li' xing" 論春秋時期烝婚制的合禮性. *Xueshu luntan* 學術論壇 2 (2006): 169–71.

Lowie, Robert H. *Primitive Society*. New York: Boni and Liveright, 1920.

Lu Hong 逯宏. *Zhoudai Yin Shang liyue jieshou yanjiu* 周代殷商禮樂接受研究. Beijing: Zhongguo shehui kexue chubanshe, 2013.

Lu Xiaona 魯小娜. "Shangdai nüjie Fu Hao yu nüxing duikang yishi" 商代女傑婦好與女性對抗意識. *Yuwen jiaoxue tongxun* 語文教學通訊 7 (2013): 94–96.

Lü Yahu 呂亞虎. "Dong Zhou shiqi 'zheng' 'bao' hun xianxiang kaobian" 東周時期烝報婚現象考辨. *Renwen zazhi* 人文雜誌 6 (2004): 138–44.

———. *Zhanguo Qin Han jianbo wenxian suo jian wushu yanjiu* 戰國秦漢簡帛文獻所見巫術研究. Beijing: Kexue, 2010.

Lü Yahu 呂亞虎 and Feng Lizhen 馮麗珍. "Dong Zhou shiqi nannü shihun nianling wenti kaobian" 東周時期男女適婚年齡問題考辨. *Shaanxi Ligong Xueyuan xuebao* 陝西理工學院學報 2 (2005): 80–83.

Luan Fengshi 欒豐實. "Shilun Yangshao shiqi zhongqi de shehui fenceng" 試論仰韶時期中期的社會分層. *Dongfang kaogu* 東方考古 9 (2012): 44–56.

Luo Hongzeng 羅宏曾. *Jianming Zhongguo gudai shi* 簡明中國古代史. Beijing: Qiushi, 1986.

Luo Kun 羅琨. "Shilun Shangdai Yindu renkou de ziran goucheng - jian tan ruhe liyong kaogu ziliao yanjiu lishi" 試論商代殷都人口的自然構成 - 兼談如何利用考古資料研究歷史. *Kaogu* 考古 4 (1995): 346–54.

Luo Yunhuan 羅運環. "Chu guo de taizi zhidu yanjiu" 楚國的太子制度研究. *Jianghan luntan* 江漢論壇 7 (2000): 70–72.

Lyons, Diane, and A. Catherine D'Andrea. "Griddles, Ovens, and Agricultural Origins: An Ethnoarchaeological Study of Bread Baking in Highland Ethiopia." *American Anthropologist* 105, no. 3 (2003): 515–30.

Ma Jifan 馬季凡. "Shangai zhongqi de renji zhidu yanjiu - yi Zhengzhou Xiaoshuangqiao Shangdai yizhi de renji yicun wei li" 商代中期的人祭制度研究 - 以鄭州小雙橋商代遺址的人祭遺存為例. *Zhongyuan wenwu* 中原文物 3 (2004): 37–44.

Ma Wei 馬薇. "Qianxi Zhongguo gudai nüxing shehui diwei bianqian" 淺析中國古代女性社會地位變遷. *Lanzhou Jiaoyu Xueyuan xuebao* 蘭州教育學院學報 28, no. 4 (2012): 23–24.

Ma Yan 馬艷. "Anhui Weichisi Dawenkou wenhua tukengmu suizangpin suo fanying de shehui xianxiang" 安徽尉遲寺大汶口文化土坑墓隨葬品所反映的社會現象. *Sichuan wenwu* 四川文物 5 (2005): 22–29.

Man, Eva Kit Wah. "Discourses on Female Bodily Aesthetics and Its Early Revelations in *The Book of Songs*." In *Overt and Covert Treasures: Essays on the Sources for Chinese Women's History*, edited by Clara Wing-Chung Ho, 113–30. Hong Kong: The City University Press, 2012.

Mao Ruilin 毛瑞林. "Huanghe shangyou de zaoqi qingtong wenming: Lintan Mogou yizhi Qijia wenhua mudi" 黃河上游的早期青铜文明: 臨潭麘溝遺址齊家文化墓地. *Dazhong kaogu* 大眾考古 3 (2013): 42–47.

McCorriston, Joy. "The Fiber Revolution: Textile Extensification, Alienation, and Social Stratification in Ancient Mesopotamia." *Current Anthropology* 38, no. 4 (1997): 517–35.

McMahon, Keith. "Women Rulers in Imperial China." *Nan Nü* 15, no. 2 (2013): 179–218.

———. *Women Shall Not Rule: Imperial Wives and Concubines in China from Han to Liao*. Lanham, MD: Rowman & LIttlefield, 2013.

Mi Yongying 米永盈. "Dong Zhou shiqi nüxing yiren shehui diwei guankui - yi youguan Qi guo nüyue de wenxian yu kaogu faxian wei shijiao" 東周時期女性藝人社會地位管窺 - 以有關齊國女樂的文獻與考古發現為視角. *Hubei shehui kexue* 湖北社會科學 8 (2014): 118–20.

Milburn, Olivia. "Gender, Sexuality and Power in Early China: The Changing Biographies of Lord Ling of Wei and Lady Nanzi." *Nan Nü* 12, no. 1 (2010): 1–29.

Miller, A.G. *Maya Rulers of Time: A Study of Architectural Sculpture at Tikal, Guatemala*. Philadelphia: University Museum, 1986.

Minnegal, Monica, and Peter D. Dwyer. "Women, Pigs, God and Evolution: Social and Economic Change among Kubo People of Papua New Guinea." *Oceania* 68, no. 1 (1997): 47–60.

Mo Di 墨翟. *Mozi* 墨子, annotated by Sun Yirang 孫詒讓. Taipei: Huazheng, 1987.

Moore, Henrietta L. *Feminism and Anthropology*. Cambridge: Polity, 1988.

Morgan, Lewis Henry. *Ancient Society or Researches in the Lines of Human Progress from Savagery through Barbarism to Civilization*, edited by Eleanor Burke Leacock. Glouster, MA: Peter Smith, 1974.

Mu Haiting 穆海亭. "Zhoudai jinwen zhong de fuming" 周代金文中的婦名. *Wenbo* 文博 5 (2007): 54–55, 15.

Mullis, Eric C. "Toward a Confucian Ethic of the Gift." *Dao* 7, no. 2 (2008): 175–94.

Mumford, T.F. "Death Do Us Unite: Xunzang and Joint Burial in Ancient China." *Papers on Far Eastern History* 27 (2008): 1–19.

Murdock, G.P. *Social Structure*. New York: Macmillan, 1949.

Murdock, George P., and Caterina Provost. "Factors in the Division of Labor by Sex: A Cross-Cultural Analysis." *Ethnology* 12, no. 2 (1973): 203–26.

Nakassis, Dimitri, William A. Parkinson, and Michael L. Galaty. "Redistribution in Aegean Palatial Societies: Redistributive Economies from a Theoretical and Cross-Cultural Perspective." *American Journal of Archaeology* 115, no. 2 (2011): 177–84.

Nanjing Bowuyuan 南京博物院, Xuzhou Bowuguan 徐州博物館, and Pizhou Bowuguan 邳州博物館. "Jiangsu Pizhou Liangwangcheng yizhi Dawenkou wenhua yicun fajue jianbao" 江蘇邳州梁王城遺址大汶口文化遺存發掘簡報. *Dongnan wenhua* 東南文化 4 (2013): 21–41.

Nash, June. "The Aztecs and the Ideology of Male Dominance." *Signs* 4 (1978): 349–62.

Nelson, Sarah Milledge. "Ancient Queens: An Introduction." In *Ancient Queens: Archaeological Explorations*, edited by Sarah Milledge Nelson, 1–18. Walnut Creek, CA: AltaMira Press, 2003.

———. *Gender in Archaeology: Analyzing Power and Prestige*, second edition. Walnut Creek, CA: AltaMira Press, 2004.

———. "Ideology, Power, and Gender: Emergent Complex Society in Northeastern China." In *In Pursuit of Gender: Worldwide Archaeological Approaches*, edited by Sarah Milledge Nelson and Myriam Rosen-Ayalon, 73–80. Walnut Creek, CA: AltaMira Press, 2002.

———. *Shamanism and the Origin of States: Spirit, Power, and Gender in East Asia*. Walnut Creek, CA: Left Coast Press, 2008.

Ngo Van Xuyet. *Divination Magie et Politique dans la Chine Ancienne*. Paris: Presses Universitaires de France, 1976.

Nishijima Sadao. "The Economic and Social History of the Former Han." In *The Cambridge History of China, Volume I, The Ch'in and Han Empires, 221 B.C.–A.D. 220*, edited by Denis Twitchett and Michael Loewe, 545–607. Cambridge: Cambridge University Press, 1986.

Nylan, Michael. "Afterword." In *Chang'an 26 BCE: An Augustan Age in China*, edited by Michael Nylan and Griet Vankeerberghen, 505–17. Seattle: University of Washington Press, 2015.

Ortner, Sherry B. "Gender Hegemonies." *Cultural Critique* 14 (1989–1990): 35–80.

Paglia, Camille. "Erich Neumann: Theorist of the Great Mother." *Arion* 13, no. 3 (2006): 1–14.

Pang, Sunjoo. "The Consorts of King Wu and King Wen in the Bronze Inscriptions of Early China." *Momumenta Serica* 33 (1977-1978): 124–35.

Pang Yaoxian 龐耀先 and Pang Ping 龐萍. "Majiayao wowen caitaoweng yongtu lice - jian tan wengguan zangsu de jige wenti" 馬家窯渦文彩陶甕用途蠡測 - 兼談甕棺葬俗的幾個問題. *Sichou zhi lu* 絲綢之路 8 (2010): 13–17.

Parker, Seymour, and Hilda Parker. "The Myth of Male Superiority: Rise and Demise." *American Anthropologist* 81, no. 2 (1979): 289–309.

Pearson, Richard. "Chinese Neolithic Burial Patterns: Problems of Method and Interpretation." *Early China* 13 (1988): 1–45.

———. "Social Complexity in Chinese Coastal Neolithic Sites." *Science* 213, no. 4512 (1981): 1078–86.

Pei Mingxiang 裴明相. "Lun Zhengzhou shi Xiaoshuangqiao Shangdai qianqi jisi yizhi" 論鄭州市小雙橋商代前期祭祀遺址. *Zhongyuan wenwu* 中原文物 2 (1996): 4–8.

Peregrine, Peter. "Some Political Aspects of Craft Specialization." *World Archaeology* 23, no. 1 (1991): 1–11.

Pines, Yuri. *Foundations of Confucian Thought: Intellectual Life in the Chunqiu Period, 722–453 B.C.E.* Honolulu: University of Hawaii Press, 2002.

Puett, Michael J. *To Become a God: Cosmology, Sacrifice, and Self-Divination in Early China*. Cambridge, MA: Harvard University Press, 2002.

Pulleyblank, Edwin G. "Ji 姬 and Jiang 姜: The Role of Exogamic Clans in the Organization of the Zhou Polity." *Early China* 25 (2000): 1–27.

Qi Fa 齊發. "Zhanguo shiqi de jiating jiegou" 戰國時期的家庭結構. *Huazhong Keji Daxue xuebao* 華中科技大學學報 2 (2003): 58–61.

Qi Hangfu 齊航福. "Cong Yinxu jiaguwen kan Shangdai funü shehui diwei" 從殷墟甲骨文看商代婦女社會地位. *Zhongzhou xuekan* 中州學刊 12 (2014): 128–32.

Qi Wenxin 齊文心. "'Fu' zi benyi shitan" 婦字本意試探. In *Jinian Yinxu jiaguwen faxian yibai zhounian guoji yantaohui lunwenji* 紀念殷墟甲骨文發現一百週年國際學術研討會論文集, edited by Wang Yuxin 王宇信 and Song Zhenhao 宋鎮豪, 149–54. Beijing: Shehui kexue wenxian chubanshe, 2003.

Qian Yaopeng 錢耀鵬, Zhou Jing 周靜, Mao Ruilin 毛瑞林, and Xie Yan 謝焱. "Gansu Lintan Mogo Qijia wenhua mudi fajue de shouhuo yu yiyi –2008 niandu quanguo shida kaogu faxian zhi yi" 甘肅臨潭磨溝齊家文化墓地發掘的收穫與意義 - 2008 年度全國十大考古新發現之一. *Xibei Daxue xuebao* 西北大學學報 5 (2009): 5–10.

Qian Zongfan 錢宗范. *Zhoudai zongfa zhidu yanjiu* 周代宗法制度研究. Guilin: Guangxi Shifan Daxue chubanshe, 1989.

Qiang Gao and Yun Kuen Lee. "A Biological Perspective on Yangshao Kinship." *Journal of Anthropological Archaeology* 12, no. 3 (1993): 266–98.

Qiao Xin 喬鑫. "Lun Yinxu 'yi xue he zang' mu de tezhi" 論殷墟異穴合葬墓的特質. *Wenxuejie* 文學界 4 (2011): 149–50.

Qiao Xinhua 喬新華 and Yang Guoyong 楊國勇. "Xian Qin funü juese bianqian de yuanyin" 先秦婦女角色變遷的原因. *Shanxi Daxue xuebao* 山西大學學報 8 (2002): 20–23.

Qin Yangang 秦燕鋼 and Sun Yingwei 孫英偉. "'Zhou Nan Guanju' he Zhoudai guizu de yinghunzhi" 周南關雎和周代貴族的媵婚制. *Zhonghua wenhua luntan* 中華文化論壇 3 (2006): 34–39.

Rao Zongyi 饒宗頤. "Fu Hao mu tongqi, yuqi suojian shixing fangguo kao" 婦好墓銅器玉器所見氏姓方國考. In *Gu wenzi yanjiu* 古文字研究 12, 299–307. Beijing: Zhonghua shuju, 1985.

Raphals, Lisa. "Arguments by Women in Early Chinese Texts." *Nan Nü* 3, no. 2 (2001): 157–95.

———. *Sharing the Light: Representations of Women and Virtue in Early China*. Albany: State University of New York Press, 1998.

Redclift, Nanneke. "Rights in Women: Kinship, Culture and Materialism." In *Engels Revisited: New Feminist Essays*, edited by Janet Sayers, Mary Evans, and Nanneke Redclift, 113–44. London: Tavistock, 1987.

Ren Wei 任偉. "Cong kaogu faxian kan Xi Zhou Yan guo Yin yimin zhi shehui zhuangkuang" 從考古發現看西周燕國殷遺民之社會狀況. *Zhongyuan wenwu* 中原文物 2 (2001): 55–59.

Robb, John E. "The Archaeology of Symbols." *Annual Review of Anthropology* 27 (1998): 329–46.

Rogers, Susan Carol. "Female Forms of Power and the Myth of Male Dominance: A Model of Female/Male Interaction in Peasant Society." *American Ethnologist* 2, no. 4 (1975): 727–56.

Rosemont, Jr., Henry, and Roger T. Ames. *The Chinese Classic of Family Reverence: A Philosophical Translation of the* Xiaojing. Honolulu: University of Hawaii Press, 2009.

Schafer, Edward H. "Ritual Exposure in Ancient China." *Harvard Journal of Asiatic Studies* 14, nos. 1/2 (1951): 130–84.

Schlegel, Alice. *Male Dominance and Female Autonomy: Domestic Authority in Matrilineal Societies.* New Haven: HRAF Press, 1972.

———. "Status, Property, and the Value on Virginity," *American Ethnologist* 18, no. 4 (1991): 719–34.

Schneider, Betty. "Body Decoration in Mozambique." *African Arts* 6, no. 2 (1973): 26–31.

Schuessler, Axel. *ABC Etymological Dictionary of Old Chinese.* Honolulu: University of Hawaii Press, 2007.

Selach, Gideon. "Marxist and Post-Marxist Paradigms for the Neolithic." In *Gender and Chinese Archaeology*, edited by Katheryn M. Linduff and Yan Sun, 11–27. Walnut Creek, CA: Altamira Press, 2004.

Service, Elman R. *Origins of the State and Civilization: The Process of Cultural Evolution.* New York: W.W. Norton & Company, 1975.

———. *Primitive Social Organization: An Evolutionary Perspective.* New York: Random House, 1962.

Shandong Sheng Bowuguan 山東省博物館. "Tantan Dawenkou wenhua" 談談大汶口文化. *Wenwu* 文物 4 (1978): 58–66.

Shang Lixin 尚麗新. "*Shijing* yingjia shi yu Zhoudai yinghun wenhua" 詩經媵嫁詩與周代媵婚文化. *Shanghai Shifan Daxue xuebao* 上海師範大學學報 31, no. 1 (2002): 65–70.

Shang Minjie 尚民杰. "Dui shiqian shiqi chengnian nannü hezang mu de chubu tantao" 對史前時期成年男女合葬的初步探討. *Zhongguoshi yanjiu* 中國史研究 3 (1991): 50–57.

Shanghai shi Wenwu Baoguan Weiyuanhui 上海市文物保管委員會. "Fuquanshan yizhi disanci fajue de zhongyao xianxiang" 福泉山遺址第三次發掘的重要現象. *Dongnan wenhua* 東南文化 3 (1987): 51.

Shanxi sheng Linfen Xingshu Wenhuaju 山西臨汾行署文化局. "Shanxi Linfen Xiajin cun Taosi wenhua mudi fajue baogao" 山西臨汾下靳村陶寺文化墓地發掘報告. *Kaogu xuebao* 考古學報 4 (1999): 459–86.

Shaughnessy, Edward L. "Chronologies of Ancient China, a Critique of the Xia-Shang-Zhou Chronology Project." In *Windows on the Chinese World: Reflections by Five Historians*, edited by Clara Wing-Chung Ho, 15–28. Lanham, MD: Lexington Books, 2008.

———. "The Composition of the 'Qian' and 'Kun' Hexagrams of the *Zhouyi*." In *Before Confucius: Studies in the Creation of the Chinese Classics*, 197–219. Albany: State University of New York Press, 1997.

———. "From Liturgy to Literature: The Ritual Contexts of the Earliest Poems in the Book of Poetry." *Hanxue yanjiu* 漢學研究 13, no. 1 (1995): 133–64.

———. "Marriage, Divorce, and Revolution: Reading Between the Lines of the *Book of Changes*." *Journal of Asian Studies* 51, no. 3 (1992): 587–99.

Sheng Ying 盛英. "Lun Zhongguo shanggu nüshen" 論中國上古女神. *Zhongguo wenhua yanjiu* 中國文化研究 4 (2012): 130–41.

Shi Tao 石陶. "Huanghe shangyou de fuxi shizu shehui – Qijia wenhua shehui jingji xingtai de tansuo" 黃河上游的父系氏族社會 – 齊家文化社會經濟型態的探索. *Kaogu* 考古 1 (1961): 3–11.

Shiga Shūzō 滋賀秀三. *Chūgoku kazokuhō no genri* 中國家族法の原理. Tokyo: Sōbunsha, 1967.

Shima Kunio 島邦男. *Inkyo bokuji kenkyū* 殷墟卜辞研究. Hirosaki: Chūkokugaku Kenkyūkai, 1958.

Shimomi Takao 下見隆雄. *Kō to bosei no mekanizumu - Chūgoku joseishi no shigi* 孝と母姓のメカニズム - 中国女性史の視座 (Tokyo: Kenbun, 1997).

Shirakawa Shizuka 白川靜. *Kōkotsubun no sekai* 甲骨文の世界. Tokyo: Heibonsha, 1972.

———. *Setsubun shingi* 說文新義. Kobe: Hakutsuru Bijutsukan, 1969-1974.

Silverblatt, Irene. *Moon, Sun, and Witches: Gender Ideologies and Class in Inca and Colonial Peru*. Princeton: Princeton University Press, 1987.

Smith, D. Howard. "Chinese Religion in the Shang Dynasty." *Numen* 8, no. 2 (1961): 142–50.

Song Hua 宋華. "Fu Hao 'kuilongwen' bianzu fangding yanjiu" 婦好夔龍紋扁足方鼎研究. *Wenwu jianding yu jianshang* 文物鑒定與鑒賞 9 (2013): 50–52.

Song Yanpo 宋艷波, Jia Jiali 宋嘉莉 and He Deliang 何德亮. "Shandong Tengzhou Zhuanglixi Longshan wenhua yizhi chutu dongwu yicun fenxi" 山東滕州庄里西龍山文化遺址出土動物遺存分析. *Dongfang kaogu* 東方考古 9 (2012): 609–26.

Song Zhenhao 宋鎮豪. "Xia Shang renkou chutan" 夏商人口初探. *Lishi yanjiu* 歷史研究 4 (1991): 92–106.

———. *Xia Shang shehui shenghuo shi* 夏商社會生活史. Beijing: Zhongguo shehui kexue chubanshe, 1994.

Soper, A. "King Wu Ting's Victory of the 'Realm of Demons.'" *Artibus Asiae* 17, no. 1 (1954): 55–60.

Sun Dehua 孫德華. "Cong *Shijing* de aiqing shi kan Zhoudai de pinhunli ji hunzhi tedian" 從詩經的愛情詩看周代的聘婚禮及婚制特點. *Changchun Daxue xuebao* 長春大學學報 7 (2007): 58–60.

Sun Hongbin 孫紅彬. "*Shijing* zhong de mei yu Zhoudai de benzhe bu jin" 詩經中的媒與周代的奔者不禁. *Wenbo* 文博 4 (2002): 24–29.

Sun Jie 孫潔. "Cong *Shijing* kan Zhoudai de chuqizhi" 從詩經看周代的出妻制. *Anhui wenxue* 安徽文學 5 (2007): 63–64.

Sun Lei 孫蕾. "Henan Shengchi Duzhong yizhi Yangshao wanqi rengu de zhigu yanjiu" 河南澠池篤忠遺址仰韶晚期人骨的肢骨研究. *Jiangnan kaogu* 5 (2014): 93–99.

Sun Lei 孫蕾 and Wu Zhejiang 武志江. "Shengchi Duzhong yizhi Yangshao wenhua wanqi rengu yanjiu" 澠池篤忠遺址仰韶文化晚期人骨研究. *Huaxia kaogu* 華夏考古 3 (2010): 1–9.

Sun Litao 孫立濤. "'Fu Xi' minghao kaoxi" 伏羲名號考析. *Qinghai shehui kexue* 青海社會科學 2 (2014): 105–11.

Sun, Yan and Hongyu Yang. "Gender Ideology and Mortuary Practice in Northwestern China." In *Gender and Chinese Archaeology*, edited by Katheryn M. Linduff and Yan Sun, 29–46. Walnut Creek, CA: Altamira Press, 2004.

Sun Zuchu 孫祖初. "Banpo wenhua zai yanjiu" 半坡文化再研究. *Kaogu xuebao* 考古學報 4 (1998): 419–46.

———. "Lun zhongyuan xin shiqi shidai zhongqi wenhua" 論中原新石器時代中期文化. *Wenwu jikan* 文物季刊 4 (1996): 39–57.

Takashima, Ken-ichi. *A Little Primer of Chinese Oracle-Bone Inscriptions with Some Exercises*. Wiesbaden: Harrossowitz Verlag, 2015.

Takigawa Kamitaro 瀧川龜太郎. *Shiki kaichū kōshō* 史記會注烤證. Tokyo: 1934; reprinted Taipei: Zhonghua shuju, 1977.

T'ang Chün-I. "The T'ien Ming [Heavenly Ordinance] in Pre-Ch'in China." *Philosophy East and West* 11, no. 4 (1962): 195–218.

Tang Jigen. "The Burial Ritual of the Shang Dynasty: A Reconstruction," in *Exploring China's Past: New Discoveries and Studies in Archaeology and Art*, translated and edited by Roderick Whitfield and Wang Tao, 173–81. London: Saffron, 1999.

Tang Jinqiong 唐錦琼. "Yinxu Huayuanzhuang dongdi M60 de sangsu ji qi tezhi" 殷墟花園庄東地 M 60 的葬俗及其特質. *Kaogu* 考古 3 (2010): 80–90.

Thatcher, Melvin P. "Marriages of the Ruling Elite in the Spring and Autumn Period." In *Marriage and Inequality in Chinese Society*, edited by Rubie S. Watson and Patricia B. Ebrey, 25–57. Berkeley: University of California Press, 1991.

Thorp, Robert L. *China in the Early Bronze Age: Shang Civilization*. Philadelphia: University of Pennsylvania Press, 2006.

Thote, Alain. "Shang and Zhou Funeral Practices: Interpretation of Material Vestiges." In *Early Chinese Religion: Part One: Shang through Han (1250 BC–220 AD)*, edited by John Lagerwey and Marc Kalinowski, 103–42. Leiden: E.J. Brill, 2009.

Tian Fu 田夫 (Xing Yitian 邢義田). "Cong *Lienü zhuan* kan Zhongguoshi muai de liulu" 從列女傳看中國式母愛的流露. In *Zhongguo funüshi lunwenji sanji* 中國婦女史論文集三集, edited by Bao Jialin 鮑家麟, 19–27. Taipei: Sanlian, 1993.

Tiger, Lionel. *Men in Groups*. New York: Random House, 1969.

Tolstoy, P. "Morgan and Soviet Anthropological Thought." *American Anthropologist* 54, no. 1 (1952): 8–17.

Tong Zhe 童哲, ed. *Han Fei zi jijie* 韓非子集解. Beijing: Zhonghua, 1998.

Trigger, Bruce G. *Understanding Early Civilizations: A Comparative Study*. Cambridge: Cambridge University Press, 2003.

Tung, Jowen R. *Fables for the Patriarchs: Gender Politics in Tang Discourse*. Lanham, MD: Rowman & Littlefield, 2000.

Turner, Victor. *The Forest of Symbols: Aspects of Ndembu Ritual*. Ithaca: Cornell University Press, 1967.

Van Auken, Newell Ann. "A Formal Analysis of the *Chuenchiou* 春秋 (Spring and Autumn Classic)." PhD dissertation, University of Washington, 2006.

Van Norden, Bryan W., trans. *Mengzi: With Selections from Traditional Commentaries*. Indianapolis: Hackett Publishing, 2008.

Vandermeersch, Léon. *Wangdao ou la Voie Royale: Recherches sur l'Esprit des Institutions de la Chine Archaïque*. Paris: Ecole Française d'Extrême-Orient, 1977.

VanPool, Christine S., and Todd L. VanPool. "Gender in Middle Range Societies: A Case Study in Casas Grandes Iconography." *American Antiquity* 71, no. 1 (2006): 53–75.

von Glahn, Richard. *The Economic History of China: From Antiquity to the Nineteenth Century*. Cambridge: Cambridge University Press, 2016.

Waguespack, Nicole M. "The Organization of Male and Female Labor in Foraging Societies: Implications for Early Paleoindian Archaeology." *American Anthropologist* 107, no. 4 (2005): 666–76.

Waley, Arthur. *The Book of Songs*, edited by Joseph R. Allen. New York: Grove Press, 1996.

Walsh, Eileen Rose. "From Nü Guo to Nü'er Guo: Negotiating Desire in the Land of the Mosuo." *Modern China* 31, no. 4 (2005): 448–86.

Wang Chaochao 王朝潮. "Zhanguo houqi Qin guo waiqi yanjiu" 戰國後期秦國外戚研究. *Bohai Daxue xuebao* 渤海大學學報 2 (2011): 107–11.

Wang Fang 王方. "Dong Zhou nüxing faxing fashi chulun" 東周女性髮型髮飾初論. *Kaogu yu wenwu* 考古與文物 3 (2011): 46–57.

Wang Fen 王芬. "Mudi kongjian jiegou yu shehui guanxi de guanlianxing sikao - yi Dawenkou shiqi mudi wei li" 墓地空間結構與社會關係的關聯性思考 - 以大汶口文化時期墓地為例. *Dongfang kaogu* 東方考古 9 (2012): 112–37.

Wang Guangming 王光明. "Shilun Dawenkou wenhua de hezangmu" 試論大汶口文化的合葬墓. *Wenwu chunqiu* 文物春秋 1 (2005): 1–9.

Wang Guofu 汪國富. "Cong Dadiwan yi, erqi wenhua yicun kan woguo gudai muxi shizu shehui" 從大地灣一, 二期文化遺存看我國古代母系氏族社會. *Tianshui Shifan Xueyuan xuebao* 天水師範學院學報 22, no. 6 (2002): 35–37.

Wang Guowei 王國維. "Nü zi shuo" 女字說. In *Guantang jilin* 觀堂集林, 163–66. Taipei: Heluo tushu chubanshe, 1975.

Wang Huajie 王華杰. "Guanyu Chuodun yizhi Majiahong wenhua muzang: Zangshi xingbie guanxi de tuice" 關於綽墩遺址馬家洪文化墓葬: 葬式與性別關係的推測. *Changjiang wenhua luncong* 長江文化論叢 (2007): 17–21.

Wang Jianhua 王建華. "Henan Yangshao shidai renkou guimo ji xiangguan wenti de chubu yanjiu" 河南仰韶時代人口規模及相關問題的初步研究. *Huaxia kaogu* 華夏考古 4 (2010): 49–57.

Wang Jiaxin 王佳欣. "Cong jiaguwen zixing kaocha Yin Shang shehui de hunsang xiguan" 從甲骨文字形考察殷商社會的婚喪習慣. *Lishui Xueyuan xuebao* 麗水學院學報 36, no. 1 (2014): 48–51.

Wang Kelin 王克林. "Taosi wanqi Longshan wenhua yu Xia wenhua - lun Huaxia wenming de xingcheng (xia)" 陶寺晚期龍山文化與夏文化 - 論華夏文明的形成 (下). *Wenwu shijie* 文物世界 6 (2001): 23–31.

Wang Lei 王磊. "Shilun Longshan wenhua shidai de renxun he renji" 試論龍山文化時代的人殉和人祭. *Dongnan wenhua* 東南文化 4 (1999): 22–27.

Wang Ningsheng 汪寧生. "Yangshao Burial Customs and Social Organization: A Comment on the Theory of Yangshao Matrilineal Society and Its Methodology." *Early China* 11–12 (1985–7): 6–32.

———. "Yangshao wenhua zangsu he shehui zuzhi de yanjiu - dui Yangshao muxi shehui shuo ji qi fangfalun de shangquan" 仰韶文化葬俗和社會組織的研究 - 對仰韶母系社會說及其方法論的商榷. *Wenwu* 文物 371 (1987): 36–43.

Wang Qimin 王啟敏. "Zhoudai zongmiao lizhi kao" 周代宗廟禮制考. *Tangshan Shifan Xueyuan xuebao* 唐山師範學院學報 37, no. 1 (2015): 50–53.

Wang Qiwei 王奇偉. "Cong 'pinji zhi chen' xianxiang kan Shangdai funü de shehui diwei" 從牝雞之晨現象看商代婦女的社會地位. *Yindu xuekan* 殷都學刊 1 (2000): 22–26.

Wang Siyuan 王泗原, *Chuci jiaoshi* 楚辭校釋. Beijing: Renmin jiaoyu, 1990.

Wang Taiquan 王泰權. *Wu diguo: cang zai jiaguwenli* 巫帝國: 藏在甲骨文裡. Taipei: Xiangshi wenhua chubanshe, 2014.

Wang Xiao 王曉. "Peiligang wenhua zangsu qianyi" 裴李崗文化葬俗淺議. *Zhongyuan wenwu* 中原文物 1 (1996): 76–81.

Wang Xiuchen 王秀臣. *Sanli yongshi kaolun* 三禮用詩考論. Beijing: Zhongguo shehui kexue chubanshe, 2007.

Wang Xuan 王璇. 'Shilun *Zuozhuan* zhong de hunyinguan" 試論左傳中的婚姻觀. *Jingji yu shehui fazhan* 經濟與社會發展 1, no. 4 (2003): 116–18.

Wang Yao 王耀. "Muquanzhi shiqi nüxing wenhua jieshuo - yi qinshu chengwei yanjiu wei zhongxin" 母權制時期女性文化解說 - 以親屬稱謂研究為中心. *Yueyang Zhiye Jishu Xueyuan xuebao* 岳陽職業技術學院學報 27, no. 2 (2012): 41–45.

Wang, Ying. "Rank and Power among Court Ladies at Anyang." In *Gender and Chinese Archaeology*, edited by Katheryn M. Linduff and Yan Sun, 95–113. Walnut Creek, CA: Altamira Press, 2004.

Wang Yonghong 王永紅. "Ganshou Shangdai Jiangnan - Jiangxi Xingan Dayangzhou Shangdai damu chutu wenwu jingpinzhan" 感受商代江南 江西新干大洋洲商代大墓出土文物精品展. *Shoucangjia* 收藏家 2 (2006): 7–12.

Wang Yuxin 王宇信, Zhang Yongshan 張永山, and Yang Shengnan 楊升南. "Shilun Yinxu wuhao mu de Fu Hao" 試論殷墟五號墓的婦好. *Kaogu xuebao* 考古學報 2 (1977): 7–10.

Wang Zhen 王珍. "Luelun Yangshao wenhua de qunhun he duiouhun" 略論仰韶文化的群婚和對偶婚. *Kaogu* 考古 7 (1962): 382–83.

Wang Zheng 王政. "Dawenkou wenhua 'wo ya' zangsu yu baya gusu de wushu wenhua neihan" 大汶口文化"握牙"葬俗與拔牙古俗的巫術文化內涵. *Yishu kaogu* 藝術考古 1 (2008): 90–95, 69.

———. "Gudai wenyan xiaoshuo yu Zhoudai de yuji qiuyu" 古代文言小說與周代的雩祭求雨. *Xiaoshuo pinglun* 小說評論 6 (2012): 52–53.

Wang Zhenzhong 王震中. "Zhongxin juluo xingtai, yuanshi zongyi yu qiubang shehui de zhenghe yanjiu" 中心聚落形態原始宗邑與酋邦社會的整合研究. *Zhongyuan wenhua yanjiu* 中原文化研究 4 (2014): 5–14.

Wang Zijin 王子今. *Zhongguo nüzi congjun shi* 中國女子從軍史. Beijing: Junshi yiwen chubanshe, 1998.

Wang Zijin 王子今 and Sun Zhongjia 孫中家. "Zhanguo Qin Han shiqi de nüjun" 戰國秦漢時期的女軍. *Shehuixue yanjiu* 社會學研究 6 (1996): 113–18.

Wang Zijin 王子今 and Zhang Jing 張經. *Zhongguo funü tongshi: Xian Qin juan* 中國婦女通史: 先秦卷. Hangzhou: Hangzhou chubanshe, 2010.

Wang Zirong 王子榮. "Shijing Guofeng nüxing xingxiang mianmianguan" 詩經國風女性形象面面觀. *Chuandong xuekan* 川東學刊 5, no. 3 (1995): 110–13.

Warner, Rebecca L., Gary R. Lee, and Janet Lee. "Social Organization, Spousal Resources, and Marital Power: A Cross-Cultural Study." *Journal of Marriage and Family* 48, no. 1 (1986): 121–28.

Watson, James L. "Anthropological Overview: The Development of Chinese Descent Groups." In *Kinship Organization in Late Imperial China, 1000–1940*, edited by Patricia Buckey Ebrey and James L. Watson, 274–92. Berkeley: University of California Press, 1986.

Wei Shou 魏收. *Weishu* 魏書. Beijing: Zhonghua, 1974.

Wen Yiduo 聞一多. "Gao Tang shennü chuanshuo zhi fenxi" 高唐神女傳說之分析. In *Wen Yiduo quanji* 聞一多全集, vol. 1, 81–116. Taipei: Liren shuju, 1993.

———. "Shuo yu" 說魚. In *Wen Yiduo quanji* 聞一多全集, vol. 1, 117–38. Taipei: Liren shuju, 1993.

Wheatley, Paul. *The Pivot of the Four Quarters: A Prelminary Enquiry into the Origins and Character of the Ancient Chinese City*. Edinburgh: Edinburgh University Press, 1971.

Whitehouse, Ruth D. "Gender Archaeology and Archaeology of Women: Do We Need Both?" In *Archaeology and Women: Ancient and Modern Issues*, edited by Sue Hamilton, Ruth D. Whitehouse and Katherine I. Wright, 27–40. Walnut Creek, CA: Left Coast Press, 2007.

Wittfogel, Karl. "The Society of Prehistoric China," *Zeitschrift für Sozialwissenschaften* 8 (1939): 138–86.

Wolfe, Donald M. "Power and Authority in the Family." In *Studies in Social Power*, edited by Donald Cartwright, 99–117. Ann Arbor: University of Michigan Institute for Social Research, 1959.

Wu Aiqin 吳愛琴. "Shuo ji" 說筓. *Shixue yuekan* 史學月刊 1 (2007): 134–36.

Wu Congxiang 吳從祥. *Handai nüxing lijiao yanjiu* 漢代女性禮教研究. Ji'nan: Qilu, 2013.

Wu Cunhao 吳存浩. "Shangdai muzang xingzhi he xiguan yanjiu" 商代墓葬形制和習慣研究. *Minsu yanjiu* 民俗研究 4 (1994): 41–46.

Wu Fei 吳飛. "Fumu yu ziran: 'zhi mu bu zhi fu' de xifang puxi (xia)," 父母與自然: '知母不知父' 的西方譜系 (下). *Shehui* 社會 34, no. 3 (2014): 1–36.

———. "Jinshi renlun pipan yu muxi lun wenti" 近世人倫批判與母系論問題. *Zhongguo zhexue shi* 中國哲學史 4 (2014): 116–25.

———. "Muquan shenhua 'zhi mu bu zhi fu' de xifang puxi (shang)" 母權神話: '知母不知父' 的西方譜系 (上). *Shehui* 社會 34, no. 2 (2014): 33–59.

Wu, Jui-man. "The Late Neolithic Cemetery at Dadianzi, Inner Mongolia Autonomous Region." In *Gender and Chinese Archaeology*, edited by Katheryn M. Linduff and Yan Sun, 47–91. Walnut Creek, CA: Altamira Press, 2004.

Wu Qi 吳祺. "Cong jiagu buci kan Shangdai zhi meieguan" 從甲骨卜辭看商代之美惡觀. *Mianyang Shifan Xueyuan xuebao* 綿陽師範學院學報 33, no. 7 (2014): 73–76.

Wu Ruowen 伍弱文. "Shouci pojie Banpo renmian yuwen zhi mi" 首次破解半坡人面魚紋之謎. *Wenshi yuekan* 文史月刊 12 (2013): 22–23.

Wu Ruzuo 吳汝祚. "Cong muzang fajue lai kan Yangshao wenhua de shehui xingzhi" 從墓葬發掘來看仰韶文化的社會性質. *Kaogu* 考古 12 (1961): 691–92.

Wu Yumei 武玉梅. "Cong *Shijing* kan Zhoudairen de hunlian shenghuo" 從詩經看周代人的婚戀生活. *Liaoning Daxue xuebao* 遼寧大學學報 1 (1996): 90–92.

Xia Mailing 夏麥陵. "Yuan shi fu yu Chunqiu hunzhi" 原氏仲惠與春秋婚制. *Zhengzhou Daxue xuebao* 鄭州大學學報 1 (1993): 68–71.

Xia Zhiqian 夏之乾. "Tantan tongxing maizang xisu" 談談同性埋葬習俗. *Shiqian yanjiu* 史前研究 4 (1984): 98–103.

———. "Was There Ever a Matriarchy?" *Chinese Sociology and Anthropology* 25, no. 4 (1983): 8–13.

Xiao Guoliang 蕭國亮. *Zhongguo changji shi* 中國娼妓史. Taipei: Wenjin chubanshe, 1996.

Xie Chenxing 謝晨星. "Cong *Chu ci Tianwen* kan Xia minzu fuquanzhi zhansheng muquanzhi" 從楚辭天問看夏民族父權制戰勝母權制. *Zhongguo chengshi jingji* 中國城市經濟 2 (2012): 300, 302.

Xie Naihe 謝乃和. "Jinwen zhong suojian Xi Zhou wanghou shiji kao" 金文中所見西周王后事迹考. *Huaxia kaogu* 華夏考古 4 (2008): 142–52.

Xie Weiyang 謝維揚. *Zhoudai jiating xingtai* 周代家庭形態. Beijing: Zhongguo shehui kexue chubanshe, 1990.

Xu Fu 徐復. *Qin huiyao dingbu* 秦會要訂補. Taipei: Dingwen shuju, 1978.

Xu Guangde 徐廣德 and He Minling 何毓靈. "Xin shiji Yinxu kaogu de zhongda faxian - ji Anyang Yinxu huayuan dong 54 hao mu de fajue" 新世紀殷墟考古的重大發現 - 記安陽殷墟花園莊村東 54 號墓的發掘. *Xungen* 尋根 4 (2001): 65–72.

Xu Haijing 徐海晶 and Hou Shujuan 侯淑娟. "Bei chao shangceng nüzi de hunlianguan" 北朝上層女子的婚戀觀. *Baicheng Shifan Xueyuan xuebao* 白城師範學院學報 28, no. 6 (2014): 97–99, 112.

Xu Jinxiong 許進雄. *Wenzi xiaojiang* 文字小講. Taipei: Taiwan shangwu, 2014.

Xu Mangui 許滿貴. "Fuqi he jin jie liangyuan lian li jiaobei shang yinhuan – gudai hunsu yin jiao bei jiu ji jiubei yuanshi chengxu jianshang" 夫妻和卺結良緣連理交杯觴飲歡 - 古代婚俗飲交杯酒及酒杯原始承緒鑒賞. *Dongfang shoucang* 東方收藏 12 (2012): 60–62.

Xu Shenzhan 許順湛. "'Yangshao' shiqi yi jinru fuxi shizu shehui" 仰韶時期已進入父系氏族社會. *Kaogu* 5 (1962): 256–61.

Xu Yihua 徐義華. "Shangdai zhufu de zongjiao diwei" 商代諸婦的宗教地位, in *Jinian Yinxu jiaguwen faxian yibai zhounian guoji yantaohui lunwenji* 紀念殷墟甲骨文發現一百週年國際學術研討會論文集, edited by Wang Yuxin 王宇信 and Song Zhenhao 宋鎮豪, 448–58. Beijing: Shehui kexue wenxian chubanshe, 2003.

Xu Yingying 許瑩瑩. "Tan Zhongguo gudai funü zhenjieguan de xingcheng yu bianqian" 談中國古代婦女貞節觀點的形成與變遷. *Xue lilun* 學理論 32 (2012): 186–89.

Xu Yuanzhe 許元哲. "Shangdai jisi de yongsheng fangfa" 商代祭祀的用牲方法. *Xinxiang Xueyuan xuebao* 新鄉學院學報 23, no. 3 (2009): 72–74.

Xu Zhaofeng 徐昭峰. "Xiajiadian xiaceng wenhua leixing bianxi - jiyu Erlitou wenhua leixing de duibi yanjiu" 夏家店下層文化類型辨析 - 基於二里頭文化類型的對比研究. *Dongbei shidi* 東北史地 2 (2010): 10–16.

Xu Zhongshu 徐中舒. "Zhongguo gudai de fuxi jiating ji qi qinshu chengwei" 中國古代的父系家庭及其親屬稱謂. *Sichuan Daxue xuebao* 四川大學學報 1 (1980): 110–12.

Xu Zhuoyun 許倬雲. "Cong *Zhouli* zhong tuice yuangu de funü gongzuo" 從周禮中推測遠古的婦女工作. *Dalu zazhi* 大陸雜誌 7 (1954): 202–05.

Xun Kuang 荀況. *Xunzi jiaoshi* 荀子校釋, annotated by Wang Tianhai 王天海. Shanghai: Shanghai guji, 2005.

Yan Ming 嚴明. *Zhongguo mingji yishu shi* 中國名妓藝術史. Taipei: Wenjin, 1992.

Yan Sun and Hongyu Yang. "Gender Ideology and Mortuary Practice in Northwestern China." In *Gender and Chinese Archaeology*, edited by Katheryn M. Linduff and Yan Sun, 29–46. Walnut Creek, CA: Altamira Press, 2004.

Yan Wenming 嚴文明. *Yangshao wenhua yanjiu* 仰韶文化研究. Beijing: Wenwu, 1989.

Yan Xiang 晏翔. "Cong Majiayao wenhua de zangsu tan want you ling guan" 從馬家窯文化的葬俗談萬物有靈觀. *Hebei Qingnian Guanli Ganbu Xueyuan xuebao* 河北青年管理幹部學院學報 3 (2010): 55–58.

Yan Yiping 嚴一萍. "Fu Hao liezhuan" 婦好列傳. *Zhongguo wenzi* 中國文字 3 (1981): 1–104.

Yang Baocheng 楊寶成 and Yang Xizhang 楊錫璋. "Cong Yinxu xiaoxing muzang kan Yindai shehui de pingmin" 從殷墟小型墓葬看殷代社會的平民. *Zhongyuan wenwu* 中原文物 1 (1983): 30–4.

Yang Guangyu 楊廣宇. "Zhenmian rensheng bubei buqu - qianlun 'Mang' zhong de qifu xingxiang" 真面人生不卑不屈 - 淺論氓中的棄婦形象. *Hefei Lianhe Daxue xuebao* 合肥聯合大學學報 9, no. 2 (1999): 26–29.

Yang Hsi-chang. "The Shang Dynasty Cemetery System." In *Studies of Shang Archaeology: Selected Papers from the International Conference on Shang Civilization*, edited by K.C. Chang, 49-63. New Haven: Yale University Press, 1986.

Yang Jiping 楊際平. "Dunhuang chutu de fangqi shu suoyi" 敦煌出土的放妻書瑣議. *Ximen Daxue xuebao* 西門大學學報 4 (1999): 34–41.

Yang Junru 楊筠如. "Chunqiu shidai zhi nannü fengji" 春秋時代之男女風紀. In *Zhongguo funüshi lunwenji* 中國婦女史論文集, edited by Li Youning 李又寧 and Zhang Yufa 張玉法, second edition, 20–38. Taipei: Taiwan Shangwu, 1988.

Yang Kuan 楊寬. *Xi Zhou shi* 西周史. Taipei: Taiwan Shangwu, 1999.

Yang Lianmin 楊連民 and Ma Xiaoxue 馬曉雪. "'Guining fumu' yu 'guining' zhidu kaolue" 歸寧父母與歸寧制度考略. *Liaocheng Daxue xuebao* 聊城大學學報 6 (2003): 13–26.

Yang Lihui 楊利慧. *Nü Wa suyuan - Nü Wa xinyang qiyuan di de zai tuice* 女媧溯源 - 女媧信仰起源地的再推測. Beijing: Beijing Shifan Daxue chubanshe, 1999.

Yang Mao 楊茂. "Churen sheng, renxun shitan" 楚人牲, 人殉試探. *Xinan Nongye Daxue xuebao* 西南農業大學學報 5 (2009): 94–97.

Yang Mei 楊美. "Qianyi jiaguwen suo fanying de Shangdai funü diwei" 淺議甲骨文所反映的商代婦女地位. *Xuexingtang yuyan wenzi luncong* 學行堂語言文字論叢 1 (2011): 370–76.

Yang Shengnan 楊升南. "Jiaguwen zhong suojian Shangdai de gongna zhidu" 甲骨文中所見商代的貢納制度. *Yindu xuekan* 殷都學刊 2 (1999): 27–32.

Yang Xiaoli 楊曉麗. "*Shijing* qifu xingxiang qianxi" 詩經棄婦形象淺析. *Dali Xueyuan xuebao* 大理學院學報 1, no. 1 (2002): 101–03.

Yang Yi 楊怡. "*Shijing* zhong 'lian' yu shengzhi chongbai" 詩經中蓮與生殖崇拜. *Qingnian zuojia* 青年作家 7 (2010): 5–6.

Yang Yun 楊允. "Zhoudai shengmu songge tanxi" 周代聖母頌歌探析. *Shehui kexue zhanxian* 社會科學戰線 1 (2009): 277–78.

Yao Dazhong 姚大中. *Huanghe wenming zhi guang* 黃河文明之光. Taipei: Sanmin, 1981.

Yates, Robin D.S. "Social Status in the Ch'in: Evidence from the Yün-meng Legal Documents. Part One: Commoners." *Harvard Journal of Asiatic Studies* 47, no. 1 (1987): 197–237.

Yi Hua 易華. "Cong Qijia dao Erlitou: Xia wenhua tansuo" 從齊家到二里頭: 夏文化探索. *Xueshu yuekan* 學術月刊 12 (2014): 134–44.

Yin Qun 印群. "Dong Zhou shiqi Qin Qi xunren mu de bijiao yanjiu" 東周時期秦齊殉人墓的比較研究. *Dongfang kaogu* 東方考古 4 (2012): 316–25.

———. "Lun Dabaozishan Qin gong lingyuan de renxun - jian tan Ying Qin xianren xiqian zhi diwang" 論大堡子山秦公陵園的人殉 - 兼談嬴秦先人西遷之地望. *Fudan xuebao* 復旦學報 6 (2014): 80–87.

Yin Shengping 尹盛平. "'Di si' yu 'si mu' kao" 帝司與司母考. *Gu wenzi yanjiu* 古文字研究 13. Beijing: Zhonghua shuju, 1986, 431–37.

Ying Yong. "Gender, Status, Ritual Regulations, and Mortuary Practice in the State of Jin." In *Gender and Chinese Archaeology*, edited by Katheryn M. Linduff and Yan Sun, 161–202. Walnut Creek, CA: Altamira Press, 2004.

Yinxu Xiaomintun Kaogudui 殷墟孝民屯考古隊. "Henan Anyang shi Xiaomintun Shangdai fangzhi 2003-2004 nian fajue jianbao" 河南安陽市孝民屯商代房址 2003-2004 年發掘簡報. *Kaogu* 考古 1 (2007): 3–13.

———. "Henan Anyang shi Xiaomintun Shangdai muzang 2003-2004 nian fajue jianbao 河南安陽市孝民屯商代墓葬 2003-2004 年發掘簡報. *Kaogu* 考古 1 (2007): 26–36.

Young, Katherine K. "Introduction." In *Women in World Religions*, edited by Arvind Sharma, 10–36. Albany: State University of New York Press, 1987.

Yu Fuwei 余扶危, Li Yuee 李月娥, and Jia Caixia 賈彩霞. "Luoyang Yangshao he Longshan wenhua shiqi muzang yanjiu" 洛陽仰韶和龍山文化時期墓葬研究. *Luoyang Ligong Xueyuan xuebao* 洛陽理工學院學報 3 (2007): 56–61.

Yu Jiang. "Ritual Practice, Status, and Gender Identity: Western Zhou Tombs at Baoji." In *Gender and Chinese Archaeology*, edited by Katheryn M. Linduff and Yan Sun, 117–36. Walnut Creek, CA: Altamira Press, 2004.

Yu Liangjie 余良杰. "Lun sanglin yu Chunqiu shiqi hunyin zhi guanxi" 論桑林與春秋時期婚姻之關係. *Jiangsu Ligong Daxue xuebao* 江蘇理工大學學報 5 (1995): 99–102.

Yu Qiangjun 余強軍. "Daojia zhexue de nüxing qizhi jiqi dangdai jiazhi" 道家哲學的女性氣質及其當代價值. *Shandong Nüzi Xueyuan xuebao* 山東女子學院學報 115 (2014): 50–53.

Yu Tingting 余婷婷. "Dong Zhou shiqi de cansang shengchan quyu tanxi" 東周時期的蠶桑生產區域探析. *Sichou* 絲綢 1 (2013): 63–66.

Yuan Yuan 袁媛. "Cong jiaguwen zhong de jige zi kan Shangdai nüxing" 從甲骨文中的幾個字看商代女性. *Xiandai yuwen* 現代語文 6 (2011): 147–48.

Zhan Shiyou and Peng Chuanhua. "Cultivation (Jiaohua, 教化): The Goal of Xunzi's Ethical Thought." *Frontiers of Philosophy in China* 2, no. 1 (2007): 25–49.

Zhang Bangwei 張邦煒. *Hunyin yu shehui (Songdai)* 婚姻與社會 (宋代). Chengdu: Sichuan renmin chubanshe, 1989.

Zhang Changan 張長安 and Yao Zhiguo 姚志國. "Shilun Peiligang wenhua shiqi de shehui jieduan" 試論裴李崗文化時期的社會階段. *Zhongyuan wenwu* 中原文物 2 (1996): 39–46.

Zhang Chi 張弛. "Shijiahe juluo xingsheng shiqi zangyi zhong de xin guannian" 石家河聚落興盛時期葬儀中的新觀念. *Kaogu* 考古 8 (2014): 68–80.

Zhang Hongliang 張鴻亮. "Dong Zhou Chu guo lianhun kaoshu" 東周楚國聯婚考述. *Jianghan kaogu* 2 (2007): 52–57.

Zhang Hongyan 張宏彥. "Weishui liuyu Laoguantai wenhua fenqi yu leixing yanjiu" 渭水流域老官台文化分期與類型研究. *Kaogu xuebao* 考古學報 2 (2007): 153–78.

Zhang Huian 張會安. "Xin'gan Dayangzhou Shangdai muzang yuqi de gongyi ji wenhua yiyun yanjiu" 新干大洋洲商代墓葬玉器的工藝及文化意蘊研. *Jinggangshan Daxue xuebao* 井岡山大學學報 32, no. 6 (2011): 124–30.

Zhang Jing 張靜. "Cong 'Mang' deng jishou minge kan Zhongguo gudai funü de xingge guangcai" 從氓等幾首民歌看中國古代婦女的性格光彩. *Xinzhou Shifa Xueyuan xuebao* 忻州師範學院學報 16, no. 4 (2000): 47–51.

Zhang Lianju 張連舉. "*Shijing* zhong de shengzhi chongbai mima dujie" 詩經中的生殖崇拜密碼讀解. *Beifang luncong* 北方論叢 2 (2001): 92–95.

Zhang Nan 張囡 and Li Yaguang 李亞光. "Lun Zhoudai de ying hun zhidu" 論周代的媵婚制度. *Liaoning Gongcheng Jishu Daxue xuebao* 遼寧工程技術大學學報 2 (2008): 170–72.

Zhang Shuaifeng 張帥峰. "Guo guo guizu de yu xiangshi wenhua" 虢國貴族的玉項飾文化. *Zhonghua wenwu huabao* 中華文物畫報 6 (2012): 114–17.

Zhang Shuyi 張淑一. "Zhoudai nüzi de xingshi zhidu" 周代女子的姓氏制度. *Shixue jikan* 史學集刊 2 (1999): 67–70.

Zhang Tianen 張天恩. "Qianlun Xiwangcun leixing jige wenti" 淺論西王村類型幾個問題. *Kaogu yu wenwu* 考古與文物 2 (1994): 70–81.

Zhang Xuechen 張雪晨. "Longshan shidai Rizhao diqu yinshi wenhua lice" 龍山時代日照地區飲食文化蠡測. *Huaxia kaogu* 華夏考古 3 (2011): 81–87, 108.

Zhang Yongshan 張永山. "Shixi 'xi duo nü zhi bei peng'" 試析錫多女屮貝朋. *Gu wenzi yanjiu* 古文字研究 16, 29–35. Beijing: Zhonghua shuju, 1989.

Zhang Zhenglang 張政烺. "Fu Hao lueshuo" 婦好略說. In *Jiagu jinwen yu Shang Zhou shi yanjiu* 甲骨金文與商周史研究, 186–95. Beijing: Zhonghua shuju, 2012.

Zhang Zhixin 張志新. "Suzhou de Liangzhu yicun ji gudai wenming" 蘇州的良渚遺存及古代文明. *Suzhou Daxue xuebao* 蘇州大學學報 1 (1997): 111–17.

Zhang Zhongpei 張忠培. "Liangzhu wenhua mudi yu qi biaoshu de wenming shehui" 良渚文化墓地與其表述的文明社會. *Kaogu xuebao* 考古學報 4 (2012): 401–22.

Zhao Cheng 趙誠. *Jiaguwen yu Shangdai wenhua* 甲骨文與商代文化. Shenyang: Liaoning renmin chubanshe, 2000.

———. "Zhufu tansuo" 諸婦探索. In *Gu wenzi yanjiu* 古文字研究 12, 99–106. Beijing: Zhonghua shuju, 1985.

Zhao Dongyu 趙東玉. "Shangdai neihun shuo boyi" 商代內婚說駁議. *Liaoning Shifan Daxue xuebao* 遼寧師範大學學報 34, no. 5 (2011): 132–34.

Zhao Dongyu 趙東玉 and Lu Cui 盧翠. "Chunqiu shiqi Qi guo guifu 'luanzheng' tanxi" 春秋時期齊國貴婦亂政探析. *Liaoning Shifan Daxue xuebao* 遼寧師範大學學報 1 (2009): 120–22.

Zhao Fulin 晁福林. "Kongzi yu Wanqiu - jian lun Zhoudai wuxi diwei de bianhua yu wunü bujia zhi su" 孔子與宛丘 - 兼論周代巫覡地位的變化與巫女不嫁之俗. *Gansu shehui kexue* 甘肅社會科學 1 (2006): 52–56.

Zhao Gaiping 趙改萍. "Huozhou shengmu miao bihua yu Nü Wa chongbai" 霍州聖母廟壁畫與女媧崇拜. *Shanxi dang'an* 山西檔案 4 (2014): 16–20.

Zhao Huili 趙會莉. "*Shijing* zhong Zhoudai hunsu tanwei" 詩經中周代婚俗探微. *Xueshu jiaoliu* 學術交流 2 (2014): 154–56.

Zhao Jianli 趙劍莉. "Jin guo furen kao" 晉國夫人考. *Nei Menggu Nongye Daxue xuebao* 內蒙古農業大學學報 1 (2012): 313–14.

Zhao Rongjun 趙容俊. *Yin Shang jiagu buci suo jian zhi wushu* 殷商甲骨卜辭所見之巫術 (revised edition). Beijing: Zhonghua, 2011.

Zhao Wenyi 趙文藝. "Cong Banpo Jiangzhai yizhi yu minzuxue ziliao kan muxi shizu gongshe" 從半坡姜寨遺址與民族學資料看母系氏族公社. In *Minzuxue yanjiu* 民族學研究, edited by Minzuxue yanjiuhui 民族學研究會, vol. 6, 22–32. Beijing: Minzu, 1985.

Zhao Yanxia 趙豔霞. *Zhongguo zaoqi xingshi zhidu yanjiu* 中國早期姓氏研究. Tianjin: Tianjin guji chubanshe, 1996.

Zhao Ye 趙曄. "Liangzhu wenwu renxun renji xianxiang shixi" 良渚文化人殉人祭現象試析. *Nanfang wenwu* 南方文物 1 (2001): 32–37.

Zhao Yi 趙翼. *Gaiyu congkan* 陔除叢考. Shanghai: Shangwu, 1957.

———. *Nianer shi zhaji* 廿二史劄記. Taipei: Shijie shuju, 1974.

Zhejiang Sheng Wenwu Kaogu Yanjiusuo 浙江省文物考古研究所 and Zhejiang Hangzhou Shi Yukeng Qu Wenguanhui 浙江杭州市余杭區文管會. "Zhejiang Yukeng Xingqiao Houtoushan Liangzhu wenhua mudi fajue jianbao" 浙江余杭星橋后頭山良渚文化墓地發掘簡報. *Nanfang wenwu* 南方文物 3 (2008): 28, 31–49.

Zhen Hongyong 甄洪永. "Shanggu Jiang shi buzu minsu yicun yu Chunqiu shiqi funü congzheng guanxi shixi" 上古姜氏部族民俗遺存與春秋時期婦女從政關係試析. *Qinghai Minzu Daxue xuebao* 青海民族大學學報 7 (2011): 77–80.

Zheng Huisheng 鄭慧生. *Shanggu Huaxia funü yu hunyin* 上古華夏婦女與婚姻. Henan: Henan Renmin, 1988.

Zheng Qun 鄭群. "You 'gui' kan *Shijing* zhong de nüxing zai hunyin zhong de juese" 由歸看詩經中的女性在婚姻中的角色. *Simao Shifan Gaodeng Zhuanke Xuexiao xuebao* 思茅師範高等專科學校學報 20, no. 1 (2004): 41–43.

Zheng Xuan 鄭玄 et al., annotators. *Chongkan Songben Yili zhushu fujiao kanji* 重栞宋本儀禮注疏附校勘記. Nanchang: Nanchangfu xuekanben, 1815; reprinted Taipei: Yiwen, 1955.

Zheng Xuan 鄭玄, annotator. *Chongkan Songben Zhouli zhushu fujiao kanji* 重栞宋本周禮注疏附校堪記. Nanchang: Nanchangfu xuekanben, 1815; reprinted Taipei: Yiwen yinshuguan, 1955.

Zhengzhou Shi Wenwu Gongzuodui 鄭州市文物工作隊 and Zhengzhou Shi Dahecun Yizhi Bowuguan 鄭州市大河村遺址博物館. "Zhengzhou Dahecun yizhi 1983, 1987 nian fajue baogao" 鄭州大河村遺址 1983, 1987 年發掘報告." *Kaogu xuebao* 考古學報 1 (1996): 111–41.

Zhongguo Kexueyuan Kaogu Yanjiusuo Gansu gongzuodui 中國科學院考古研究所甘肅工作隊. "Gansu Yongjing Qinweijia Qijia wenhua mudi" 甘肅永靖秦魏家齊家文化墓地. *Kaogu xuebao* 考古學報 2 (1975): 57–96.

Zhongguo Kexueyuan Kaogusuo et al. 中國科學院考古研究所. "Beijing fujin faxian de Xi Zhou nuli xunzang mu" 北京附近發現的西周奴隸殉葬墓. *Kaogu* 考古 5 (1974): 309–21.

Zhongguo Shehui Kexue Xueyuan Kaogu Yanjiusuo 中國社會科學院考古研究所. "Henan Yanshi Shengcheng Shangdai zaoqi wangshi jisi yizhi" 河南偃師商城商代早期王室祭祀遺址. *Kaogu* 考古 7 (2002): 6–8.

Zhongguo Shehui Kexueyuan Kaogu Yanjiusuo Anyang Gongzuodui 中國社會科學院考古研究所安陽工作隊. "Henan Anyang Shi Yinxu Liujiazhuang beidi 2008 nian fajue jianbao 河南安陽市殷墟劉家莊北地 2008 年發掘簡報." *Kaogu* 考古 7 (2009): 24–38.

———. "Henan Anyang Yinxu Huayuanzhuang dongdi 60 hao mu" 河南安陽殷墟花園庄東地 60 號墓. *Kaogu* 考古 1 (2006): 7–18.

———. "Yinxu Dasikong M303 fajue baogao" 殷墟大司空 M303 發掘報告. *Kaogu xuebao* 考古學報 3 (2008): 353–94.

Zhou Haixia 周海霞. "Chunqiu shiqi de liangxing xisu yu zhenjieguan" 春秋時期的兩性習俗與貞節觀. *Hanshan Shifan Xueyuan xuebao* 韓山師範學院學報 1 (2008): 55–59.

Zhou Mi 周蜜 and Huang Yuhong 黃玉洪. "Yun Xian Qiaojiayuan mudi Dong Zhou - Xi Han jumin yachi de xingtai guancha yu celiang" 隕縣橋家院墓地東周 - 西漢居民牙齒的型態觀察與測量. *Jiang Han kaogu* 江漢考古 3 (2010): 106–12.

Zhou Yanliang 周延良. "*Shijing* yinghun shi yu yinghun wenhua" 詩經媵婚詩與媵婚文化. *Wenyi yanjiu* 文藝研究 3 (2002): 63–73.

Zhou, Yiqun. *Festivals, Feasts, and Gender Relations in Ancient China and Greece*. Cambridge: Cambridge University Press, 2010.

———. "Virtue and Talent: Women and *Fushi* in Early China," *Nan Nü* 5, no. 1 (2003): 1–42.

Zhu Fenghan 朱鳳翰. *Shang Zhou jiazu xingtai yanjiu (zengding ban)*. 商周家族型態研究 (增訂本). Tianjin: Tianjin guji, 2004.

Zhu Honglin 朱紅林. "Zhanguo shiqi youguan hunyin guanxi falü de yanjiu – zhujian Qin Han lü yu 'Zhouli' bijiao yanjiu (si)" 戰國時期有關婚姻關係法律的研究 - 竹簡秦漢律與 '周禮' 比較研究 (四). *Jilin Shifan Daxue xuebao* 吉林師範大學學報 3 (2011): 46–50.

Zhu Liuyu 朱柳郁. "Cong yingqie zhengbao zhidu kan Zhoudai zhengzhi hunyin" 從媵妾蒸報制度看周代政治婚姻. *Tianjin Shida xuebao* 天津師大學報 4 (2000): 42–45.

Zhu Naicheng 朱乃誠. "Xin Zhongguo diyibu xin shiqi shidai mudi fajue zhuankan de tedian ji qi xueshu yingxiang – chongdu 'Dawenkou' you gan" 新中國第一部新石器時代墓地發掘專刊的特點及其學術影響 - 重讀大汶口有感. *Nanfang wenwu* 南方文物 3 (2011): 1–7.

Zhu Xiaoding 朱曉汀, Lin Liugen 林留根 and Zhu Hong 朱泓. "Jiangsu Pizhou Liangwangcheng yizhi Dawenkou wenhua mudi chutu rengu yanjiu" 江蘇邳州梁王城遺址大汶口文化墓地出土人骨研究. *Dongnan wenhua* 東南文化 4 (2013): 53–64.

Zu Jingran 祖晶然. "Cong Shuihudi Qin jian kan Qin guo funü de hunyin zhuangkuang" 從睡虎地秦簡看秦國婦女的婚姻狀況. *Suzhou Keji Xueyuan xuebao* 蘇州科技學院學報 28, no. 5 (2011): 54–58.

Zuo Qiuming左丘明. *Chongkan Songben Zuozhuan zhushu fujiao kanji* 重栞宋本左傳注疏附挍堪記. Nanchang: Nanchangfu xuekanben, 1815; reprinted Taipei: Yiwen yinshuguan, 1965.

Zurndorfer, Harriet. "Polygamy and Masculinity in China: Past and Present." In *Changing Chinese Masculinities: From Imperial Pillars of State to Global Real Men*, edited by Kam Louie, 13–33. Hong Kong: Hong Kong University Press, 2016.

Index

ASIAN VOICES
An Asia/Pacific/Perspectives Series
Series Editor: Mark Selden